THE
TEABO
MANUSCRIPT

THE LINDA SCHELE SERIES IN
MAYA AND PRE-COLUMBIAN STUDIES

THE
TEABO
MANUSCRIPT

Maya Christian
Copybooks, Chilam
Balams, and Native Text
Production in Yucatan

MARK Z.
CHRISTENSEN

UNIVERSITY OF TEXAS PRESS, AUSTIN

Requests for permission to reproduce material from this work should be sent to:
    Permissions
    University of Texas Press
    P.O. Box 7819
    Austin, TX 78713-7819
    http://utpress.utexas.edu/index.php/rp-form

♾ The paper used in this book meets the minimum requirements of ANSI/NISO
Z39.48-1992 (R1997) (Permanence of Paper).

Design by Kimberly Glyder

Library of Congress Cataloging-in-Publication Data
Christensen, Mark Z., author.
The Teabo manuscript : Maya Christian copybooks, Chilam Balams, and native text
production in Yucatan / Mark Z. Christensen.
First edition. | Austin : University of Texas Press, 2016.
Includes bibliographical references and index.
 LCCN 2015049526
 ISBN 978-1-4773-1081-6 (cloth : alk. paper)
 ISBN 978-1-4773-1082-3 (library e-book)
 ISBN 978-1-4773-1083-0 (non-library e-book)
LCSH: Chilam Balam de Teabo (Manuscript) | Manuscripts, Maya. | Mayas—Religion. |
Christianity and culture—Mexico—History. | Mayas—Medicine—Early works to 1800. |
LCC F1435.3.R3 C47 2016 | DDC 299.7/842—dc23
LC record available at http://lccn.loc.gov/2015049526

doi:10.7560/310816

TO CARTER

who if he found a Maya
manuscript would simply
roll it up and use
it as a sword

CONTENTS

Maps and Figures

Tables

Acknowledgments

For many years now, Matthew Restall has encouraged and supported my work, and this project has benefited greatly from his guidance and scholarly influence. I still consider myself fortunate to have been his student. John F. Chuchiak also deserves my most heartfelt thanks. His expertise in Maya manuscripts and Church history, particularly in Yucatan, opened new insights and challenged me to see the Teabo Manuscript in new ways, and I am profoundly grateful. When I came across particularly puzzling words and passages, David Bolles proved most generous with his time and talents in the translation of Yucatec Maya, and I am grateful. Finally, Victoria Bricker and Timothy Knowlton provided their time and expertise whenever I had questions or was in need of other scholarly opinions.

Of course, many deserve my sincere appreciation for both their scholarship that paved the way and their assistance through various conversations, emails, and advice. My thanks in particular to Louise Burkhart, Fr. Roger Corriveau, Jaime Lara, Brian Murdoch, Michel Oudijk, Stafford Poole, C.M., Frauke Sachse, Sabine Dedenbach-Salazar Saenz, Amara Solari, and David Tavárez. A few existing works include discussions and translations of various versions of the Genesis Commentary and other texts that proved helpful in my own translation process. I am particularly grateful for Victoria Bricker and Helga-Maria Miram's work on the Kaua, and Gretchen Whalen's work on the Morley Manuscript. Moreover, portions of this book benefited from the comments of those attending the 2013 roundtable at the Käte Hamburger Kolleg at the Center for Religious Studies, Ruhr-Universität. I also am indebted to the staff at Brigham Young University's L. Tom Perry Special Collections, including Cindy Brightenburg, Kohleen Jones, and Russ Taylor, for their assistance and the generosity of the library for allowing a full reproduction of the text. This project has also benefited from the financial support of the National Endowment for the Humanities and Assumption College.

As always, the largest debt is held by those most close: my family. My wife is always willing to listen to me ramble on about translations and new ideas for the book, and my kids help me to smile and laugh after long days in front of a computer. I could not have asked for a more beautiful family.

Conventions of Transcription and Translation

This book draws heavily from Maya, Nahuatl, and Spanish sources, and all English translations are my own unless stated otherwise. In all instances I strive to make the translations readable and oftentimes favor a figurative rather than a literal translation of the texts. Maya authors did not conform to modern conventions of punctuation, spacing, and paragraphing, so I have included them in the translations. However, to the extent possible I have transcribed the Teabo Manuscript and other documents as they appear in their original form, employing the occasional "..." when water damage or wear renders the text unreadable. For purposes of readability, I employ modern standards for determining line breaks and do not parse the transcription into phrase-segments as is sometimes done to highlight potential poetic devices in the text. The manuscript typically separates paragraphs with a decorative drop cap, and such are represented in the transcription. In instances of possible confusion in the translation, I use parentheses to convey intended meanings and brackets for omitted words. Moreover, in the transcriptions I occasionally comment on the reading of a word, and such are found in the notes.

As is common practice, I employ "ɔ" for the backwards "c" used by the colonial Maya—today written as "dz"—and "dz" for those instances where a "ɔ" appears in personal or place-names. Moreover, the colonial Maya often marked glottal stops with horizontal strokes through "h" and "p," and such are represented here as "ch" and "p". The Maya word *yetel*, "and or with," often appears abbreviated as a "y" with a horizontal stroke, seen here as "y". Throughout the main text, Maya, Nahuatl, and Spanish words appear in italics upon their first appearance only. Finally, all biblical citations are from the New American Bible (NAB) as it is employed in English-speaking American Catholic churches today.

Introduction

[I]T IS IN THE COLONIAL LITERATURE OF
YUCATAN THAT WE MUST SEARCH FOR THE MAIN
CLUES TO THE LITERARY PAST OF THE FIRST
RANKING CIVILIZATION OF THE AMERICAS.
—MUNRO S. EDMONSON (1971)[1]

For years the Maya and their writings have captured the attention of the general public and scholars alike. The drawings of nineteenth-century explorer Frederick Catherwood depicting the great buildings and monuments of the ancient Maya laced with hieroglyphs ignited the Western world's fascination with this "lost culture." It seemed as though the Maya had been busily writing for centuries, but what did they write about? Although scholars have since made astounding achievements in "breaking the Maya code" to read the hieroglyphs, today the question remains in the minds of scholars and the public alike and even provided fodder for the recent 2012 doomsday craze.[2]

Although forced to share the Yucatan Peninsula with the Spaniards, the colonial Maya nevertheless continued their tradition of writing, albeit in the Roman alphabet.[3] Scholars have made important inroads into understanding what the colonial Maya wrote, uncovering documents ranging from the mundane bill of sale to the seemingly esoteric writings found in what have been termed the Books of Chilam Balam (Maya-authored manuscripts relating various topics important to Maya culture). Yet despite such progress, whenever a scholar approaches a Maya document, the basic question resurfaces: "What did they write about?" It was this question that bounded throughout my head as I held a curious Maya manuscript in the summer of 2012.

While visiting family in Utah, I decided to spend some time at Brigham

Young University to see some of my undergraduate professors and explore the L. Tom Perry Special Collections. I was particularly interested in a collection titled "Biography of William E. Gates, 1863–1940" (MSS 279). Throughout his career studying the Maya, Gates collected an impressive amount of material that included Maya manuscripts from the colonial period. During his lifetime and upon his death, Gates's collection found its way into various universities, including Princeton, Tulane, and Brigham Young. In 1946 BYU purchased a portion of the collection, which today consists of 117 boxes of documents, manuscripts, photocopies, grammars, personal correspondence, and other materials. Included in this collection is a forty-four-page manuscript written in Yucatec Maya that was originally (mis)cataloged as a "Christian doctrine." Upon closer examination of the text to see what its Maya author(s) was saying, I discovered that it was much more.

Like many manuscript copybooks of its time, this particular manuscript is a collection of discourses written on large sheets of paper. The dimensions are certainly not uniform, but the rough size of the eleven sheets is 21 cm x 33 cm. The sheets are folded in half to create a sewn gathering of 22 folios, or 44 pages, with each folded page measuring approximately 21 cm x 16.5 cm.[4] The sheets are composed of a handmade laid paper, likely made from linen fibers, with no watermarks present. The ink is brown and appears to be iron gall ink written in several hands using various ink recipes. Water damage has caused severe tidelines (stains) on nearly every page. The head conservator for rare books and manuscripts at Brigham Young's Harold B. Lee Library, Kohleen Jones, confidently places the manuscript in the eighteenth or early nineteenth century.

The manuscript has various thematic sections. The first contains a redaction of the creation of the world and the Fall of Adam and Eve. Following this section is the genealogy of Christ taken from the Bible and eschatological material including a Maya rendition of the European apocalyptic text *The Fifteen Signs before Doomsday*. The manuscript then contains a devotional anthem and invocation to both Mary and Christ—discourses that readily appeared throughout European books of hours—and a passage on indulgences that loosely resembles the "Papal instructions for avoiding purgatory" found in the Chilam Balam of Kaua. Finally, the manuscript concludes with a few medicinal remedies for common ailments that seem to have been appended in the early twentieth century, one of which includes the entry "Teabo 8 de Enero de 1911."

This book brings to light this unstudied Maya manuscript, referred to hereafter as the "Teabo Manuscript," through a translation and analysis of its contents. At its heart, this book reveals what the Maya of Teabo deemed important enough to write about and preserve. In the process, the study employs the Teabo Manuscript as a platform from which to explore various topics including the evangelization of the Maya, their literary compositions, and the aspects of Christianity they contained. The study also utilizes the Teabo Manuscript to expose, in many cases for the first time, connections between other religious texts, both European and Maya, and their authors, thus sharpening the scholarly image of colonial writing among the Maya. Finally, the manuscript's death record and medicinal remedies illuminate further the dualistic nature of such texts and their authors, the texts being products of both the individual and corporate realm, and the authors as oftentimes being responsible for maintaining both the spiritual and physical well-being of the *cah*, or Maya town (plural *cahob*). In the end, this book endeavors to analyze and contextualize the Teabo Manuscript in a way that contributes valuable elements to the elusive, fluid, and multifaceted answer regarding what the colonial Maya wrote about and why.

Colonial Maya Texts

Although Spaniards had contact with the Yucatec Maya with some regularity beginning in 1517, the military conquest of Yucatan was a lengthy process involving various *entradas* that did not end until the establishment of Yucatan's capital, Merida, in 1542. This is not to say that the Maya were then "conquered" or that subsequent "revolts" were not actually products of an unfinished conquest, or even that the Yucatan Peninsula was entirely secured by the Spanish. Much of the area would remain unconquered, or what the Spanish preferred to refer to as territory *despoblado* ("uninhabited") to disguise their inability to subdue the area's population.[5]

This delay in military subjugation also delayed evangelization efforts. The Franciscans dominated such efforts and waited until 1545 to obtain a firm foothold in Yucatan, although their numbers remained low throughout the colonial period, with Yucatan receiving only 2.9 percent of all friars sent from Spain by the crown.[6] Once there, they immediately began establishing convents and schools, the latter constituting an essential component in converting the Maya.[7] In his *Historia de Yucatán*, Juan Francisco Molina Solís poetically stated:

> In the shadow of the cathedral, and in each one of the monasteries scattered throughout all the territory of the peninsula, schools (for the Maya) were opened; and this was not an accidental or isolated work, but premeditated and carried out with a thoughtful and shrewd plan.[8]

Larger convent schools established where ecclesiastics resided—first in Campeche, Merida, and Mani—recruited the sons of the Maya nobility of the surrounding region to reside in their schools as boarders. Molina Solís further claims that even the smaller towns, the *pueblos de visita*, had day schools equipped, among other things, with a Maya instructor or *maestro*.[9] In the colonial schools, the youth of the Maya nobility were taught to read and write in the Roman alphabet and also instructed in the Christian doctrine.[10]

Some of the Maya trained in the schools left to become maestros in the towns, charged with the responsibility of instructing the youth in the Catholic doctrine and even of serving as surrogate priests in the frequent absence of the ecclesiastic.[11] Indeed, scattered throughout the late sixteenth-century reports of *encomenderos* given in response to Philip II's questionnaire, and known as the *Relaciones Geográficas*, is the general phrase, "In this town there is a school for young boys where they are taught to read and write and who have their maestro."[12] Furthermore, documents from the early Franciscans and ecclesiastics testify to their reliance on these native assistants, whose responsibilities could include baptizing the sick and dying infants, hearing confessions of those in their last extremity, delivering sermons and conducting church business on Sundays, and the general policing of the community's spiritual nature.[13] The maestros served as intermediaries and "go betweens" among the foreign religious/colonial hierarchy and the native town. These trained maestros also assisted ecclesiastics in composing religious texts in Maya such as catechisms, sermons, and doctrinal treatises.[14] Perhaps the most famous example is Gaspar Antonio Chi, who in a *probanza de mérito* (proof of merit) sent to the king of Spain stated:

> [I have] performed great services for God and Your Majesty in order to bring about the conversion of the natives of this province . . . and, as requested by the said friars, translated and wrote sermons in the Indians' language in order to preach to them.[15]

Prior to the arrival of the Spanish, the Maya nobility maintained the spiritual and physical well-being of their cahob through various positions, including that of the *ah kin* (traditional Maya priest) and *ah dzib cah* (town scribe). Many of the nobility saw opportunity in the new colonial structure to maintain these positions of religious and intellectual authority, oftentimes as maestros and *escribanos* (scribes) respectively in the local town council, or *cabildo*. In the eighteenth century, ecclesiastical officials would even complain that many towns had too many native officers, stipulating that there should be only two instructors of the doctrine and both over the age of fifty.[16] Regarding the escribano, the Maya endowed the position with a rank equal to that of the local native leader, or *batab*. Interestingly, this deviated from Spanish practice where the escribano held the lowest position in the cabildo hierarchy and thus illustrates the important position of the literate Maya in their communities. Once trained in literacy, the nobility of each town continued to monopolize the positions of maestro and escribano—the only two cabildo positions that required a knowledge of writing—teaching the necessary skills to hand-picked successors.[17]

Despite their training in and close connection to a Spanish worldview, maestros and escribanos were not simple partisans. Some became diligent followers and enforcers of the Faith, others rebelled against it, and still others (perhaps the majority) strove to negotiate between the old and the new. As one scholar states, "The Franciscans had formed a Maya youth, but they did not consider that the environment to which they returned had not changed."[18] Put another way, upon returning to the Maya town, the trained Maya reentered a life vastly different from the one experienced in the friars' boarding schools, and this often required negotiating the old with the new. Armed with the tools of both literacy and a general autonomy from direct ecclesiastic supervision, both maestros and escribanos would play a large role in determining the written record and religious experience of many native towns, particularly those lacking a resident ecclesiastic.[19]

Overall, the schools instructed the next generation of Maya rulers in the doctrine and details associated with a Spanish/Catholic colonial world. The Maya students learned how to compose bills of sale, testaments, and even religious texts. They became versed on how to maintain reports, keep financial records, and create petitions. Moreover, they had access to European texts—the extent of which depended on the size of the church's and ecclesiastics' personal libraries. Perhaps most importantly, these schools endowed the Maya with the tools to negotiate a world filled with new actors, rules, and religious beliefs. And these tools helped construct a Maya Christian worldview evinced in the documents, both religious and mundane, that they would produce.[20]

Elsewhere I have grouped native-language religious texts into three general categories.[21] Category 1 texts are printed texts composed by either ecclesiastics, native aides, or both and intended for a readership of ecclesiastics and natives alike. To ensure their orthodoxy, such texts underwent strict review and a process of licensing that required the approval of various ecclesiastical and civic authorities.[22] Category 2 texts concern handwritten texts authored by ecclesiastics, native aides, or both and designed for the use and local readership of primarily ecclesiastics and at times natives. Category 3 regards texts written largely by natives for natives. Although it is possible that some ecclesiastics, certainly those of a more lenient nature, were aware of such texts or even assisted in their composition at some stage, they were not the intended users or audience, nor did they play a role in the texts' preservation, recopying, and iteration. Because of the strict editorial scrutiny of printed texts in Category 1 and the involvement of ecclesiastics as either authors or audience for Category 2 texts, the literary products of these categories generally contained little or no unorthodox content. However, the general autonomous nature of Category 3 texts afforded them greater opportunity to deviate from the standard messages as a product of either cultural adaptations, personal/local preferences, or both.[23]

Ecclesiastical authorities, however, were not naïve to this, and they took steps to try and regulate the content and quality of religious texts. Indeed, they were aware of the potential errors and alterations that could arise from allowing native assistants too much autonomy in translating and composing religious texts. Thus, the initial leniency granted toward native involvement in the translation and composition of Christian texts ended. The First and Second Mexican Provincial Councils of 1555 and 1565 respectively both restricted severely the natives' involvement in the translation process and even their possession of native-language Christian texts. Indeed, the First Council stated:

> We have found grave mistakes that continue in the native language sermons, as from not understanding them and from the errors and mistakes they (the natives) make when they translate them. Therefore, we state and order that from now on no sermons be given to the Indians to translate, neither to have in their possession, and those that have them are to be taken away. And when some good documents or sermons have to be given to them, let them be such that their (the natives') capacity can comprehend and understand, and carry the signatures of the religious or minister who gave it to them, so that they (the natives) cannot falsify nor corrupt them.[24]

Generally speaking, natives were not to translate or possess any handwritten religious text without direct authorization from an ecclesiastic, and they were not to create their own religious texts.

Reflecting this concern of natives writing autonomously and possessing religious texts is a 1570s Inquisition questionnaire regarding, among other things, whether or not to prohibit the natives' possession of translated texts. The questionnaire was given to a few select ecclesiastics chosen for their lan-

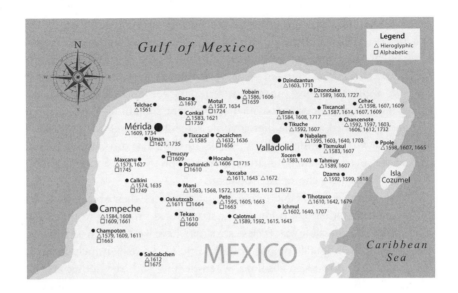

MAP 0.1. Hieroglyphic and Alphabetic Maya Texts Confiscated, 1560–1750 (after Chuchiak 2004)

guage abilities. Regarding the possession of religious texts, fray Domingo de la Anunciación responded by saying, "handwritten [books] should be totally prohibited from them because we have experience that all of the native-authored handwritten books have a thousand errors both in the writing and in the material they relate." However, ecclesiastics were more trusting of Category 1 printed texts, and Anunciacíon states that certain ones, such as Molina's confessional manuals and his own large and small *doctrinas* (cate-chisms), could "confidently" be left among natives.[25] In a word, natives were not officially authorized to compose and maintain autonomously their own Christian texts, those of Category 3, because, as William Hanks argues for the Chilam Balams, they were written "*outside* the spheres of governance and mission."[26]

But this does not mean that such texts ceased to exist. In reality, Yucatan and its evangelization depended heavily on native-authored and handwritten manuscripts—an understandable trait when considering that, unlike Mexico City, a printing press would not be available until 1813.[27] Religious authori-ties reported confiscating a wide variety of unauthorized texts ranging from hieroglyphic codices to Maya-authored religious texts of a Category 3 nature (see Map 0.1). Late sixteenth-century Inquisition reports from Yucatan in-dicate that translated religious texts were found "in the possession of some

Indians who know how to read."[28] Diego López de Cogolludo and Pedro Sánchez de Aguilar both recount instances where Maya-authored *cartapacios* (copybooks) were confiscated from the Maya. And fray Diego de Landa mentioned that he had collected various handwritten sermons in Maya whose contents displeased him.[29] The same occurred in the highlands of Guatemala, where the K'iche' Codex—a colonial manuscript containing three calendar sequences modeled after the hieroglyphic screenfold books of the Maya—was penned. Commenting on the author of the Codex, Pedro Cortés y Lárraz, who served as archbishop of Guatemala from 1766 to 1779, stated, "I am informed that he was a choirmaster (maestro)."[30]

Such texts are invaluable to modern scholars for their ability to reveal a Maya interpretation of a colonial Christian world. In regard to the Teabo Manuscript, it is possible that ecclesiastics may have worked alongside native aides during the original composition of some of the texts it includes (it is always difficult to speak in absolutes when dealing with the unofficial). Yet the natives ultimately owned the texts' preservation, emendation, and iteration throughout the years with an eye toward a local native audience. It was they who determined decade after decade what the manuscript would contain, what to record, or, better, what aspects of Christianity they deemed important enough to preserve and incorporate. Thus, I agree with Hanks when stating that the function of the writers or copyists of such unofficial texts which lay beyond the supervised sphere of *reducción* "was authorlike insofar as they chose the themes, words, and sentiments expressed."[31] Today, such Category 3 texts are limited in number, but to this corpus the Teabo Manuscript adds one more.

Maya Texts, Ethnohistory, and Purposes of This Book

Having established that the Maya composed a wide variety of colonial texts, including those religious, we now return to the question we began with: "What did they write about?" Beginning in the 1830s and 1840s and proceeding into the early twentieth century, various scholars including Charles Étienne Brasseur de Bourbourg, Carl Hermann Berendt, Crescencio Carillo y Ancona, and William Gates strove to answer such a question by collecting, transcribing, and translating a variety of Maya writings. Particularly prolific, Ralph Roys produced transcriptions and translations of myriad colonial Maya texts that enabled him to author numerous articles and books between 1920 and 1965. His transcriptions and translations of colonial Maya documents ranging from medicinal and botanical treatises to mundane land sales are still employed by scholars today.[32]

Anthropologists such as Munro S. Edmonson and Victoria Bricker at Tulane took up the torch and employed "the [Maya's] literary documents of the sixteenth century and later" as a "primary window open on the America of aboriginal times."[33] The Books of Chilam Balam attracted the most attention during this time—particularly in the 1980s.[34] Although such studies furthered the use of colonial Maya texts, the texts were largely used, as Edmonson's quote at the beginning of the chapter illustrates, as a source of information on the precolonial past, with the colonial era receiving secondary attention. Emphasis was placed on Maya science, medicine, and calendrics. Linguistic and anthropological studies dominated this era, and pioneering breakthroughs occurred in our understanding of colonial Yucatec Maya as a language and writing system and its relationship to the past and present generations.[35] Yet a social history of the colonial Maya obtained primarily from their sources had yet to be achieved.

To be sure, the colonial period won attention from scholars throughout the 1970s and 1980s, resulting in a variety of seminal works on Maya colonial society such as Robert Patch's 1979 dissertation that would later become his 1993 *Maya and Spaniard in Yucatan, 1648–1812*, Nancy Farriss's *Maya Society under Colonial Rule* (1984), and Grant Jones's *Maya Resistance to Spanish Rule* (1989). Yet the focus largely remained on Spanish sources. An important analytical re-creation of colonial Maya culture through their colonial texts appeared with the 1978 dissertation of a Bricker student, Philip C. Thompson. His study utilized a large corpus of Maya testaments and bills of sale originating from the eighteenth-century town of Tekanto to produce a documentary ethnography of the town and its people. Thompson used the sources to uncover inheritance patterns, kinship terminology, and class structure and its relationship to political office.[36]

Thompson's study was seminal in another way: it cast a brighter spotlight on the importance and utility of mundane Maya texts. Certainly scholars knew of their existence—Roys made this clear with his 1939 *Titles of Ebtun*. Yet, generally speaking, they were overshadowed by more monumental, seemingly more interesting works such as the Chilam Balams or the Ritual of the Bacabs. Like Thompson, Matthew Restall exploited the benefits of mundane documentation in his 1992 dissertation "The World of the Cah," later to become *The Maya World* (1997). Whereas Thompson examined Tekanto, Restall expanded his scope to employ a wide variety of documentation from various regions throughout Yucatan to expose the centrality of the

Maya's sociopolitical unit, the cah, in the lives of the colonial Maya. It represents the first social history employing native-language sources to encompass the colonial Yucatec Maya as a whole, or as James Lockhart would put it, to "see the general within the particular."[37]

Twenty-first-century studies utilizing Maya documents involve a wide range of documentation from Chilam Balam texts to testaments, and although the precolonial Maya still receive attention, particularly from anthropologists, the colonial Maya increasingly appear. For example, Victoria Bricker and Helga-Maria Miram's important study on the Chilam Balam of Kaua (2002) and Laura Caso Barrera's work on the Chilam Balam of Ixil (2011), while detailing colonial connections to the precolonial past, also explore a colonial world in which Spanish systems had significantly influenced Maya culture.[38] Along with the continued ethnohistorical works of Restall, John Chuchiak has also made good use of both Spanish and Maya texts to produce an impressive collection of articles and book chapters detailing the contributions of the Maya in colonial society.[39] Moreover, the increase of known and accessible Maya texts has allowed for comparisons among the texts themselves; the works of Timothy Knowlton (2008, 2010) and myself (2013, 2014), among others, both fall into this category. Finally, in 2010 Hanks produced his seminal *Converting Words*, which examines the formation and spread of a *Maya reducido* or Christianized Maya. Connections with his work in general are made here throughout, but, significantly, his chapter examining the Chilam Balams "reverses a long scholarly tradition in which these works are read for their pre-Columbian content, not for their value as an index of colonial transformation."[40]

It is in this general vein of thought that I place this book. Although precolonial connections are noted, this book concentrates more on what the Teabo Manuscript can tell us about the colonial Maya, their writing, and their religious worldview. To achieve this, I have divided the translation of the manuscript into chapters with substantial introductions. Traditionally, studies on colonial Maya codices contain a single lengthy introduction followed by the entire translation, albeit with extensive footnotes. However, in the case of the Teabo Manuscript, dividing the translation into specific sections with separate introductions followed by a translation of the Maya text, as will be done here, reveals better the contributions and insights the manuscript has to offer on the colonial Maya. In addition, while I employ philological analyses on occasion to reveal specific insights, particularly in the notes, this book's overall focus is more historical than linguistic and thus, in general, I leave a thorough linguistic study to future works whose scope include such.

The following chapters explore the Teabo Manuscript and its connections with other Maya and European texts that served as archetypes in the hope of achieving two broad purposes. The first concerns the exposure and recognition of the existence of Maya Christian copybooks, their cognate texts,[41] and the valuable and uncommon insight they provide into the Maya Christian worldview the colonial Maya chose to record and preserve. As mentioned, many extant studies on Maya texts concern the Books of Chilam Balam.[42] To be sure, these works are important, but they should not eclipse the other significant works the Maya composed in their communities. The comparative examination of the Teabo Manuscript with other Maya-authored works provides new insights into colonial text production and the shared yet distinct experience the colonial Maya had with Catholicism while further exposing the role of the Maya, particularly the authors and copyists of such works, in determining what that experience entailed.

The second purpose regards exposing in new ways the impact and influence of European texts on those the Maya composed. Bricker and Miram truly illustrated the potential for this type of work with their examination of the Kaua (2002). Certainly, the fascination of religious texts in native languages can limit studies to the boundaries of New Spain to overlook European antecedents.[43] Moreover, the exact European texts employed often remain nebulous, although cultural, philological, and orthographic clues indicate their influential presence.[44] None of the Maya texts of the Teabo Manuscript occurred in an intellectual vacuum, and all received inspiration, either direct or indirect, from both Maya and European cultural and textual antecedents. As such, the genealogies of many of the texts included in the Teabo Manuscript expose with greater clarity the need to examine New World texts in light of their Old World originals. Only then can we truly begin to appreciate how the Maya made Christianity their own and the rich history, context, and cultural adaptation contained within native-language texts.[45]

The chapters follow the thematic sections of the manuscript and further develop various concepts introduced here.[46] Chapter 1 concerns a redaction of Genesis and the creation of the world, and partial cognate texts can be found in the Chilam Balams of Kaua, Chan Kan, and the Morley Manuscript. In fact, the Teabo Manuscript offers the most complete translation of this redaction, and the four separate accounts allow for an uncommon opportunity for comparative analyses. The chapter also employs this commentary on Genesis to examine its presence in various works and to discuss further colonial text production and text sharing and iteration among Maya texts. Although scholars have recognized the trend among the Books of Chilam Balam, little or nothing exists discussing text sharing outside those famous texts. Here, the chapter engages Hanks's work (2010) on the creation and dissemination of a Maya reducido to add further insight. Finally, the chapter exposes the important role the Creation played in evangelization and the various influences European texts and worldview had on the Maya account.

Chapter 2 addresses the manuscript's subsequent Christocentric material that includes a genealogy of Jesus Christ taken from Matthew 1 in the Bible and an apocalyptic discourse inspired by the parable of the sheep and goats found in Matthew 25. In regard to the latter, the Tusik and, to a lesser degree, Chumayel contain similar texts, thus further exposing the presence of text sharing among Maya documents. Chapter 3 continues the apocalyptic theme with the translation of a popular European text: *The Fifteen Signs before Doomsday*. Gretchen Whalen's work on the Morley Manuscript provides an important yet preliminary discussion of the signs, stating that they were similar to those in the Tusik. Moreover, she reported not having seen the signs in Nahuatl texts. Fortunately, I succeeded in finding the signs in various Nahuatl texts, and this chapter provides an extensive analysis of the signs as they appear in Maya, Nahuatl, and European works that allows for new insights on the adoption of Christian eschatology into native cultures and text sharing.

Chapter 4 examines the next section of the Teabo Manuscript, which contains a supplication to both Mary and Christ for their mercy and divine aid. This chapter also discusses what appears to be a Maya discourse on indulgences and places it in the historical context of colonial Yucatan and New Spain, where such bulls experienced great popularity. Finally, Chapter 5 examines the various annotations and entries appended during the twentieth century that appear throughout the manuscript. This includes a death record and various medicinal remedies for common ailments. The chapter provides an analysis of both death and medicinal record keeping among the Maya to better understand the contributions of the Teabo Manuscript in this regard. Moreover, the entries themselves provide additional insight on the paradoxical individual- and cah-specific nature of these copybooks and their maintenance over the years.

A Chilam Balam or a Maya Christian Copybook?

Among its other contributions, this book calls attention to a category of Maya manuscripts I term the "Maya Christian copybook." Most cah-preserved manuscripts containing various religious or historical entries have fallen into the nebulous category of Chilam Balam texts. Scholars differ in their qualifications of what makes a text a "Chilam Balam." Originally, the term applied to colonial Maya manuscripts that contained the prophecy of a Maya prophet, or *chilam*, with the surname Balam who lived during the eve of the Spanish arrival, an event he reportedly prophesied. Certain works, such as the Chilam Balams of Tizimin and Chumayel, contain the prophecies of the prophet. Yet over the years, the term became applied to most of the town-preserved codices scholars discovered, regardless of whether or not they contained the prophecy of Chilam Balam.[47] As a result, the majority of manuscripts granted the name "Chilam Balam" make no mention of the prophet whatsoever.

The Teabo Manuscript itself provides an apt example of the tendency to award the Chilam Balam label to such codices. Although Teabo produced the Chilam Balam of Na[48] and perhaps even the Tekax, which, in another example of text sharing, served as a model for the Na,[49] rumors have long existed of Teabo having produced other unknown Chilam Balams. In the 1920s, Jean Genet and Pierre Chelbatz described a Chilam Balam for Teabo of twenty pages that contained historical accounts and whose location is unknown.[50] In their 1948 work examining the Chilam Balams, Alfredo Barrera Vásquez and Silvia Rendón indicated that rumors existed regarding the possible existence of lost Chilam Balams of Teabo, Peto, Nabula, Tihosuco, Tixkokob, Hocaba, and Oxkutzcab.[51] Moreover, at one point Munro Edmonson commented that while examining the Gates material—from whence came the Teabo Manuscript—he had come across several Chilam Balam texts from Teabo.[52] Although it is uncertain what specific texts these scholars were referring to when making such claims, it is likely, particularly in the case of Edmonson, that the Teabo Manuscript was initially referred to as a Chilam Balam.

So what, then, are the Books of Chilam Balam? Simply put, they are manuscript compilations of various topics deemed important enough by their authors, likely including maestros, and cah to record in writing. In a way, these books are bound portions of a larger archive of material—indigenous, European, or both—available to the Maya authors and/or cah.[53] This, then, allows for a cah to have multiple copies of any given text circulating in various manuscripts. Due to the central nature of the cah in producing these texts, most Chilam Balams carry the name of the town in which they were found (see Map 0.2). Because the Maya rewrote and amended the manuscripts multiple times throughout the colonial period, the versions available to scholars today are commonly late eighteenth- to nineteenth-century issues of early colonial originals.[54]

The content of the Chilam Balams vary from text to text and can include anything from town histories to calendrics, medicinal remedies, or doctrinal tracts.[55] Many Chilam Balams derived their content from similar sources, allowing, for example, the Teabo and Morley Manuscript and the Chilam

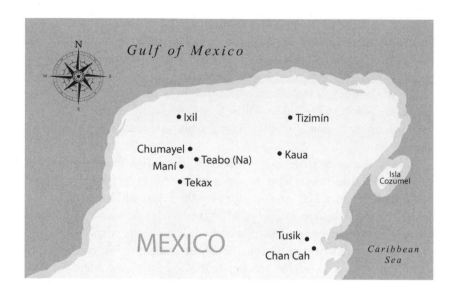

MAP 0.2. Towns Where Extant Books of Chilam Balam Were Found (after Hanks 2010)

Balams of Kaua and Chan Kan to all share cognate passages on the creation of the world.[56] Because ecclesiastical officials technically forbade natives from possessing and creating their own religious texts, these manuscripts remained hidden from questioning eyes, and only nine are known to scholars today.[57]

Yet not all texts compiled and preserved by Maya towns can or should be classified as Chilam Balams.[58] In recent years, scholars have increasingly recognized the existence of handwritten religious manuscripts that contained compilations of selected religious texts deriving from Christianity. Maya trained in writing and the Christian religion in the schools compiled these religious copybooks that were subsequently rewritten and amended over the course of the colonial period. Interestingly, some of the material in such works also appears in Chilam Balam texts. Perhaps the most well-known religious copybook is the Morley Manuscript initially examined by Gretchen Whalen.[59] Timothy Knowlton describes the work as "sort of a 'missing link' between the Books of the Chilam Balam and Christian doctrinal works produced by the Franciscans."[60] Due to their importance and maintenance by local Maya within the cah, the copybooks occasionally contain annotations in the final pages or the margins of the book detailing death records and, at times, a few medicinal remedies. Just as someone might record the baptismal date or death of a loved one in the first or last pages of their Bible, so too did the Maya utilize these texts for such purposes.

Although it is tempting to define these Maya-authored religious copybooks as Chilam Balams, particularly when considering their various cognate passages with existing Chilam Balam texts, it would not tell us much about them due to the wide variety of texts the Chilam Balam category encompasses. Moreover, although the compilers of Maya Christian copybooks were surely aware of the Chilam Balam manuscripts, they chose to select and include in their works only texts of a religious nature, thus differentiating them from Chilam Balam texts.

And there are other manuscripts besides that of the Morley and Teabo which likewise testify to a genre of Maya Christian copybooks distinct from Chilam Balams (see Table 0.1). The Garrett-Gates Mesoamerican Manuscripts Collection at Princeton University (GGMM) contains several examples, all of which date from the eighteenth to nineteenth centuries. Two are Maya books containing various prayers and texts; one—no. 71—is from Teabo, the other—no. 72—has death records from Tekom and makes references to Chichimila. The latter contains a section with instructions written in a Maya hand on how to help someone in the last extremity. The Maya reader is instructed to immediately call for a priest authorized to confess, and that if it were an emergency he should read the prayers included in the text.[61] Although escribanos likewise contributed to the creation and preservation of such copybook texts, the instructions appear to be for a Maya maestro charged with such duties. In fact, in his instructions to ecclesiastics, the sixteenth-century bishop of Yucatan, fray Francisco de Toral, outlined the role of maestros, who he calls in Maya *ah cambeçah* (he who teaches), in helping other Mayas to die well. Due to their importance in this regard, he stated, "And the ah cambeçah and others who likewise help [the sick] to die well are highly valued before our lord God."[62] This role for maestros continued throughout the colonial period.[63]

Another example, but from an unknown town, is a likely eighteenth-century copybook (GGMM no. 65, hereafter referred to as "Maya Sermons") of seventy-two folios containing a variety of Christian texts that includes a "libro de matrimonio de predicasiones de pariende" and portions of the *Flos sanctorum*, a popular hagiography in Spain. One of the texts is a Maya version of the *The Fifteen Signs before Doomsday*. Interestingly, similar passages of this text can also be found in the Teabo and Morley Manuscripts and the Chilam Balam of Tusik. Also fascinating, pages five through eighteen of this manuscript of more than 140 pages correspond very closely with the first

Table 0.1. Examples of Maya Christian Copybooks

Manuscript	Origin	Religious Texts	Death Records	Author
Teabo Manuscript	Teabo	Genesis Commentary, Fifteen Signs, other	Yes	Unknown
Morley Manuscript	Unknown	Genesis Commentary, Fifteen Signs, other	No	Unknown
"Maya Sermons," GGMM no. 65	Unknown	Exempla, Fifteen Signs, other	No	Unknown
"Passion Text," GGMM no. 66	Teabo	Passion, discursos sobre la missa, indulgence	Yes	Baltasar Mutul
GGMM no. 70a	Teabo	Arte de bien morir,	Yes	Unknown
GGMM no. 71	Teabo	Various prayers, other	Yes	Unknown
GGMM no. 72	Tekom (Chichimila?)	Various prayers, other	Yes	Unknown
Harvard Manuscript	Unknown	Passion	No	Unknown

twenty-three pages of the Tusik that recount the moralistic tales of "A Soldier," "St. Julian," "Coronado," "Pilate," and "St. Paul," as well as *The Fifteen Signs* and a subsequent discussion of the Final Judgment. The Maya stories and eschatological discussion derived from hagiographies and texts popular throughout the Middle Ages such as Jacobus de Voragine's *The Golden Legend* (ca. 1260)—with the *Flos sanctorum* being the Spanish version—and the Bible.[64]

An additional Maya Christian copybook from Teabo is a manuscript that consists of a Maya redaction of the Passion (GGMM no. 66, hereafter "Passion Text"), followed by instructions for the Mass that has cognate texts in the Kaua and Chan Kan.[65] Still another small manuscript text from Teabo is a leather-bound Maya translation of the seventeenth-century *Ramillete de divinas flores* (Bouquet of Divine Flowers) (GGMM no. 70a), which is an *Arte de bien morir* by don Bernardo Sierra that apparently experienced some popularity among the Maya.[66] The final pages contain death records from mid to late nineteenth-century Teabo, and some, including one from 1882, contain the name and signature of Secundino Na—most definitely the same person as José Secundino Na, who with his father, José María Na, helped compose the Chilam Balam of Na from Teabo, and who was an active author in that town until his death on May 15, 1885.[67] Indeed, the rubrics are an exact match. One final example is a manuscript of unknown provenance of which various images were found among the Mayanist Ian Graham's papers at the Peabody Museum in Harvard.[68]

As mentioned, many of these manuscripts have cognate texts with various Books of Chilam Balam. But do they belong under the same category? In discussing the matter with David Bolles, he commented,

> There really should be a separate classification for this sort of literature because little or none of it is based on Pre-Columbian thought, which is what I think the term "Book of Chilam Balam" should be applied to . . . Naming everything that is written in the Yucatecan Mayan language as "The Book of Chilam Balam of . . ." doesn't tell us much about the work anymore because it is used to name a wide variety of books with not all the same subject matter.[69]

Thus, I have classified such manuscripts as the Teabo, Morley, and those mentioned above as "Maya Christian copybooks." Of course, I realize that such classifications and distinctions were not employed by the colonial Maya in such a way and that they are for the main convenience of modern researchers who, like myself, have an insatiable need to categorize everything. The content matter of both Chilam Balams and Maya Christian copybooks appeared equally important to the Maya and oftentimes flowed freely between one genre of texts to the other. Yet the fact remains that Maya manuscripts containing purely Christian content exist today, and for the sake of convenience, I have chosen to classify them as Maya Christian copybooks.

These copybooks provide valuable information on colonial text production, culture, and religion. Their compilers, preservers, and audience were certainly Maya, thus making them Category 3 texts. However, it cannot be said for certain that local ecclesiastics were not aware of their existence. Hanks recently challenged the idea that Chilam Balam texts were kept "hidden" from priests.[70] Regarding Maya Christian copybooks, I would offer the possibility that such texts were kept hidden from "certain" priests, but perhaps allowed to be seen by those more lenient.[71] Regardless, because they were technically forbidden and maintained by local Maya within their communities, these copybooks provide an uncommon insight into the aspects of Christianity that the Maya deemed important enough to record. With rare exception, these copybooks have gone largely unstudied and represent a significant gap in the historiography concerning Maya evangelization, religion, and text production in the colonial period.[72] This book endeavors to begin to fill that gap.

General Observations about the Teabo Manuscript

The surviving corpus of Maya texts, particularly Maya Christian copybooks, points to Teabo as an active producer of colonial manuscripts (see Table 0.2). The town resides in the Tutul Xiu territory and was a visita town of Mani in 1582, eventually becoming a *cabecera de doctrina*, the principal town of a district, by 1610.[73] By 1617 the Franciscans established a modest church for native worship and later in the seventeenth century completed the convent church of San Pedro y San Pablo, which housed eight resident friars in 1808 and stands today, albeit with a fairly recent coat of red paint.[74] Teabo was the

Table 0.2. Known Maya Texts from Teabo

Manuscript	Date	Location
Teabo Manuscript	19th–20th Century	LTPSC, MSS 279, box 74, folder 3
Tekax?	19th Century	Copies in LTPSC, MSS 279, box 24, folder 4
Na	19th Century	Tozzer Library, Harvard
Cuaderno de Teabo	Copy by Berendt, 1868	Berendt-Brinton Linguistic Collection, no. 49, pp. 93–96.
"Passion Text"	19th Century	GGMM no. 66
Arte de bien morir	18th–19th Century	GGMM no. 70a
"Yucatec prayers"	19th Century	GGMM no. 71

residence of the eighteenth-century ecclesiastic fray Pedro Beltrán de Santa Rosa María, who himself was involved in producing Maya works, including a doctrina and a novena in 1740 and a Maya grammar in 1746.

Although larger sites such as Merida, Campeche, and Izamal boasted more resident priests, the ecclesiastic presence in 1808 of Teabo's convent appears comparable for the time with towns such as Mani, Conkal, Motul, Oxkutzcab, and others having a similar number of friars. Thus, it seems unlikely that the number of texts available today from Teabo was due to any additional ecclesiastical presence. Nor was it exceptional for its religious devotion. Indeed, as late as the 1790s fray José Perdomo, the Guardian or religious superior of the Franciscans in Teabo, imprisoned a native for idolatry.[75] And in the 1980s, a select population of Teabo—primarily the elderly—still continued its agricultural rites to precontact deities.[76] In the end, it is likely that Teabo produced similar quantities of texts to that of other cahob, but collectors, such as Gates, had the most luck in acquiring those from Teabo.

Regarding the Teabo Manuscript itself, the paper appears to be that of the eighteenth or early nineteenth century, but the orthography extends into the twentieth century. Moreover, a number of dates appear throughout the text from 1802 to 1925. Thus the manuscript has been copied and amended multiple times, the final occurrence being in the twentieth century, until somehow it fell into Gates's possession. Fortunately, the line "Teabo 8 de Enero de 1911" appears in the final pages of the manuscript to confirm its origin.

Concerning its author(s), many Maya Christian copybooks and Books of Chilam Balam lack an identifiable author. As Hanks states, "If by 'author' we designate the starting point in the production of a text—its source—then few of the major works have neatly defined authors. Rather, they are the product of recopying and reworking over long periods."[77] Some authors, like José Secundino Na and José María Na in the Na, openly took responsibility for their role. Others invented their sources out of whole cloth, or simply alluded to them. The Ixil provides examples of both. The book declares that its medicinal remedies were "given by a moor, by his own voice, Ruy Díaz de Vivar (El Cid)."[78] El Cid was a Spanish nobleman and the great military leader of medieval Spain and his published legend was popular, although prohibited, reading throughout New Spain. Here, the Maya of Ixil obviously knew of the legend and elected the Campeador as the source of the remedies while obscuring the true author. Moreover, inserted at the bottom of one of its pages is the line, "yo proveye junn yPolito Pech (rubric), (I supplied the paper/book, Hipólito Pech).[79] Although we cannot be certain as to the specific role of Hipólito, the insertion indicates the role of the Pech *chibal* (lin-

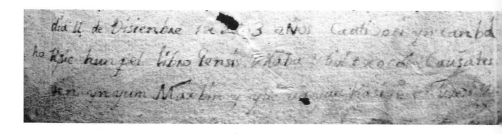

FIGURE 0.1. Entry of Unknown Author in the Teabo Manuscript

eage) in the book's composition. In the end, when no clear assertions are available, we are left to surmise the identity of the author(s). However, analyses of orthography, prose, and hand can be used to assist in making observations, and such is the case with the Teabo Manuscript.

The following appears at the end of the Teabo Manuscript's redaction of *The Fifteen Signs before Doomsday*:

> *dia 11 de Desienbre de 1803 años caa ti ɔoci yn canbal hoksic hunpel libro Gensis u kaba u tial txocol Ca u sates ten yn yum Max bin y ylic ua yan Kasite ten u . . .*[80]
>
> (The 11th of December 1803, when I finished learning to bring forth a book called Genesis in order for it to be read. That he forgives me, my lord who will see if there are errors, I the . . .)

An extremely similar phrase is also found in another Teabo text, the "Passion Text":

> *Teabo y Nobi 22 de 1803 años Ca ti ɔoci yn canbal hoksic hunpel Libro fasion u kaba u tial txocol Ca u sates ten yn yumob hemax bin ylic ua yan Kasite ten u ɔeɔil u Palilob Uay ti Cah Teabo lae Baltḥaseʳ Mutul* (rubric) *esno*
>
>> *Ten Baltasar Mutul tialtic libro fasion lae esno* (rubric)[81]
>
> (Teabo, November 22, 1803, when I finished learning to bring forth a book called Passion in order for it to be read. That they forgive me, my lords who will see if there are errors, I who am the least of their servants. Here in this cah of Teabo. Baltasar Mutul, notary [rubric]
>
>> I who am Baltasar Mutul possess this Passion book, notary [rubric])

The incomplete statement from the Teabo Manuscript lacks its author. Although the statement by Baltasar Mutul in the Passion Text is a near verbatim match to that in the Teabo Manuscript, the handwriting differs, suggesting a different author and the use of a common concluding statement (see figures 0.1 and 0.2). Given that the entry in the Teabo Manuscript appeared less than one month after that in the Passion Text, and that both originate from Teabo, it seems very plausible that Baltasar Mutul was aware of the Teabo Manuscript's compilation although his hand is difficult to locate in the manuscript itself. That said, changes in orthography, prose, and ink throughout the text suggest the hands of various contributors. Although inconsistencies in any given author's calligraphy and orthography make such analyses an inexact science, it appears that at least two Maya authors penned the doctrinal texts of the Teabo Manuscript. Moreover, the death record and the random medicinal remedies appear in different hands.

Thus, like other Maya Christian copybooks, the Teabo Manuscript had multiple contributors. That such copybooks were preserved by the cah and exchanged hands is also made clear by the "Passion Text." Although Baltasar

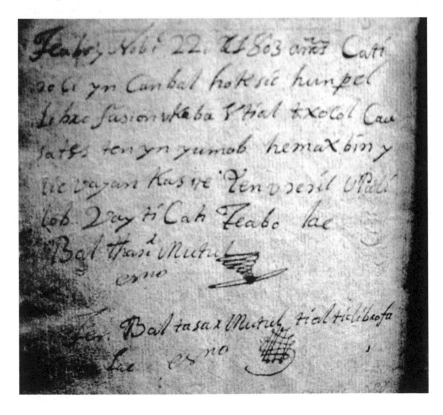

FIGURE 0.2. Entry of Baltasar Mutul in the Passion Text

Mutul was the self-proclaimed author and owner, death records amended in the final pages range throughout the late nineteenth century. Two entries recording the 1875 death of "Ma Bictoriana Na" (María Victoriana Na) and the 1882 death of Juan Pech were signed by Secundino Na, certainly the same person as the José Secundino Na who helped compose the Chilam Balam of Na from Teabo and who added some death records in the previously mentioned Maya translation of *Ramillete de divinas flores* also from Teabo.[82] It would seem likely that Mutul and his successor, Na, both composed and had access to a variety of Maya Christian copybooks in their town of Teabo.

In sum, the Teabo Manuscript was one of several Maya Christian copybooks extant today from Teabo. Two or more Maya authors likely compiled the work in the early nineteenth century from various existing sources, and it was then preserved and appended throughout the early twentieth century until it fell into the possession of Gates. The intention was seemingly to compile a work of Christian texts that the authors and/or the cah deemed important. The texts and topics worthy of preservation in the Teabo Manuscript are the subjects to which we now turn.

Creating the Creation

IT BEGINS, THE RENOWN, THE NEWS, THAT THE
WORLD WAS CREATED BY OUR LORD GOD, RULER;
ALL OTHER THINGS, HE CREATED THEM WELL IN SIX
DAYS, ALL WAS FINISHED AND WELL MADE;
AND HE MADE OUR FATHER, ADAM, AND OUR FIRST
MOTHER, EVE. —TEABO MANUSCRIPT[1]

THE REPORTS AND NEWS BEGIN WITH HOW THE
HEAVEN AND THE EARTH WERE CREATED BY GOD,
THE TRUE RULER, WHICH HE PERFECTED WITH THE
OTHER REMAINING THINGS WITHIN SIX DAYS,
UNTIL HE FINISHED PERFECTING EVERYTHING.
AND HE MADE OUR FIRST FATHER ADAM
AND OUR FIRST MOTHER EVE.
—CHILAM BALAM OF KAUA[2]

THE FOUNDATIONS OF THE AWARENESS OF EXIS-
TENCE: HEAVEN WAS CAUSED TO BE AND EARTH BY
GOD, THE RULER. THE MULTITUDE, IT WAS
COMPLETED, HE PERFECTED IT IN SEVEN DAYS.
EVERYTHING [THERE WAS], HE COMPLETED MAKING:
THE FIRST FATHER ADAM AND MOTHER EVE.
—CHILAM BALAM OF CHAN KAN[3]

ONE COMMON THREAD connects the myriad cultures of the world together no matter how different they may appear: the creation story. They are inscribed on stone walls, written on forms of paper, and spoken on the tongues of many different cultures. From the Romans to the Egyptians, the Norse to the Greeks, Christians to Buddhists, each group maintained stories of their origin. Why? The complicated answer to that question lies far beyond the scope of this chapter. But perhaps it is sufficient to say that creation myths slake our inherent thirst to understand our role and place in the world, where we came from, why we are here, and what happens next. In other words, we want to know the beginning, middle, and end of the plot, or as Aristotle would have it, the *mythos*, of life. However, creation myths go far beyond the satisfaction of curiosity. Indeed, creation myths define a culture's place and purpose in both the world and the overall cosmos. They explain and justify a culture's belief system and worldview while ultimately validating the existence of such in the presence of others.[4]

Both before and after the arrival of the Spaniards, the Maya maintained various versions of the creation of the world. Much of what we understand of these creation myths derives from colonial documents. Yet hieroglyphic writing from the precontact era, although terse, suggests a "larger body of cultural knowledge about creation events."[5] Moreover, as Knowlton aptly illustrates, such precontact writing and iconography informs our understanding of and gives additional meaning to the creation myths found in the Chilam Balams and those recorded by Spaniards.[6]

Like colonial documents, precontact recordings of the creation underscored sociopolitical, familial, religious, and local identity, thus preventing a single, monolithic Maya creation story. Commenting on hieroglyphic texts recounting the creation, David Stuart notes, "[W]e see that the Creation was very local in its flavor, with different kingdoms and cities claiming different supernatural origins, each a center of the cosmos in its own way."[7] Notwithstanding, creation myths across Mesoamerica do share general similarities. For example, many shared the concept of an evolving creation with cosmogonic ages or suns, each with different versions of human beings, preceding the current era that too will eventually end in disaster to produce a new era. Humans had the responsibility to maintain the order of these cosmos through rites and sacrifices, thus creating a symbiotic relationship between man and the divine.[8]

The *Popol Vuh*, a colonial manuscript relating a creation narrative in K'iche' Maya, illustrates many of these elements. In his translation of the manuscript, Allen Christenson states: "It is important to remember that the *Popol Vuh* was written by representatives of the Nima Quiché nobility and there was little attempt at objective 'history' in the modern sense. The authors' purpose in compiling this record is, at least in part, to bolster the legitimacy and traditions of their own lineages, often at the expense of their neighboring rivals."[9] Thus, like many Maya creation myths whether recorded on precontact stelae or eighteenth-century paper, the *Popol Vuh* is *a* Maya version of the creation as told by a specific lineage, not *the* Maya version—the importance of which is discussed later.[10]

In this version, the evolutionary efforts of the gods in creating humans is evident. Following various failed attempts, they succeeded in creating man from maize dough. The purpose of man was to care for the earth and provide for the gods and honor them. In return for their creation, the first men declared to the Framer and Shaper, "Truly we thank you doubly, triply that we were created, that we were given our mouths and our faces. . . . We thank you, therefore, that we were created, that we were given frame and shape."[11] At the request of the gods, this appreciation would take on the form of sacrifices for later generations. Yucatec Maya creation myths found in the Chilam Balams of Tizimin, Chumayel, and Códice Pérez share these concepts of destruction, renewed creation, and birth.[12]

In general, all Maya accounts serve the purpose of a creation myth: they legitimate and explain the role of man on the earth and in the cosmos. Perhaps the scribe of the Chilam Balam of Chumayel stated it best when declaring that these creation myths "are for the Maya people here when inquired if they know how they had been born and the founding of the world here in this peninsula."[13] The translation in this chapter provides an additional example of a Maya creation myth found in the first twenty-four pages of the Teabo Manuscript, one that contributes sections not found in other redactions of the commentary. Preceding the translation is a discussion on the role of the Creation story in evangelization, an account and comparison of the appearance of the Genesis Commentary throughout various Maya texts, and an analysis of the commentary as found in the Teabo Manuscript to reveal its various European and Maya elements.[14] In all, this chapter offers additional insights into the Maya-Christian colonial dialogue that created the Creation in Maya texts.

The Importance of Genesis in Evangelization

For Spanish ecclesiastics, and indeed all Christians today, the Creation is fundamental to explaining and validating the primary tenets of Christianity. According to the biblical account, God created the cosmos and the world in six creative periods, called "days." On the sixth day, God formed the first man,

Adam, and gave him dominion over the earth and its inhabitants. He placed Adam in a paradisaical garden in Eden wherein also were placed two specific trees: the Tree of Life and the Tree of Knowledge of Good and Evil, the latter of which Adam was commanded not to partake. Adam then begins the task of gathering and naming all creatures, but among these "none proved to be the suitable partner for the man."[15] Rectifying this, God formed a female companion for Adam from one of his ribs. Both Adam and Eve lived naked in the garden as they were in a state of innocence.

After a time, Lucifer, the serpent, beguiles Eve into eating the fruit of the Tree of Knowledge of Good and Evil. Subsequently, Eve brings the fruit to Adam, who also partakes. With knowledge having replaced their innocence, they recognize their nakedness and sew aprons from fig leaves and hide from God. When he discovers their transgression, God curses Lucifer, Eve, and Adam. To Eve God declares, "I will intensify the pangs of your childbearing; in pain shall you bring forth children. Yet your urge shall be for your husband, and he shall be your master."[16] For the sake of Adam, God curses the earth; "thorns and thistles shall it bring forth to you," and, after clothing them, God evicts Adam and Eve from Eden to toil in the world for their subsistence.[17] Following their eviction, Adam and Eve procreate, and the remaining pages of the Bible relate their posterity's successes when properly venerating and obeying God, and their failures when neglecting to do so.[18]

For neophytes in the Faith, the Creation introduces themes important to Catholicism. As the being who created the earth, its inhabitants, man, and the cosmos, God reigns supreme. No other deities are mentioned, thus enforcing monotheism and the almighty power of God.[19] Indeed, when speaking of the Creation and the power of God, the sixteenth-century fray Luis de Granada commented, "Who will not be humbled and prostrate and become a worm in the presence of such great majesty? Who will dare to offend such a powerful monarch and lord of heaven and earth?"[20]

Through "The Fall," or Lucifer's successful temptation of Eve, the Creation also introduces the opposing forces of good and evil. Here, the subtlety of the devil becomes evident, and his conquest over Eve allowed the Church to proscribe women as frail and morally abased. The Fall also introduces sin largely as a result of Lucifer's deceit—a concept useful to ecclesiastics when trying to invalidate native deities—and the subsequent need for a savior, Jesus Christ. Having established the fallen state of man and his reliance upon the grace and mercy of God and Christ, the Creation story allows ecclesiastics to further elucidate how mankind may earn such grace and mercy through various works as attending Mass, confession, living according to *policía cris-*

tiana, "Christian civility," and so on.[21] In many ways, the Creation story is the keystone in the arch that is Catholic doctrine.

Various native-language religious texts composed by early ecclesiastics bear evidence of the importance of the Creation in instructing the natives. In general, the Creation appears in these texts as either its own topic, or included in a discussion on the fourteen Articles of Faith, the fifth of which proclaims a belief in God as the maker of heaven and earth, or in the explanation of the Apostles' Creed, wherein the first statement likewise asserts a belief in God as creator of heaven and earth. Regarding texts in Nahuatl, in 1564 the Franciscan Bernardino de Sahagún produced his *Colloquios*, which re-created the conversations that allegedly took place between the first twelve Franciscans sent to evangelize the Nahuas in 1524 and the native nobles and priests.[22] In these, their initial efforts to explain the Catholic faith, the friars recount the Creation, including the creation of the angels and the heaven of God's abode, Empyrean.[23]

The Dominican Martín de León begins his 1611 Nahuatl *Camino del cielo* with the Creation to explain not only the omnipotence of God, but also his power over the devil and the latter's role in deceiving mankind.[24] A 1548 Nahuatl *Doctrina* commissioned by the Dominicans begins with a discussion on the Articles of Faith and, thus, a significant discussion of the Creation. The doctrina also contains a few sermons dedicated to the Creation.[25] And the 1759 Nahuatl *Promptuario* of Ignacio de Paredes places the explanation of the creation and purpose of mankind at the beginning of his voluminous work.[26]

Due to the dearth of religious texts printed in Yucatec Maya, fewer examples exist. In fact, the only text that truly addresses the topic is arguably the most renowned printed work in Maya: fray Juan Coronel's 1620 *Discursos predicables*.[27] The work is a collage of texts Coronel collected and edited to form his large volume. The Articles of Faith provide the structure for the first few sections, which contain a lengthy redaction of the Creation.[28] Yet this redaction largely adheres to the biblical account and, importantly, differs from that found in Category 3 Maya texts. What we see in Coronel is an ecclesiastic-endorsed, printed version of Genesis, although other nonofficial versions likewise circulated as evinced in the following manuscripts. Indeed, Coronel himself stated that he printed his work so that such teachings "do not run in handwritten copybooks where many lies are found."[29]

In all, both Maya and European cultures valued the importance of creation stories, with the latter employing them frequently in their didactic religious texts. We may safely assume, then, that the Creation was an important topic covered in the convent schools designed to train the indigenous noble youth. Ecclesiastics employed various European works, including the Bible, to convey the Creation.[30] As evinced by the Genesis Commentary in the Teabo Manuscript and others, the Maya then took this eclectic understanding of the Creation, adopted it to their culture, and made it their own again and again as they recopied and reinterpreted the story over the centuries.[31] Indeed, perhaps the Genesis Commentary in Maya texts, and all Maya Christian creation myths, are best seen as another link in the long chain of works attempting to make sense of Genesis along the lines of contemporary science, knowledge, and everyday life. Following in the footsteps of Augustine and Aquinas, the Maya contributors confronted and smoothed out potential conflicts between biblical and culturally contemporary understandings of the cosmos to create a Creation that best suited local needs.

The Genesis Commentary in Maya Texts and Text Sharing

As mentioned above, Category 3 Maya texts and their unofficial nature afford an uncommon insight into the worldview and beliefs of the colonial Maya.[32] Simply put, they illustrate which aspects of Christianity the Maya chose to record and preserve over the centuries of colonial rule. Because the Maya had a well-established tradition of creating and preserving creation myths long before the Spanish arrival, it is not surprising that their colonial writings continue this tradition.[33]

Of all the aspects of Christianity the Maya could have recorded, what appears most frequently are texts concerning the creation and end of the world—the latter will be discussed in chapter 2. Precontact Maya creation myths, the most common of subjects among hieroglyphic codices, emphasized period beginnings and endings, creation and re-creation, so this allure toward a Christian counterpart is understandable. Time and time again Mayas (and Nahuas) more readily adopted those aspects of Christianity—and the colonial world in general—that contained preexisting parallels. Regarding the matter, Matthew Restall and Amara Solari stated, "[T]here must have been some kind of comfort in finding links between their traditional worldviews and those being forced upon them by Catholic priests."[34] Thus, it is due in large part to precontact parallels that the Maya awarded the Genesis Commentary its popularity.

As found in Maya texts, the Genesis Commentary details the Creation along six days and gives the location in the heavens and earth of each creation according to a geocentric Ptolemaic model of the universe often found in Spanish almanacs or *reportorios de los tiempos*.[35] Although these Maya texts,

FIGURE 1.1. Spherical Model of the Universe

such as the Teabo Manuscript, date from the late eighteenth and nineteenth centuries (some with annotations made in the twentieth century), they still contain a geocentric model of the universe. Admittedly, the Catholic Church prohibited a heliocentric model due to its seeming conflict with the Bible, and works expressing such ideas—including those of Copernicus, Kepler, and Galileo—found themselves on the *Index Librorum Prohibitorum* until 1758 and beyond.[36] This, coupled with the lack of a university in the province, greatly limited the teaching of heliocentrism and the "new sciences" despite their general acceptance elsewhere. Regardless, the nineteenth- and twentieth-century Maya of Teabo appeared indifferent to, or perhaps uninformed of, such shifts in the scientific understanding of the cosmos and preserved the original geocentric model established centuries before. This, then, suggests an important characteristic of many Maya Christian copybooks: their authors seemed more concerned with the story and its preservation than whether or not it was doctrinally correct or scientifically up to date.

The Teabo Genesis Commentary has three self-designated parts where it proclaims "u pectzil ɔibanil" (the news that has been written). The first details the widely accepted European geocentric model with the earth representing the first of eleven heavens or spheres (see figures 1.1 and 1.2).[37] These spheres would then rotate to produce the movement of the stars and planets. The single exception to this was the highest heaven or sphere called Empyrean—the fiery and brilliant domain of God and his angels. The tenth sphere belongs to the second heaven, the Prime Mover, which the Teabo Manuscript accurately describes as "the first heaven that revolves."[38] Because the earth

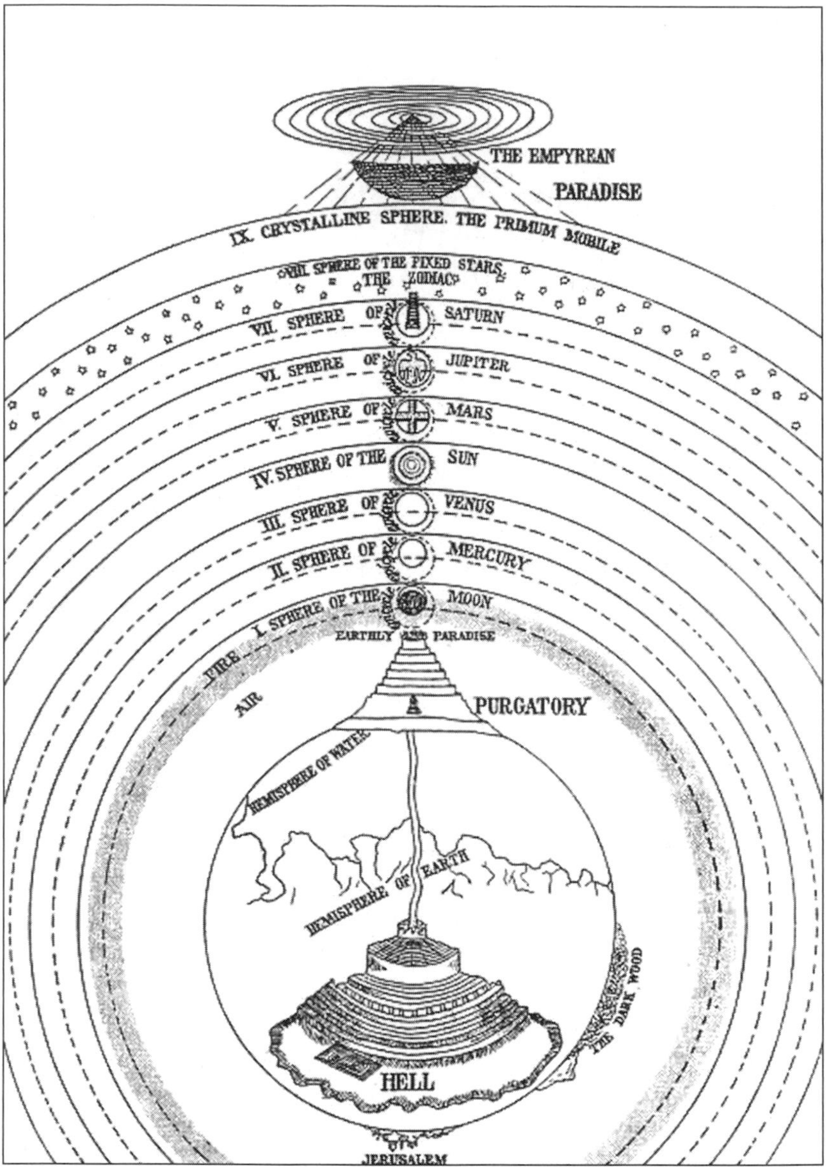
THE EMPYREAN
PARADISE
IX. CRYSTALLINE SPHERE. THE PRIMUM MOBILE
VIII. SPHERE OF THE FIXED STARS. THE ZODIAC
VII. SPHERE OF SATURN
VI. SPHERE OF JUPITER
V. SPHERE OF MARS
IV. SPHERE OF THE SUN
III. SPHERE OF VENUS
II. SPHERE OF MERCURY
I. SPHERE OF THE MOON
EARTHLY PARADISE
FIRE
AIR
PURGATORY
HEMISPHERE OF WATER
HEMISPHERE OF EARTH
THE DARK WOOD
HELL
JERUSALEM

FIGURE 1.2. Michelangelo Caetani's Diagram of Dante's Layered Cosmos

was thought to be stationary with the cosmos rotating around it, a moving force was needed to rotate the heavens. This, then, was the role of the Prime Mover and the single angel that rotated it daily as "he comes from the east and arrives in the west, one day in twenty-four hours."[39]

The ninth and eighth spheres are called Crystalline and Firmament respectively. Medieval and early modern interpretations of Genesis 1:6–9 and Psalm 148:4 that describe the "waters that be above the heavens" assigned such waters to the Crystalline layer. Yet here, the heavenly waters have been changed into solid matter to block the earth from the overwhelming resplendence and glory of Empyrean. The Firmament layer holds the stars, which are fixed and stationary. Below the Firmament are the planets, which according to the Maya manuscript "do not exist among the stars, as was said, because each one exists in a heaven."[40] The remainder of this first discourse concerns what God created on which day and where it was placed. For example, on the fourth day God created the stars and placed them in the eighth layer of heaven, Firmament. The second part of Teabo's Genesis Commentary expounds upon God's creative works on the earth, focusing specifically on Adam and the Garden of Eden, or earthly paradise, and the third part explains the creation and temptation of Eve, some details of which are discussed further below.

Certainly the Genesis Commentary was not the only creation myth in circulation during the colonial period. For example, as mentioned previously, another myth found in the Chumayel, Tizimin, and Códice Pérez tells of the destruction and subsequent re-creation of the world in Katun 11 Ahau. Here the main protagonists are the battling deity complexes Oxlahun Ti Ku and Bolon Ti Ku, with the former emerging as victors. After the battle, a flood destroys the world in order for it to be repopulated and, as is related in the Chumayel, eventually destroyed again by another flood to usher in the Second Coming of Jesus Christ and the earth's rebirth.[41] Although the myth is rife with connections to the cosmologies of the Postclassic Yucatec Maya, it also contains colonial influences from Christianity. Moreover, the Chumayel contains a passage Edmonson (1986) calls the "Birth of the Uinal" that represents a Maya creation narrative infused with Christian elements.[42] In the end, and similar to the precontact era, the Maya circulated various creation myths, adhering to those that best suited personal, local, and sociopolitical needs. Just as a homogenized Maya culture failed to exist, so too did a single creation myth either pre- or postcontact. For its part, the Genesis Commentary served as one of the myths circulated in the colonial period and beyond, and from the high number of texts within which it circulated, we can surmise it was popular. Not even the 1620 publication of Coronel's very different, yet "official," version of the Creation in his *Discursos* could supplant the commentary.

Text sharing was not uncommon among the Yucatec Maya, as is demonstrated by the Genesis Commentary, the Maya Christian copybooks mentioned in the previous chapter, and various other texts. A form of text sharing appears as early as the Classic period (c. AD 300 to 850), when particular glyphic spellings or phrasing disseminated among the Maya.[43] In 1567 various Maya rulers helped compose and sign nine letters to the king supporting the Franciscans after Diego de Landa's tortuous campaign in 1562. Although the Maya signatures represented some seventy-five different cahob, the majority of the letters are nearly identical. Moreover, the primordial titles—local histories designed to promote the sociopolitical interests of the cah and its dominant lineage—of two separate cahob, Chicxulub and Yaxkukul, contain many long, cognate passages.[44] In short, cognate discourses have a long and diverse history in Yucatan.

The cognate passages among the Chilam Balams have not gone unnoticed. Barrera Vásquez and Rendón (1974) examined the phenomenon and posited the existence of a single, original master text, derived from hieroglyphic books, from which all other Chilam Balams drew their native religious and historical content. As copies circulated among various towns and as others recopied and amended the work, the original text became corrupted and varied through scribal error. Others such as Gunsenheimer (2000/2001, 2006), Hanks (2010), and Knowlton (2010) complicated and further developed the discussion. Hanks suggests that "either many texts circulated independently or there was some other discourse, probably oral, that circulated and was absorbed into writing in different places where books were maintained."[45] Here, Hanks's thesis on reducción and its design to reform the social space, conduct, and language of the Maya can be useful in understanding commonalities among religious texts. Hanks exposes the importance of discourse production to that of reducción and the intention of doctrinal language to be iterative. Doctrinal words and phrases developed within the religious sphere of reducción circulated through repetition and spread to become common occurrences within a more general colonial worldview of belief and practice. Thus, similar phrases, glosses, and sentences found in the first grammars and dictionaries appeared throughout notarial documents and religious texts, both official and unofficial.[46] A similar comparison can be made with those religious texts likely produced in the sphere of reducción that later appeared among Chilam Balams and Maya Christian copybooks, as they too fall into a larger pattern of iteration that lay at the heart of both a precontact and colonial doctrinal discourse.

Table 1.1. Cognate Passages of the Genesis Commentary

	A	B	C	D	E	F	G	H
Teabo	1–5	—	5	—	5–8	8–11	11–22	23–24
Morley	178–85	—	185	—	185–89	—	194–213	—
Kaua	146–51	151–53	153	153–54	154–57	—	—	—
Chan Kan	26–33; 50–52*	52–55	55	55–56	56–61	—	—	—

Note: all page numbers refer to the manuscript text.
* In between the pages of the Chan Kan commentary is a discourse on planetary influences on the body and various medical tracts. The commentary then resumes.

Establishing a chronological sequence to the Chilam Balams and copybooks is also difficult due to the recopying of these texts, the process of which oftentimes included a more modern vernacular and orthography, and the lack of dates identifying the original composition. That said, comparison among cognate texts is not a fruitless exercise.[47] Indeed, the various cognate texts among colonial Maya texts are not verbatim copies but creative compositions that expound, paraphrase, and vary the narrative according to personal and local preferences.[48] Identifying and examining such instances among the texts better illustrates both the existence of common and popular Christian discourses and the ability to modify such discourses. Moreover, such an analysis reveals those aspects of Christianity certain towns/authors deemed sufficiently significant to expound upon, and those more suitable to paraphrase. This in turn exposes more clearly the evolution and devolution of specific concepts in an ever-evolving Maya-Christian worldview.

Regarding the Genesis Commentary, I have located portions of it in four colonial manuscripts: the Chilam Balams of Kaua, Chan Kan, the Morley Manuscript, and now the Teabo Manuscript. As illustrated in Table 1.1, the common Christian discourse of the Genesis Commentary appears in both similar and dissimilar ways throughout Maya texts. The moments of confluence and divergence among the texts are illustrated in the table with sections A through H. Examining the commentary through these sections better exposes trends and authorial preferences not seen otherwise. Generally speaking, and in regard to omissions and additions to the commentary, the Teabo and Morley Manuscripts largely parallel each other, with the Kaua and Chan Kan having more in common.

Section A is the longest span of text where a harmony exists between all four works. The section describes the first day of creation with an emphasis on the Empyrean, Prime Mover, and Firmament layers and a general description of the other bodies in the cosmos. A description of the second day of creation then begins focusing on the properties of the Crystalline layer. The text declares the veracity of the commentary up to this point, citing St. Augustine and astrologers who "manifest publicly and bring to light" this information.[49]

Immediately following, the Teabo and Morley Manuscripts break and start a new section, indicated by a drop cap or a series of dashes, while the Kaua and Chan Kan continue citing various authorities including St. Jerome and St. Augustine (section B in Table 1.1). The examples derived from these saints deviate from the Creation narrative and focus more on the difficulty of man in attaining reason and understanding. Included in this extended discourse is a subsection of sorts titled "discursus sagrada iscritura," or sermons on the Holy Scriptures.[50] The compilers of the Teabo and Morley Manuscripts seemingly were unaware of this extended discussion or deemed it too ancillary and omitted it altogether.

All four texts resume their harmony, however briefly, in section C. The creation of the Sun and Moon are mentioned along with the fall of Lucifer and his followers from heaven on a Monday. Here again the Kaua and Chan Kan include an extended narrative (section D) that explains how the followers of Lucifer entered into various plants and other natural phenomena to afflict man. All four texts then reunite (section E) to reiterate that "*Lunes* (Monday) is not a good day because it is the principal day Lucifer sinned and created evil and the rest of the bad angels fell behind him."[51]

Section E then continues to discuss the creative events that occurred on days three through six. As the biblical creation of the cosmos occurred over a six-day period, ending the Genesis Commentary after a discussion of the sixth day is logical, and indeed occurs in the Kaua and Chan Kan. However, the Teabo and Morley Manuscripts continue with a commentary focused more on the creation of mankind than the cosmos. With its focus on the creation of Adam, section F represents this continuation, but only for the Teabo Manuscript; Gretchen Whalen notes that the Morley Manuscript is missing three pages at this point, which no doubt contained parallel material.

Both manuscripts begin their harmony again in section G, which starts by announcing "the second part of the news that has been written where it has been taught and declared the creation of the body of our first father, Adam, by our lord God, and the way our first mother, Eve, was born."[52] This section is lengthy, as both manuscripts describe in detail the creation of Adam and Eve, the Garden of Eden, the Tree of Knowledge of Good and

Evil, and Lucifer's temptation and Eve's subsequent transgression of eating of that tree. Although there is a striking similarity between the two texts, the Teabo Manuscript occasionally shortens, condenses, or rearranges passages or series of events.[53] The harmony of section G ends abruptly as a result of missing pages from the Morley Manuscript. Yet the Teabo Manuscript continues (section H) a bit further to describe God's censure of Adam and Eve for their disobedience and their expulsion from the Garden to "[begin] the work of their penance until the final day of their lives here on earth. Amen Jesus."[54]

This analysis of Table 1.1 enables some interesting observations. Although the Genesis Commentary experienced obvious popularity among the Maya, it circulated in various tailored versions. When compared to those found in the Kaua and Chan Kan, the commentaries contained in the Teabo and Morley Manuscripts prefer a shorter discussion of the cosmos and a lengthier treatise on the creation and fall of mankind. Moreover, the section breaks found in the Teabo and Morley texts possess a striking similarity.

What are we to make of the similarities between the Teabo and Morley Manuscripts, between the Kaua and Chan Kan, and among all four in general? These cognate texts did not occur by chance, so how were they produced? My sense is that, as Hanks suggested regarding Maya reducido, such religious texts as the Genesis Commentary and others originated within the reducción and the schools used to train the Maya noble youth, perhaps even with some minor assistance from the friars. The trained Maya then brought these written and/or oral archetypes back to the cahob, where they were disseminated, recited, edited, and reworked over the centuries.

Colonial chroniclers and ecclesiastics also provide some clues as they documented how Maya maestros wrote and preserved creation myths perhaps similar to that found in the Genesis Commentary. Diego López de Cogolludo makes note of fray Juan Gutiérrez, who reportedly saw copybooks written in the Roman alphabet containing Maya creation myths.[55] Moreover, the priest Pedro Sánchez de Aguilar himself confiscated a copybook detailing the Creation from a maestro. He commented, "It would be very useful to have printed books in the language of these [Maya] about Genesis and the creation of the world because they have fables, or very harmful histories, and some of these *they have written, and they preserve them and read them in their meetings* (emphasis mine)."[56] That such meetings occurred is further confirmed by a separate request from Aguilar that "the Indians (Maya) do not hold meetings at night."[57]

Such statements offer the likely scenario in which Maya maestros and other cah officials held meetings where copybooks containing the Genesis

Commentary were read aloud and shared. This would encourage not only the continuation of written versions of the commentary in a particular cah, but also their preservation in oral history as a possible example of "recitation literacy."[58] In the end, we may safely surmise that iterations of written or oral versions (or likely both) of various texts of this kind circulated within a cah and beyond to facilitate cognate versions.

The frequent copying, recopying, and editorial redaction of such texts as they circulated in one form or the other makes any firm chronological or genealogical history of a particular text extremely problematic. The geographic location of the cahob possessing cognate texts does not seem to have much impact on the texts themselves. Texts bearing striking similarities can be found among cahob both proximate and quite distant from each other. For example, Bricker and Miram's work on the Kaua (2002) included a treatise they titled "The Meaning of the Mass," which relates the Mass to the Passion of Christ, and which they also identify in the Chan Kan located less than thirty miles from Kaua. Recently, I discovered a close cognate version of this text in the "Passion Text" from Teabo, which is over sixty miles from either cahob. Although each occurrence contains unique orthographic preferences, all three texts are extremely similar despite the distances among their cahob of origin. The creation myths found in the Chumayel, Tizimin, and the Códice Pérez, while distinct in their own ways, also share close similarities, particularly the Tizimin and Pérez, despite their wide geographical distribution.[59]

Regardless, the Genesis Commentary and other examples discussed later expose the familiar presence of cognate texts among the Maya in a practice that extended beyond the Chilam Balams and occurred more frequently than perhaps previously thought. Although evidence exists to demonstrate text sharing among the early Franciscan friars in central Mexico, whose works often included components of previous works, to my knowledge I am not aware of Nahuatl-authored texts containing significant cognate passages from texts of other *altepetl* (Nahua sociopolitical unit).[60] Yet such seemed to be the case among the Maya and their Christian copybooks.

Some Orthographic and Textual Observations about the Four Commentaries

Although the four commentaries are similar, they are far from facsimiles, and each betrays specific content and orthographic preferences. The following examines passages from all four texts discussing the creation of the layers Firmament and Crystalline. As previously noted, Crystalline was the layer assigned to designate the "heavenly waters" mentioned in the Bible that had been changed into a solid in a process, as the texts describe, similar to how Moses's staff became a serpent and the Host becomes transubstantiated into the body of Christ during Mass. The following passages illustrate both the similar and different ways each text interprets this passage, and the insights multiple renditions of the same text provide in understanding its content and variation.[61]

Teabo Manuscript

Tu capel u kinil lay firmamento U cuchil ɔaanil tulacal u sihsal babil ca yumil ti Dios tu tan chumuc haa kaknal y ekobe heix haa lae christal u kabae
haa yalabale yoklal bay hach yiyipnacil haa lay christalino lae yoklal hail cuchij yoklal bay ilic U yalabale ychil kulem ɔibobe cuchi bay u ca U serpiente
moysen bara yalabale yoklal Barail cuchij bay u cah cilich Sacramento yan
ti altarle Uah u yalabale yoklal uahil cuchi heuac hetun tu yalabal cicithan
yokole lay consagracion U kabae minan u boc uahi bla[62] maixtan U minantal mac alic ca ilic kulem ɔib lae ti yan ti molcab tu uactas caan lae bay nen
yilabale bay bidroe bay plomoe U pixmail Uba ca macac u pot chcanhal[63] ca
pactic hi ba yantac tu tane

Morley Manuscript

Bala oheltabac helel lae = hijbal lic yalic kulem Dzib = U sihsah Dios = tu cappelil = u kinil = lay firmamento = eDzaannil tulacal = u sihsah babalil = Ca
u Dzaah tu tan chumuc haa = kaknab ykabe = hex haa lae = lay christalino =
christal u kaba = ha yalabal = yoklal bay hach yibyibnacil hae = lay christal lae
= yoklal ha cuchi = bay tachil yalabal = ychil kulem Dzib = U kaba = ti bayli
cuchie = bay u caah = u serpiente = moysene = Vala yalabal = yoklal barail =
cuchie = bay u cah u cilich sacramentoyl altale = Uaah yalabal = yoklal uahil
cuchi =heuac hetun tu yalabal. cicithan yokole = lay consagraçion = u kabae
manan u booc Uahij = bala mayx tan u mananhal. mac alic haa = lic yalic kulem Dzib lae = ti yan ti molcab = tu uactas caan lae = bay nen yilabale = bay
bidroe = bay promoe = pixic - yt. balpahebal = ca pacat = ca maac u potchi-
canhal = tac pacat = hijbal yantac tu tanne =

Kaua

bla oheltabac y. natabac tun helelae hi bal lic y alic kulem ɔibob u sihsah dios
tu ca pel u kinil lai firmamento eɔlic t u lacal u sihsah babalil ca u ɔaah tan
chumuc hà kaknab y. ekobe he ix ha lae lay christalino christal u kabae haa
y alabal y oklal hach yiyibnacil haa lay christale y oklal haa cuchi baiyilie te
chil y alabale ychil kulum ɔib u kaba babal ti baylie cuchie bay u cah u serpiente moysene bara y alabal y oklal barail cuchi bai u cah u culich sacramen-
toil altare bai y alabal y oklal vahil cuchi heuac he tun t uy alable cici than y
okole lay consagracion u kabae minan u boc uahi bla ma ix tan manahal ma
c alic he hàe lic y alic kulem ɔibob ti yan ti molcabil t u uac tas caan loe uac
tas caan yanil bay nene y liable bai uidroe bay plomoe pixic y. balic ca pacat
ca mac u potchacanhal tac pacat hi bal yan tac t u tane

Chan Kan

BLA oheltabal ỵ. natalbal ỵ ylabal hibal c yalic ah Kulen dziib boob uzih-zah, Dios tu cap'el ukinil lay firmamento, edzlic tulacal u zihzah babaliloob catudzah tan chumuk kanaa .ỵ. ekoob, kanabe christalino, christal u kaba, haa yalabal yoklal hach yiyiib nac bay haa lay christal cuchie, bayilitechil yala-bal ychil kulen dziib ukaba, bayili, che, bay u caah zerpiente, Moycese bara yalabal tumenel bara cu chi, bay cliich Sacrameto yantii Altare, tu menel uah yalabal cuchi, hebac cudzocol u kuyan cutal ỵ. lay cilich tan. u kaba Minan u boc uah tii, Bla, maixtan u minantal Mac alic he, lay kake, cu than kulem dziboob, ti t yan tu mool cabiloob tu uactaaz, caan loe, uactaaz yanil bay nen y yilabale bay vidro bay plomo pixic ỵ. balic upacat camacac u pot chicaan pahal, c pacat ti hebal ya tac tutan

Teabo Manuscript[64]

On the second day, this Firmament, the place where all the creations of our lord God are combined in between the ocean and the stars, and here, this water is called crystal; it is called water because this Crystalline is like water that really spreads, because formerly it was aquatic, because such is seen as its name inside the Holy Scriptures formerly, just like the serpent of Moses is called a staff because in the beginning, it was a staff; just like the holy sacra-ment there on the altar is called bread because it was originally bread, but when the blessing is said over it, consecration is its name, it no longer has the smell of bread. Thus, neither is there anybody who calls it as we see in the Holy Scriptures, it is there, it is joined in the sixth layer of heaven. It appears like a mirror, like glass, like lead, it covers itself so that it blocks the clear view we see of whatever is in front of it.

Morley Manuscript[65]

So this has been known now, this which the Sacred Scripture says, that God created on the second one of His days, this Firmament, having put in place all His created things, then He placed it in between, in the middle of the waters; notice thus, the oceans, but as for this water here, it is the Crystalline; Crystal is its name; it is called water, because it is like really molten water. This Crystal here, because it was water formerly, thus its name is said in Holy Scripture, still as it was before. Thus it is like the serpent of Moses, said to be a staff because it was a staff before. Thus it is like the blessed sacrament of the altar, called bread because it was bread before, but whenever a blessing is said over it, the name of this is Consecration, it no longer has the scent of bread. Therefore, neither is there no one who would call it water, as this Holy Scripture says, that is there, gathered in this sixth layer of heaven. Like a mirror it is seen, like vidrio - the glass - like plomo - the lead - that it covers, and our sight becomes covered, so that it may not become clearly visible to our gaze, whatever may be in front of it . . .

Kaua[66]

Well, it may be known, and it may be understood then, now, that which the Holy Scriptures say: God created this Firmament on the second day; all the objects that He created were established, and He placed them in the middle of the sea with stars. And this water here, this Crystalline, Crystal is its name. It is called water because it spreads out all over like water, this Crystal, because it was originally completely water. It was there in it, it is said, in what is called the Holy Scriptures. Something that is perpetually, originally, such as Moses' serpent, it is called a staff, because it was originally a staff. [Or] such as the holy sacrament of the altar. Thus it is said because it was originally bread. But as soon as the blessing is said over it, whose name is consecration, it no longer smells like bread. Well, it is not that it no longer exists. We do not say it, the water here as the Holy Scriptures say, that it is collected in that eighth heaven; the eighth heaven exists like a mirror. It looks like glass; it is just like lead, which covers and hides our sight; that our sight may be shielded from the clarification of whatever exists in front of it . . .

Chan Kan[67]

[By] inference it is known and understood, and it is seen that which the evangelists say. God created on the second day this firmament. He established all created things. Then he placed the sea in the middle and the stars there. As for the sea, it is crystalline. Its name is crsytal [sic]. It is called water. In order that over everything was much water, in this way water, this "Crystal" occurred. Thus it was there within what was said. Within the holy writ. [sic] as it is called. Thus it was it occurred thus in the place of the serpent. Moses' rod it is called because of the rod it happened: thus the holy Sacrament which is on the altar. By means of bread it is said to occur, but when consecration is finished, He comes, and this is the holy word as it is called. Without the scent of bread there it is inferred. Nor is it made to be without someone saying: "Here is the fire," the holy writs say. It is there in their unification. There in the sixth level of heaven. The sixth layer is like a mirror and it is seen like glass, like lead, covered and hidden. He surveys what may have been covered. The manifest revelation there appears what has been opened. Right before him . . .

To be sure, preferences in and individual styles of translation and interpretation will always produce varied results. That said, examining specific elements of the cited text provides revealing insights. To begin, the texts differ in how to begin this passage. The Kaua, Chan Kan, and Morley Manuscript all begin with some variation of "Bala oheltabac helel lae hijbal lic yalic kulem Dzib U sihsah Dios tu cappelil u kinil lay firmamento" (So this has been known now, this which the Sacred Scripture says that God created on the second one of His days, this Firmament).[68] Yet the Teabo Manuscript uses the first part of this sentence to conclude the previous section that it ends with an "Amen," and begins the next section with "Tu capel u kinil lay firmamento . . ." complete with a decorative drop cap.

This deviance is unusual among the four texts. Generally speaking, all four texts contain similar section breaks that appear along thematic lines. The final lines of the Kaua and Chan Kan's commentary provide one of many examples. Both the Kaua and Chan Kan end the commentary with a statement on the ability of the Holy Scriptures to explain the Trinity and Creation. Although the Morley Manuscript does not contain this sentence due to missing pages, the phrase is found in the Teabo Manuscript, which, instead of ending the commentary, uses a section break indicated by a series of dashes and begins the next section with a drop cap. This generally consistent correlation between section beginning and endings is remarkable and again suggests a system of circulation that included textual and/or oral accounts of the commentary.

Multiple renditions of the same passage also assist in understanding its content—to a degree. After describing Crystalline, all four texts place it in the "uactas caan," the "sixth layer of heaven." Yet by the texts' own previous admission, Crystalline is the ninth layer of heaven, not the sixth, which is inhabited by Jupiter. Those scholars familiar with such texts have offered various explanations for this error. Bricker and Miram (2002) suggest that both appearances of *uac* in the Kaua passage be read as *uaxac*, or eight, to reflect the Ptolemaic diagram of the cosmos included in the Kaua that lists Crystalline, however erroneously, as the eighth layer.[69] Whalen posits that "perhaps [the author] was looking at a diagram of the cosmogram numbered with Arabic numerals, and misread 6 for 9 from the side or upside down."[70]

The presence of *uac* in all four texts firmly attests to its intentional reading as *uac*, "six." Yet the reason for this perpetuated error over the centuries and among four cahob scattered throughout Yucatan remains elusive. Occasionally, the European almanacs from which the commentary derives inspiration refer to the heavens in reverse order. For example, the Firmament is the fourth heaven from God's perspective, but the eighth from ours here on earth and could be referred to as either.[71] But even that scenario fails to explain the error, as Crystalline would either be the third or ninth heaven. To my knowledge, the only time the almanacs use the number six in reference to Crystalline is in their statement that Crystalline helps move the six planets.[72]

Certainly, confusion of the esoteric Ptolemaic-Christian model of the universe occurred, as seen in the diagram included in the Kaua. Furthermore, when describing the layers of the planets, the author of the Teabo Manuscript placed both Saturn and Jupiter in the "uuctas caan" (the seventh layer of heaven).[73] These and other errors are not hidden or difficult to find; any superficial study of the text reveals their presence. So why were they not corrected? Perhaps there is a meaning within the lines that escapes us. Or, perhaps the errors suggest another insight into the Genesis Commentary: that it was preserved more for its ability to connect the Maya to the cosmos in a Christian world rather than its use as a faithful replica of European thought or a doctrinally correct text. We are left to wonder how many members of the cah truly understood this Ptolemaic-Christian-Maya worldview, or even cared to. For that matter, how many Christians today could recite the Creation as dictated in Genesis or explain it? Today various Maya communities continue to preserve colonial religious texts. Although they are oftentimes unaware of such texts' content, they are respected for their connection to the past as an artifact of historic and cultural importance. The Genesis Commentary would eventually fade from the understanding of the Yucatec Maya and perhaps it began earlier in the colonial period than we realize.

The European and Maya Elements of the Genesis Commentary

Because Knowlton (2010) admirably illustrates many of the precontact influences evident in the colonial redactions of the Genesis Commentary, and the work of Bricker and Miram (2002) expertly addresses the European influences on the account as it appears in the Kaua, this section strives to contribute to these previous works by illustrating what the Teabo Manuscript can add to these conversations. In addition, further exploration of medieval religious theory and belief allows for new insights into the intended meanings of the occasionally esoteric prose of the commentary; such insights are found often in the notes accompanying the translation.

To begin, the Genesis Commentary in the Teabo Manuscript is highly Europeanized, perhaps making it easier to extract obvious Maya elements from its pages. Yet because Mayas trained in the Roman alphabet and Christianity composed the vast majority of what we understand to be the Maya's creation myths, it is difficult in most cases—such as with the *Popol Vuh*—to say with authority which elements in such myths existed prior to their exposure to Christianity. As Allen Christenson notes, the Maya were not concerned with writing an objective or even "orthodox" history. In many ways, they saw creation myths for what they were: stories. And stories can change according to the narrator's preferences.

Such modifications should not be forced into the defined categories of resistance or conformity. In truth, religion has always included resistance and conformity in a fluid, constant negotiation. For example, although most Christians today may attend church, they might also profane a little, cheat a little, and therefore "resist" full compliance in order to create a version of religion best suited to personal needs and preferences. Surely such individuals see themselves as good Christians overall despite such vagrancies that "resist" the prescribed ideal. We should not begrudge the Maya the same by claiming that their versions of the Creation represent either open resistance to the Church or complete capitulation.

As I have argued elsewhere, what seems to have mattered most to the Maya in creating these accounts was not producing a facsimile of Catholic doctrine, but presenting a story that would best resonate with a Maya audience.[74] The production of such stories involves a fluid conversation between precontact, European, and colonial cosmogonies. The Genesis account here is a result of such a conversation.

Regarding European influences, the commentary is an eclectic text from a variety of sources, none of which seemed to have been copied verbatim. Thus, various possibilities exist. Sixteenth-century Spanish reportorios, or almanacs, may have guided the first section of the Genesis Commentary in the Teabo Manuscript, and evidence exists to illustrate their popularity in New Spain, particularly that of Rodrigo Zamorano published in 1585 in Seville.[75] Simply put, these reportorios represented Europe's attempt to explain the cosmos and their effects on man. Bricker and Miram's study of the Kaua illustrates how images that appear in this Maya text were copied from such reportorios, while Laura Caso Barrera (2011) does the same for the Ixil. Interestingly, the native Andean chronicler, Guaman Poma, utilized such a reportorio in his early seventeenth-century *Nueva corónica y buen gobierno* to create a list of the five ages of the Western world—a common section of Spanish reportorios—that harmonized with the Andean past.[76] And the College of Tlatelolco—the sixteenth-century focal point for Nahua-ecclesiastic collaboration in text production—held various copies of reportorios in its library.[77] Yet the Genesis Commentary in Maya works is far from an exact translation of any reportorio. Indeed, although the European almanacs informed the descriptions and model of the cosmos, the structure of the commentary (arranged around the six days of creation) deviates significantly from the reportorios (arranged around the heavens and their constellations).

Yet reportorios were not the only possible inspiration for the Genesis Commentary. Biblical commentaries emerged from the earliest Christian writers, and by the Middle Ages many such commentaries were joined together in the *Glossa ordinaria*—a twelfth-century work that served as the standard collection of exegetical materials for centuries. Commentaries on Genesis enjoyed particular popularity. From Flavius Josephus's *Antiquities of the Jews* to St. Augustine's *The City of God* to Peter Comestor's *Historia scholastica*, commentaries on Genesis abounded. Brian Murdoch's work on medieval apocrypha demonstrates how vernacular commentaries in Europe often employed "other literary forms—verse or drama—than merely straightforward prose" to engage their readers, who were oftentimes nonecclesiastic.[78] The European authors of such vernacular interpretations of biblical text often composed their works from memory of the Bible and not directly from the text itself. The resulting work, then, was typically a creative construct of memory and existing commentaries. The Genesis Commentary found in various Maya works, including the Teabo Manuscript, seems to follow a similar pattern of drawing from various existing sources and memory to create a vernacular interpretation riddled with verse and drama so familiar and appealing to its native audience.

The lack of a printing press in Yucatan only encouraged the region's participation in the transatlantic book trade, and numerous European works found their way to Yucatan.[79] Biblical commentaries continued their popularity in the early modern era. Various commentaries on Genesis and the Creation made their way across the Atlantic, including those of the popular Augustino Eugubino and Benito Pereira.[80] Indeed, the Teabo Manuscript itself references the teachings of the great "miyatzob Doctoresob" (wisemen, doctors [of the Church]). Those who contributed greatly to the theology or doctrine of the Church were awarded the title of "Doctor." Of the select number bearing this title, a few are of particular importance here.

Quoted twice, the influential work of St. John of Damascus should certainly be considered. The saint, generally regarded as the last great figure of Greek Orthodox patrology, wrote the eighth-century *Fountain of Wisdom*— in many ways, the first *Summa theologica*—and various sermons. Although the *Fountain* contains a discussion of the Creation and various teachings of its text are found in the Maya commentary, another of his texts, a sermon on Holy Saturday, includes a lengthier exposition on the Creation and the Fall that could also have provided inspiration for the Genesis Commentary or another European text from which it borrowed.[81] Interestingly, St. John of Damascus was the patron saint of the San Juan barrio in Teabo. As noted later, various indirect references to his work and teachings appear throughout the Teabo Manuscript and suggest him as an important source.

The work of this saint would influence many theologians, including St. Thomas Aquinas, whose *Summa theologica* is also extremely palatable throughout the Genesis Commentary of the Teabo Manuscript. The commentary cites Aquinas three times—more than any other—as St. Thomas. This is not surprising when considering his lengthy expositions on the Creation and his general popularity in sixteenth-century Spain. Indeed, book inventories detailing shipments from Spain to the New World frequently included Aquinas's works, including his treatises on the Creation.[82] Other Doctors of the Church cited are St. Augustine and St. John the Evangelist, with each having one specific reference.

After the Kaua and Chan Kan conclude their commentaries, the Teabo and Morley Manuscripts continue to discuss the creation and fall of Adam. Here, the Teabo Manuscript occasionally contains sections not found in the Morley (sections F and H). In the first part of his *Summa*, Aquinas relates the differences between the body of Adam and those of other animals. Animals have claws, hides, feathers, and walk with their faces to the ground, reflecting their primary concern for food and sex. Man's equability and good temperament prevents him from needing claws or horns and allows him to make his own clothes. Moreover, he walks erect so that his gaze "may freely survey the sensible objects around him, both heavenly and earthly, so as to gather intelligible truth from all things."[83] The Teabo Manuscript captures these distinctions between man and animal. After describing the animals with their faces to the earth, the text states, "However, this man is not like this, he is erect and raised high, his gaze is marvelous, it examines his soul and what he sees. Nor did he receive true hair on his body, nor was he given much carnal desires, or feathers as pertains to the rest of His (God's) creations."[84]

Section H continues this narrative but illustrates in particular the consequence of Adam and Eve's transgression. Here, the punishment for Eve having caused Adam to sin is meted out as follows: "For this reason, with great suffering you will give birth, this principal duty, and your affliction and the pain that exists in your death and life also."[85] Aquinas's *Summa* likewise discusses the pain of pregnancy as Eve's consequence for having caused Adam to sin, although this concept was well known throughout Catholic belief and not isolated to Aquinas.[86] That said, the whole of the discussion relating Adam and Eve's consequences for having transgressed God's commandment closely parallels that of Aquinas's discussion.

Thus, following the creation of the cosmos, which possibly draws from existing reportorios and commentaries, the Genesis Commentary draws from other works to create its narrative. Similar to historical and prophetic passages in the Chilam Balams that ground their veracity in the citation of Maya prophets, the Genesis Commentary quotes various theologians and scholars known historically for their efforts in reconciling scripture with the cosmologies of the Bible, Aristotle, and Ptolemy, including Saints Thomas Aquinas, John of Damascus, Augustine, John the Evangelist, and King Alfonso X of Castile and his astrologers.

Certainly the Genesis Commentary drinks deeply from the fountain of European cosmogony. Yet it also betrays its Maya influences. In various places throughout the commentary, the text concludes a creative period or event with its "seating." In the Maya calendar and when transitioning from one division of time to another, a "seating" took place. This "seating" also applied to marking significant transitions between rulers or other events. This symbolism appears throughout precontact Maya hieroglyphs, the colonial Chilam Balams, and also in the Genesis Commentary. For example, after God established the dawning and setting of light on the first day, "it was perfected and this first day was seated." Later, God "desired to seat the beginning of the days which is Sunday."[87]

Another modification regards the Maya's use of *ah/ix bolon pixan* as a translation for "blessed" when referencing the saints. In literal terms, the phrase means "he/she of the nine souls" or the "nine-souled," and it is consistently found in reference to Catholic saints.[88] For example, the Teabo Manuscript references Saint Augustine as "Ah bolon pixan San Agustin" (he of the nine souls, Saint Augustin), and similar occurrences exist throughout myriad Maya texts.[89] The number nine held significant meaning throughout Mesoamerica; possibly it represented the number of layers in the Maya underworld, and it still appears in modern incantations performed by local Maya leaders.[90] Moreover, the names of various deities in the Maya pantheon employed the ah bolon phrase such as Ah Bolon Tzacab, Ah Bolon Yocte, and Ah Bolon Caan Chac, and a section of the Vienna dictionary—a colonial Spanish-to-Maya dictionary—describes Ah Bolon Ahau and Ah Bolonil as idols of deities worshipped in precontact times.[91] When presented with saints containing attributes and abilities similar to their gods and demigods, the Maya seemingly continued to employ the ah/ix bolon phrase to familiarize these foreign but powerful figures.

Other examples of native influences on the commentary exist that concern Maya rhetoric. Both the Maya and Nahua employed parallel constructions where the author rephrases what has been said in a slightly different form. Examples of these constructions abound in the hieroglyphic inscriptions of the Classical Maya and the writings of the colonial Maya including the Teabo Manuscript.[92] Using a bilingual triplet construction, the commentary tells the reader how it is necessary to understand how the cosmos was explained by "U yah miyatzilob astrologosob hach canaltac U miyatzob" (the wise men, the astrologers, the most esteemed wise men). The oral aspect of Maya texts, which were more often performed than simply read, is also revealed. Here the audience is frequently referenced and told what they will hear and see and what they are to understand of the discourse. One example of many reads, "Now then, you Christian, listen to the news, the meaning of how the body of our first father Adam was formed, by our lord God."[93]

The interactive nature of the commentary deepens significantly in its discussion of the creation and fall of Adam and Eve, where the commentary reads more like a script than a summary of events you would expect to find in a printed European text. Reflecting upon the matter, Lockhart made a comment in reference to Nahua orality that could as easily be applied to the Maya:

> The Nahua manner of oral narrative was to give a far more fleshed-out, dramatized version than the succinct third-person paraphrases preferred by Europeans for most nonliterary purposes, and this mode was faithfully reduced to writing in many alphabetic documents of the sixteenth century and later.[94]

By way of illustration, consider the conversation that ensues after God created Eve from Adam's rib and awakened him saying, "'Delight in hearing, seeing the person there at your side,' thus was said by our lord God. And then Adam answered, 'Lord, this here is of my rib, of my bone also. Now Virago[95] is the name of this virgin,' so spoke Adam to our lord God."[96] The dialogic nature of Maya texts is especially evident in the commentary's explanation of how the devils counseled to deceive Adam and Eve, and when God confronts the pair about their transgression. Regarding the latter, the dialogue changes frequently, as it would in a play or performance:

> "My holy father, I fell into error because of this woman here," thus spoke Adam.

Again to the woman [God said], "Why did you cause your husband to fall into error?"

"My holy father, the devil beguiled me," thus spoke Eve.

I am not suggesting that the commentary was a play or even acted out in such a way, but rather that the text contains numerous examples of the oral and dialogic aspect commonly found throughout so many Maya and Nahua texts.

The Genesis Commentary also includes symbolic figures, events, and phrases familiar to the Maya. In the text, God declares that his greatest creation, prior to Adam, was the *u yax chel cab* (the first tree of the world). The world tree of the Maya is found inscribed throughout various precolonial sites and served as an *axis mundi* extending from the underworld through the middleworld, with its branches reaching the upperworld. In their study of the yax chel cab, Knowlton and Gabrielle Vail state it as the product of both precontact and colonial belief systems, "a colonial amalgam, a world tree at the center of a hybrid cosmology."[97] In the text, however, the yax chel cab unconventionally represents both the Tree of Knowledge of Good and Evil and the Tree of Life—two separate trees in the biblical commentary.[98] Indeed, the Teabo narrative frequently refers to this conflated version of both trees as "U cheel cilich grasia yetel cuxtal yetel toh olal" (the tree of holy grace, of life, and peace). In the account the tree is a holy and sacred thing full of mystery, and God commands Adam and Eve, "Do not touch nor eat of the fruit because it is very solemn, you are not worthy to touch it."[98]

Another example of Maya influence in the narrative occurs later in the commentary. When Adam and Eve are ashamed to appear naked before God, they hide underneath a *che habin* or Dogwood tree native to Yucatan. The leaves and bark of this tree were common elements used in precontact and colonial idolatrous rituals, and its bark is frequently used in medicinal remedies.[99] And when tempting Eve to eat of the forbidden fruit, Lucifer exclaims that the fruit will enable her vision to reach from "hun xaman y hun chikin" (the north to the west).[100] This Maya phrase also appears in the Tizimin, the Morley Manuscript, and in Coronel's *Discursos* and is a metonym for "everywhere."[101] This is simply one example of many where Maya phrases and symbols are included to familiarize a European cosmogony.

Furthermore, the commentary's progressive creation of man resonates with other Maya creation myths where speechless, senseless beings are improved and/or replaced until finally achieving a version of mankind capable of venerating the deities.[102] In the Teabo Manuscript, after God formed Adam, Adam could not move until he received the breath of life. Then, through a series of sequential actions taken by God, Adam received his sight, speech, hair, and skin. Interestingly, and admittedly to a lesser degree, the Bible recounts the formation of man in a similar progressive way, with Adam being formed, then made to sleep while Eve was created from his rib, only later to awaken and then later still receive knowledge, thus, in a way, completing his creation.

When analyzing the Genesis Commentary as a whole, certain characteristics of the text become evident. The first part of the narrative is replete with obvious references to European cosmology, biblical treatises, and citations of the saints. Undoubtedly, the Maya author(s) derived heavy inspiration from these European sources. However, beginning with "the second part of the news" on page eleven, the text largely ceases from citing the saints and other theologians, the orality of the prose increases even more, and the content begins to stray from orthodox or standard versions of the Creation. Regarding the latter, Adam's creation becomes protracted and takes on a Maya persona with creative additions such as when God says to a sightless Adam, "Ephphatha," a Greek form of the Aramaic word meaning "be opened." This phrase was spoken by Jesus to a deaf and dumb man in Mark 7:34 whom Christ had anointed with his spittle. Although not associated with the Creation, it seems that the Maya creatively selected this New Testament action and placed it into an Old Testament commentary.[103] Perhaps this was done due to the inclusion of the Ephphatha rite in baptism. During this part of the ceremony, the priest touches the recipient's ears and mouth with his thumb to "open" them to the words of God and to give him praise. It is possible that this rite associated with the birth of one's soul was then used to describe the birth of Adam by the Maya(s) authoring the work, who no doubt was familiar with the ceremony.

Another possibility concerns the sermons of St. Anthony of Padua, an important medieval figure in the Franciscan order. In his *Sermones dominicales*, St. Anthony uses the Creation to equate the six creative days and a seventh for rest with the six Articles of Faith and the promise of eternal rest in the seventh. At one point the discourse compares metaphorically the spittle of Christ opening the eyes of the blind to wisdom that opens the eyes of Adam and his descendants.[104] Perhaps this or a similar passage also served as inspiration in the Genesis Commentary. Regardless, it appears to be an uncommon inclusion into the Creation story.

Other additions that could be considered nontraditional at best would be the devils organizing themselves in an *audiencia*, or court, to decide how to best deceive Adam and Eve — reminiscent of how the Lords of the Underworld in the *Popul Vuh* conspired against the Hero Twins. These devils are the angels cast out from heaven for their rebellion. As a result, they lost their place in heaven, and the medieval and early modern belief was that God created man to take their place.[105] For the Maya, this "place" in heaven was represented by seats, as, similar to the Nahuas, the Maya associated seated figures with rulers.[106] Here in the Teabo commentary the devils counsel with one another, saying, "What will be done now if these ascend to the chairs, seats, given to us formerly? How can their hands be removed from them (the chairs) in your opinion?"[107]

Such additions reflect the preferences of the Maya inserting storylines, events, and dialogue that best told the desired story. In short, the second and third parts of the Genesis Commentary stray from what might be a more traditional European format to the storyline. Although the voice of the Maya author(s) can be heard throughout the commentary, the voice increases in volume considerably as the tale progresses and moves away from outlining the Ptolemaic-Christian model of the cosmos.

In 1990, Ana M. Juárez collected a story from Doña Docia Catzin Chan, a Maya woman living in the town of Tulum in Quintana Roo. The story is an oral account of Adam and Eve and their experience in the Garden of Eden. Although the events are biblically grounded, the story takes on many Maya elements. The devil in the form of a snake appears in a cenote (limestone cave or sinkhole), Adam and Eve are given a book of evil reportedly employed by sorcerers today, and linguistic couplets and triplets abound throughout the account.[108] It would appear that various creation myths continue to thrive within the Maya Christian worldview of many in Yucatan.

Determining the origin of colonial Maya texts is a difficult and often-times speculative affair. What I offer here are some thoughts on the origins of the commentary in hopes that they will spark discussion and debate that might bring us closer to a firm conclusion. It is possible that the first part of the commentary already existed, in some form, as a presently unidentified European treatise or as a series of texts the Mayas and/or their instructors drew from to create the commentary that the Maya used and modified to better suit an indigenous audience. Moreover, it is possible that the second and third parts either derived from a European antecedent or, more likely, were an original creation of a Maya author(s). Because this creative summary is so similar in structure among the four texts, it is possible—even probable—that it was created in the sixteenth century by a Maya author(s) with ready access to various European religious texts, perhaps in some convent where the Maya noble youths gathered to receive their instruction. From there, the commentary circulated to influence various cahob and their copybook texts, including the ones examined here. Regardless of its origins, the commentary's continued existence and preservation among "forbidden" texts reveals its importance and significance to the Yucatec Maya, and the Teabo Manuscript contributes another intimate glimpse into an ever-evolving Maya-Christian worldview that created a variety of creation myths.

The Genesis Commentary, p. 1–24[109]

(P. 1)

+

Chunpahal[110] U cah u pectzil u yan[umal sih]sabci[111] balcah tumen ca yumil
ti Dios ah tepal u chayan balob y utzcin°hob ychil uacpel ti kin ti lahi to lah
yutzcintci y u metci ca yum ti Ada[m] y ca yax na ti eva Genesis
  8 enero de 1802
  año H 16–4521[112]

Ɔiban tumen cilich bolon ah miyatz moysen ti yunil miyatz henesis u kaba
ti lic y alic u sihsa caan[113] y luume hohochil hanpiken Maix bal yan yokol ti
hunkul heuac he caane ma bay loe yokol bay licil u canticob Bolon miyatzob
Doctoresob ti lic y alicob he caan lae lici tac u nak u ɔocol u sihsabal tumen
ca yumil ti Diose ca tu chupah u pictanil Angelesobi u hach cichcelemtacil
sihsabilob yx ma xulumte ix cuxtal ɔaan tiob tumen ca yumil ti Dios Ah tepal
ti ɔocan can tun u sihil angelesobe bay licil u cantic y yalic u yunil miyatz
consilio u kabae y Doctoresob bayx licil u cantic yetel yalic ca yᵘmilan San
Juan Damaseno u kabae heklay caan yan ynfireo u kabae u yax chun can y
culic ca yumil ti dios ah tepal lo[e] y caan Pirmero mouir u kabae ti ~~may to~~
u yax chun can cu[114] sut y caan christarino U kabae ti

(P. 1)

+

It begins, the renown, the news, that the world was created by our lord God, Ruler; all other things, He created them well in six days, all was finished and well made; and He made our father, Adam, and our first mother, Eve. Genesis
    January 8, 1802
    año H 16–4521

It has been written by the very wise man, Moses, in a book of wisdom, Genesis is its name, in which it says that the heaven and earth were created pure, clean, nothing ever existed on it. But heaven was not that way because of how the great wise men, the doctors, relate it in which they say, "Regarding these heavens, as soon as the horizon[115] was finished, had been created by our lord God, then it was filled with a throng of angels, they were very beautiful creations, and eternal life was given to them by our lord God, Ruler."[116] When the birth of the angels was finished, as relates and says the book of wisdom, Council is its name, and the doctors, and as our patron named St. John of Damascus relates and says, "This heaven is called Empyrean, it is the first heaven, and our lord God, Ruler sits there." And the heaven called Prime Mover is the first heaven that revolves,[117] and the heaven called Crystalline[118]

. . . may to yana sasil ekhochen to cuchi ca tun U sihsa Dios sasil Ca haui ekhochenile heix ekhochenil ca cuchie Ca u kabatah akabil heyx sasilite Ca yalah kinil caix U ɔah u sashal yetel U tħubul Bay tun ɔoc lukanhic yt cuᵐ-lahic yax chun kin lae helay sasil lae Cu tħan Santo thomas hunpel muyalae lembanachij yutzcinaah Ca yumil ti Dios heix muyalae lay oci y utzcinabci kin ca ɔocie ti ɔabi y ti culcinabi ti pirmero mouil U yax chun caan cu sut ti yalahe ca tun yilah ca yumil ti Dios hach cici ɔoc lukanile tulacal U sihsah balile ca tun yoltah U cuntcint U chun U kinil hek lay Domingoe tu capel hij tun U kinil ca yutzcintah ca yumil ti Dios firmamento helay caā yanhebal y taklahebal tulacal hi bahun U sihsah balil tulacale lay u uaxctas can esPeras U kabae heklay uohanil y takun taklic tulacal lae

---

Heix Uchebal U hach lemb y U pot chicanhal tulacal bal loe lay yan U hach uilal ca oheltic hibicil tzolanil tumennelob U yah miyatzilob astro-logosob hach canaltac U miyatzob bay U cah Rey D.ⁿ Alonso yan ti castillae Ah miyatz yalabal he caanob lae buluc tasili tu baab onse sielos heix u nohol yan hach canale lay ymPireo lae U babalil kak bolon pixanob

. . . before there was light, when darkness covered, then God caused light to be born, then the darkness stopped. This darkness back then He called night, and this light we call day; and He set its dawning and setting. As such, it was perfected and this first day was seated. Regarding this light, St. Thomas says that a resplendent cloud (light)[119] was created well by our lord God, and this cloud entered[120] and perfected the day. Then it was completed, it was placed and seated in Prime Mover, the first heaven that revolves, as was said. Then our lord God saw that all His creations were very glorious and perfected. Then He desired to seat the beginning of the days which is Sunday. Then, it was on the second day that our lord God created well the Firmament which is the heaven where all His created things,[121] however many, exist and are placed, all of them. This is the eighth heaven, called Spheres, of which is written and preserved, all of them are fixed [to it].[122]

And so that all things really shine and are really visible there. It is very necessary that we understand how it was organized by the wise men, the astrologers, the most esteemed wise men such as King Don Alfonso there in Castile, called "The Wise." Regarding these heavens, there are eleven layers in them, eleven heavens, and the greatest is very high, this Empyrean that is covered with fire; the nine-soul

Santosob y̱ Santaob yanie ti ix lic U paclampactic [ob u baob u glo]¹²³ riai-
lobo bolon pixanobie heix caan ympireo lae ch[icil] . . . n chich eᴐlic matan
U pec maixtan U cut gi ti hunkulil hetun lahuntas caane yan yalan ympireo
lae lay primero mouil U yax chun caan ca sutic u [ka]bae yoklal lay cu sut
tumen huntul Angel tuba tu hunal tal ti lakin kuchuc ti chikine hunp̱el u kinil
ti can tu kal oras U kintzil¹²⁴ yalabale tilic U suttob tu pach laobi esperas U
kabaobe heix caan loe minan ekobi baix yan yalan xan maix bal yani lay bolon tas cane christarino U kabae hetun uaxac tas caane firmamento U kaba
lay yanilob taklic ekob ti bay tatakilob ᴐipit kabe helay loe tu uich lembanac
u sasilil u pacattob yanilobe
    AMen Jesus

H euac hetun planetasob ma ti llanob¹²⁵ ychil ekobi ti yalah lae yoklal
hun hun tzuc caan yanilob bay licil tzoliccob ti hun tzol u binelob y̱
yalic planetasob lae saturno tu uuctas caan yan supiter tu uuctas¹²⁶ caan yan
marte tu hotas caan yan sol tu cantas caan yan Venus tu yoxtas caan yan
mercurrio tu catas caan yan luuna lay naᴐpul cokol lae tix yantac U chayan
U sihsah babalil ca

male and female saints are there; and here they reward each other the glory of the nine-souled. And this heaven, Empyrean, is glued, firmly established; it does not move nor does it ever rotate. But then the tenth heaven that is below Empyrean is the Prime Mover, the first heaven that rotates is its name, because this one rotates by one angel by himself, alone,[127] he comes from the east and arrives in the west, one day in twenty-four hours it is said. Meanwhile, it rotates behind these things called "spheres," and there are no stars in that heaven (Prime Mover). Similarly, in the one that is below it, there is also nothing there. This is the ninth layer of heaven, called Crystalline, and here the eighth layer of heaven is called Firmament. This one has stationary stars like stationary rings; the light, the brilliance of the faces of those there shine.

Amen Jesus.

But the planets do not exist among the stars, as was said, because each one exists in a heaven. This is how they are arranged: they go in single file and are called planets; Saturn exists in the seventh layer of heaven; Jupiter exists in the seventh layer of heaven; Mars exists in the fifth layer of heaven; the Sun exists in the fourth layer of heaven; Venus exists in the third layer of heaven; Mercury exists in the second layer of heaven; the Moon is there close above us and there is fixed.[128] And there existed the rest of every single creation of our

yumil ti Dios u sihnalis kaki bay licil yalic Astrologoso caanob hatzantacob
ti mobimientosob yoklal licil u nana olticcob ti ekob y̱ ti planetasob tilic U
ha^{tz}lamticob Asentricosob consentricosob u kabaob ychil u Romanseil tħa-
nil sutbessob ci U tħan lae hek lay ychil u maya tħan lae episielos U kabaob
xane bay u cah esperasob mehentacobe eɔecnac U ximbalobe bayx ua bic y̱
olahilobe Bla oheltabac y̱ natabac helelae hibal lic yalic kulem ɔib U sihsah
ca yumil ti Dios lae

    amen

Tu caꝑel u kinil lay firmamento U cuchil ɔaanil tulacal u sihsal babil ca
yumil ti Dios tu tan chumuc haa kaknal y̱ ekobe heix haa lae christal
u kabae haa yalabale yoklal bay hach yiyipnacil haa lay christalino lae yoklal
hail cuchij yoklal bay ilic U yalabale ychil kulem ɔibobe cuchi bay u ca U serpiente moysen bara yalabale yoklal Barail cuchij bay u cah cilich Sacramento
yan ti altarle Uah u yalabale yoklal uahil cuchi heuac hetun tu yalabal cicitħan
yokole lay consagracion U kabae minan u boc uahi bla[129] maixtan U minantal mac alic ca ilic kulem ɔib lae ti yan ti molcab tu uactas caan lae bay nen
yilabale bay bidroe bay plomoe U pixmail Uba ca macac u pot chcanhal[130]
ca pactic hi ba yantac tu tane hex yayax u pactabale lic ylic loe tumenel bay
yollahmail Dios u beltic

(P. 4)

lord God, the creations of fire. In this manner the astrologers say the heavens are divided into movements, for this is how they understood them, the stars and the planets being each one divided. "Acentricos" and "concéntricos" are their names in the Romance language, "rotations" as they say in the Maya language. Also, epicycles, as they are called, are like spheres, they travel calmly according to the manner of their desires. It is assumed that now it has been known and understood that which the Holy Scriptures say of the creations of our lord God.

Amen.[131]

On the second day, this Firmament, the place where all the creations of our lord God are combined in between the ocean and the stars, and here, this water is called crystal; it is called water because this Crystalline is like water that really spreads, because formerly it was aquatic, because such is seen as its name inside the Holy Scriptures formerly, just like the serpent of Moses is called a staff because in the beginning, it was a staff; just like the holy sacrament there on the altar is called bread because it was originally bread, but when the blessing is said over it, consecration is its name, it no longer has the smell of bread. Thus, neither is there anybody who calls it as we see in the Holy Scriptures,[132] it is there, it is joined in the sixth layer of heaven.[133] It appears like a mirror, like glass, like lead, it covers itself so that it blocks the clear view we see of whatever is in front of it. And here what should be seen first will be seen according to the desire of God; He does

yoklal ca tiac U xulel U lemba caan ympireo ye[tel U]¹³⁴ lemba U pacat U
cillich Uinicil Ca yumil ti Jesuchristo y U lemba U pacat u cilich Colel Suhuy
Santa Maria y U chayan Santob yetel Santaob cicithan U uinicilobe bay San
Juan euangelista uucten lembanacil ma U chayanil he tulacal ɔiban ychil ku-
lem ɔibobe U hach hah hach tohil xan tulacal bay licil yalic Ah bolon pixan
San Agustin he cilich kulem ɔibobe U naat uinic bin kuchuccie ma kuchan
U hach naate yoklal hach hah y hach tohi xan bay licil yaliccob Astrologosob
lic u potchicancunicob ti mahancenil y tan sahsasil ti bay lae

He kin tu cantas caan yan he lunae lay naɔpul c okol lae lic yalic y ah
miyatzil llanumal¹³⁵ yetel u pectzil lae tij tu kinil lunes lae hach hatz-
cab cuchi ca lubi lusifer likul ti caan huntaɔhij ti metnal Ca tohlabie y U chay
anangelob U cetbesah U than yetelobe bayix U than xan he U kinil lunes lae
ma yutzil kini tumen laili U kinil sipci y yutzcintci ma tibilil lusifer y chayan
U lobol angelesob lubiob te tu pache

(P. 5)

this so that there is an end to the resplendence of the heaven Empyrean and the resplendence of the view of the holy body of our lord Jesus Christ, and the resplendence of the view of the holy lady, virgin St. Mary and the rest of the male and female saints; their bodies are blessed, like St. John the Evangelist, seven times brighter than the rest.[136] This is all written in the Holy Scriptures, it is really true, really correct also all that which he of the nine souls, St. Augustine says, "The understanding of these Holy Scriptures a man will arrive at is not the true understanding because it is really true and really correct also." Thus say the astrologers which they manifest publicly and bring to light, in this way.[137]

The Sun here exists in the fourth layer of heaven. The moon here is close above us, of which speak their[138] wise men of its character and reputation; that on this day Lunes (Monday) it was in the morning when Lucifer fell from heaven straight to hell, when he was cast out with the other angels that followed his words. And thus they say also that the day Lunes (Monday) is not a good day because it is the principal day Lucifer sinned and created evil and the rest of the bad angels fell behind him.

Tu yoxpel U kinil chipahi luume tumen ca yumil ti Dios yol pixan ti ha yokol cuchi ca u haɔah uba haa nachil Ca u tzucah Uba helay Kaknab U kaba lae ca ti cinhij tun lume Uchebal U hoklahal xiuob yetel cheob y̱ U chayan U yanal balob hokiob yokkol luume bay bic yanil tac helelae cicithanbil ix luume tumen Ca yumil ti Dios hun suthix U pixchahal luᵘme tumen xiuob y̱ cheob y̱ nicteob y̱ chahuctaccob ti helan helan ix tulacal xane heuac minan Uchucili tiob lae Tu yoxpel U kini lae tu yutzcinah Ca yumil ti DS: parayso terenar

---

Tu canpel U kinil tu yutzcinah Dios luuminaria helay kin y̱ ue lae ca u takcunah ti caan kin y̱ ue he kin lae luuminaria Mayor U yalabal lay oci lae u nohochil tichkak yoklal lay tichkaktic yetel U sahcunic yokol cab lae heix Ue luuminaria menor U yalabal yoklal Uɔil tichkak yoklal lay tichkak yetel sasil cunic akab lae ─────────────────────

Bayxan yutzcinah ekob ca yumil ti Dios ca ɔahob tu uaxactas can heixi Ue lay naɔpul c okol hetun kine tu cantas caan yan tix yanhij U uilal U cutalie yoklal ti yanhi yetel sihsab lay muyal hach lembanac occi tu uinicil kin lae Ca tiac

(P. 6)

On the third day, the earth was born because our lord God had previously covered it over in water, then the water removed itself, then it reduced itself into a smaller part, now its name is "ocean." Then the earth was dried, water was removed so that plants and trees could grow and the rest of the other things could manifest on the earth as they are today. This earth became a blessed thing through our lord God; in an instant the earth was covered with plants, trees, flowers, and sweet things each one different from the other also, but lacking power among them [to be like the others].[139] On the third day, our lord God created well eternal paradise.

On the fourth day, God created well the light, the Sun and Moon here. Then He affixed the Sun and Moon in heaven. The Sun, this greater light it is called, this means the great illuminator because it illuminates and gives light on earth. And the Moon, the lesser light it is called regarding the small illuminator, because it illuminates and gives light to the night.

Likewise, our lord God created well the stars, then He placed them in the eighth layer of heaven. And this Moon is close above us. However, the Sun exists in the fourth layer of heaven, and this situation is a necessary thing from here on because here it existed and was created. This truly resplendent cloud (light) entered into the form of the Sun.[140]

Ca tiac yan tu tan chumuc caan U chebal U yan[tal u][141] sasiltiob cuchie
heuac Ma yoltah Ca yumil ti Ds. ah tepali lay tux yan sihic yetel topi tix
culhi xane

L ic ix yalic huntul Doctor he kin y Ue ca sihiobe Ma ya thabo Ma ya hopi
U kakil U pacatob heuac tu canpel U kinil tun sihsabcob cuchi ca hopi
u leMba u pacat u kakilob tix U chaah U lembaob yetel U sasililob ti hunpel
Muyal yan sihsabi tumen Ca yumil ti Ds bay uchic au uyicex y Manic a xoc-
cex samee ti tun likul u sasilil tulacal ekobi yetel planetas ti kin lae

---

T u hopel hi tun u kinil u sihsah Ca yumil ti Ds balcheob lay chihobe
ychil haa hi tub sihi cayobe nuctacob yetel chichantacobe heix cayob
lae ti yanhobi ychil haa ca eMiob Cabalil tu hach taMil haa Ca totop hokiob
ti xiknalob uchuc canob canal ti yk Caiix cicithantabiob tuMen Ca yumil ti
dios U tial ca yabacob hach yan hiix U uilal u sihilob ychil huunpel Kin lay
chichobe y lay cayobe tumenel he lay cay y chichobe chach y onel U baob lae
tu xiknalilob y baob tic Cu banal U xikobe

(p. 7)

This, then, exists in front of the middle of heaven so that everything had light back then, but our lord God, Ruler did not desire this where it was first born, and blossomed, and seated also.[142]

And as one doctor says, when the Sun and Moon were born, they were not lit, they did not begin their fire, their light. But finally on the fourth day when they were created back then, then began their illumination, their light, their fire. And they received their resplendence and their light from a cloud previously created by our lord God, as you previously heard and just read about, from whence comes the light of all the stars and planets on this (fourth) day.

On the fifth one, day, our lord God created the animals: the birds born under the water, the fishes large and small. And these fishes here that existed in water descended into the very depths of the water. Then they quickly emerged with wings reaching the heavens high in the air. And then they were blessed by our lord God so that truly many existed. And it was a necessary thing that they were born in one day, these birds and fishes because the fish and birds are related to each other as flying things and those that sink themselves with their fins.

T u uacpel hic U kinil U sihsah Ca yumil ti Ds balcheob tu uich lum y
chuyan balcheob ti bay u nahmaile tu pachi tune yetel ɔochij tu ɔochix
u xulci u Meyah ca yumil ti Ds^e yoltah Mente y yutzcintci uinici ylex to hunkul Ma yoltah ca yumil ti DS unicil u Meyahi ti babahuni U nahehek lay tu
yanal bale heuac yoltah Ca yumil ti Dios ah tepal ti U uxul u Meyah y ɔoc U
Meyah yok tu ba tu hunale bacacix ɔocan u sihsic tulacal u bal caane y luume
yetel tulacal U bal caan yetel luume y tulacal bal tu sihsah cuchie heuac Ma
heli ^u yoli¹⁴³ yetel ma chachi yol Ca yumil ti Dios ah tepal lae Ua Ma lahi
tu lah U tuMtic cilich SantisiMa trinidad hunnab Dios ti oxtul U persona-
sil yuMbil Mehenbil espiritu Santo bay licil U cici patcanti kuleM ɔib lae¹⁴⁴

T u kin hijx yul oltah ca yumil ti Dios U Mente y u pale yax uinic Ca yumil ti Dios Ca hopi U kaak cunicob yetel U multunticob cilich oxtul
personas Santissima trinidad Ca thanahij Dios yumibil Dios Mehenbil Dios
espiritu Santo tilic yalic tu batanbaob Ca Ucutzcinte huntul Uinic ti baytac
kohbilane y tac Uinicile tialtic cayob yanob ti Kanab yetel chichob

(p. 8)

On the sixth day, our lord God created the animals on the face of the earth and the rest of the animals as He saw fit. Finally, at the end and when our lord God had finished completely the end of the fruits of His labors He desired to make, and having created well man that you see forever hereafter, our lord God did not desire the labors of man to be as miserable as with other things. Instead, our lord God, Ruler desired to end and finish His work by Himself alone. Although He finished creating all things in heaven and earth and all things born back then, our lord God Ruler did not desire to rest and relax. Nor did they completely finish deliberating, the blessed Holy Trinity, one God in three persons, the Father, the Son, the Holy Spirit, as is well explained in the Holy Scriptures.

On this day, our lord God desired to make and conceive[145] the first man, our lord God. Then they began to inquire and deliberate, the blessed three persons, the Holy Trinity we call God the Father, God the Son, and God the Holy Spirit. Meanwhile, they said among themselves, "We will create well a man like our image and our form to have dominion over the fishes that exist in the ocean and the birds

chichobe yan ti yke yetel balcheob yan tuuich lum cu than tu baob y lex toh-
hil bahun U hach nohil U tiplic uinic Ca yumil ti Dios tilic U hach U noh
canabal tuMen cilich oxtul U personas Santissimo Trinidad tilic U Multunticob Ua bic u nah U menticob yax uinic uay lokol cabe U noh layli tan ylilic
Dios yumbil U hochob U kohbilanob y yet pisantic hahal hach bay U uinicil
Ca yumil ti Diose tilic U . . . pisic U uanan U uinicil ti canal tilic u pacat ti
caan Ca u ɔibol te binel yt nacalie heklay Ma u ɔaahob ti u chayan U sihsa-
hob balilob chibal U pacalob yokol luuMe tulacale ti takan U uichob ti luum
U earante¹⁴⁶ U hanalobe hetun huntul uinic lae Ma bay lae Canal U uaan y
likan U pacat cha kax thantzil tumtabi u pixan y u pacat Maix u ɔaah U tzo-
tzotzel hali U uinicil yokole Maix ɔab u ɔibɔibal hal U kukMel xane ti bay
Unamal ti U chuyan¹⁴⁷ U sihsabilobe ɔaah yoc ti uaan U talel y U yabal yah
Miyatzilil yetel U cux olal cu than

(P. 9)

that exist in the air, and the animals that exist on the face of the earth," thus they spoke among themselves.[148] You will see how much justice, the very greatness to which our lord God elevated man as the utmost highest of the blessed three persons, the Holy Trinity.[149] Meanwhile, they discussed how to make well the first man here on earth the greatest that is seen as the image, the representative of God the Father, and similarly true and great as the body of our father, God, being similarly erect, His standing body. When he (Adam) looked at heaven, then he desired to go and rise up—something not given to the other created beasts that they placed on the earth, all of which have their faces to the earth in front of their food. However, this man is not like this, he is erect and raised high, his gaze is marvelous, it examines his soul and what he sees.[150] Nor did he receive true hair on his body, nor was he given much carnal desires, or feathers as pertains to the rest of the creations. He received feet and from standing comes the greatest good wisdom and judgment. So says

than Santo thoMas yk U pixanil sihnal ti Dios U yonel U batanbaob y angelesobe yokol he pix yicnal Ca yumil ti Diose bayxan yannix U cici chach
U nohil sihnal ti Ca yumil ti Dios xan he ca yumil ti Dios ah tepale yumbil
tumen tulacal bal cah tusinil bay ti caan yetel ti luume yetel ti Metnal tulacal
tu sihsah caan baabaix uinic lae utzcinab tuMen Ca yumil ti Dios lae U yumil
te sihsabilob lay ix u tzicimaob Cuchij xan bay licil yalic San Juan Damasenoe
hach bay u yet pisan dios cuchie hach ah tepal yetel Justislla u tohil ti chich
olal yetel oksah ych yantic Cu than San tomas he U sicsah Ca yax yum aDan
lae lay sipci tuMen u kebane lay U kinamtic u tzicile lay tuMen Matan u tzicile tuMen sihsabil babalob helelae heuac hetun U baylan yetel U kohbilan
Ca yumil ti Dios yan ti cuchie Ma bahun Sat Uini lae bacacix kebanchahie
bay bic tu hunali Dios ti yuchucile y tepalil ti oxtul u personas bayx tu uinic
loe hunpelili U pixan ti yanix uchucil ti kahsah u kul

(P. 10)

St. Thomas,[151] "The blessed soul is of God, the parent among them and of the angels that revolve here above with our lord God." Likewise, the great creation of our lord God also has to be really grasped. Our lord God, Ruler is father of all the entire world, as in heaven and on earth and in hell, all that was created in heaven and likewise man was well made by our lord God. These the Father created and perfected back then. Also, as St. John of Damascus truly says, "It (man) was similar to God back then, the true Ruler and Justice, justice, in having grace and compassion."[152] Thus says St. Thomas, "This our first father Adam was disheveled for he sinned, because of this his sin, he damaged his honor, because of this he is not obeyed by the created creatures but they are as they are now; and the image of our lord God he had back then never at any time will man lose it other than (if) he will sin." Just as the sole God of power and majesty is in the three persons, likewise the soul of each man has the power and the divinity

ti Dios yumbil naat likul ti Dios espiritu santo Bayxan hebic tu hunali Dios yan yetel yet has tu yukul bal Cah tusinile Matub Minan Dios bayix u pixan uinic xane ti yan tiix ɔeecbalcah heklay cucutile tulacal yoklal yanil Matub Mynan U pixan yoklal lay cuxlic layix xiMbansic layix pecsicic xane

---

U[153] capel u pectzil ɔibanil licil U cantabal yetel U nuucbesabal patci U uinicil Ca yax yuM ti aDan tumen Ca yuMyl ti Dios y U nucul sihsabci ca yax Naa ti eva

---

Ɔiban y alahan ti yunil Mayatz Genesis u kaba Cu than tuchi ca ɔoci U multuncob cilich santisima trinidad bay ɔibanil ychil cilich kulem ɔib lae ca emiob caix talob parayso terenar tu hach ciotzilil cuchi yet pisan U uenbai[154] yahaulil caan ʰekelay yanil tuMenel ca yumil ti Ds U hach yabal Mactzictac ti bahun bale tiix yantac U yabal U sihsah babalil tusinil U nohlail U yax chel cab lae lahCaten U uichancal hunppel hab hunhunpel U yantal U uich cu than San Juan evangelista yoklal yilah etsabi ti tuMen huntul angel heix taccob parayso lae lahcapis U tulumil U hool ti lembanac ti sasac takin yetel kankan takin y lahCatul angel Uaantaccob tutuluMil U hool cha Kux[155] than-

of God the Father, understanding from God the Holy Spirit. Likewise, just as God alone exists and all parts of the entire world are united in all parts of God, likewise He is in the soul of man also, and it has been preached much regarding all bodies because the soul exists in all its parts, because of this it lives and walks and moves also.[156]

The second part of the news that has been written where it has been taught and declared the creation of the body of our first father, Adam, by our lord God, and the way our first mother, Eve, was born.

It has been written and stated in the book of wisdom called Genesis that when they finished deliberating, the blessed most Holy Trinity, as is written in the blessed holy scriptures, that they descended and came to earthly paradise which was a really beautiful place back then, similar to the image of the kingdom of heaven, where there is how many really great miraculous things because of our lord God. And of all the many creations there, the greatest is the first tree of the world. This fructifies twelve times a year, once each moon it bears fruit, thus says St. John the Evangelist for he saw it, it was revealed to him by an angel.[157] Here also are obstacles in this paradise, twelve walls, gates shining with silver and gold, with twelve angels appointed to the walls, gates, it is a wonder

thantzil[158] U yilabal tiix catox yalil hunpel sayab hach ti likul tu chun U silla U kanche Culic dios ah tepal yalan yoc ca yumil ti Jesuchristo Cu hokol Sayab lae hach cha kux thantzilil yetel U ci otzilil U cuchil U pakal Ca yumile ti Dios te parayso tenerar sihsahcij[159] Ca yax yuM ti aDan lae

---

helel tun a uilic cex christiano U yanuMal u Nucul bic Patci U uinicil ca yax yuM ti aDan tuMen ca yumil ti Dios lae

---

Ca tun uol heb tan chumuc parayso terenar cilich santisima trinidad oxtul personassob tilic U Multumticob tu batanbaob Ds yuMbil Ds Mehenbil Ds espiritu Santo cu thanob Malobe utzcinte yetel c Mente Uinic tac koh-bilan tac Uenbail tialtic yetel U yuMilte yn sihsah baba. . . yano yokol cab ti luum yoklal laix canantic U pach y u tialtic U yabal kanche U yabal silla U satahob yetel pati tuMen u tzitzicbail U lobol angelobe cu than ca yumil ti Dios ti ɔocan tun yalic thanob lae Ca binob citanil tu pach paraiso terenar U chaob U hokesob U hach Utzil U ɔu luum taMil u hach Mabenil luum ti hunlukul lahCa sap tu U hoksah Dios Yutzil luum lae Damaseno U kaba hokcij luum tuMen ca yumil ti dios lae Ca tali

to be seen,[160] and there water flows from a spring whose origin is truly the chair, the seat where God the Ruler sits; this spring emerges from below the foot of our lord Jesus Christ,[161] it is truly the wonder and beauty of the place, the garden of our lord God. There in early paradise He created our first father, Adam.

Now then, you Christian, listen to the news, the meaning of how the body of our first father Adam was formed, by our lord God.

Then together in the middle of earthly paradise the holy, most Holy Trinity, three persons, while they deliberated among themselves—God the Father, God the Son, and God the Holy Spirit—they said, "We will make well and create man after our appearance and image to possess and be the lord of my creations on the earth, the land because he will care for the place; to him belongs the many chairs, the many seats the bad angels lost and left because of their pride,"[162] so said our lord God. When they finally finished saying these words, then they went to another part of earthly paradise. They took, they withdrew the very good, core of the earth from the depths, the really enclosed, eternal earth, twelve arm lengths, from which God extracted the best earth. Damascene is the name of this earth removed by our lord God.[163] Then He came

ca tali caix U cicithantah U uinicil huntul xiblal U cichcel . . . mil uinic tance-
lem hach cichicelem U kohbilan chaua U uaan yan U pol yan U xicin yan U
uich yan U chi yan U kab yan Y yoc ti chilan tu cilich tan ca cilich yum May
to oCooc haa yokol may to pacatnac May to pecsas ɔocan tun U cici pattal
Uenbail lae ca ustabi tu yikil cuxtal tumen ca yumil ti Ds Ca tun Cuxlahij
may to pacatnac Ca tun tu yala Ca yumil ti Dios than lae Epeta pacatnen
caix pacatnahij ti hach cichcelem ti hunlukul Ah Miyatz ca tun hopi U hokol
u . . . Ca hopi U hokol U tzotzel u pol caix hopi u yothal y[okol] ca u pesah
Uba ca ɔabi tub tu chij tuMen ca yumil ti dios ca hechahi u chi ca hopi u
than tilic u niptic u pixan Ca yumil di Ds yah sihsahule tilicil nacsic U pacat
canal tanMuk U yilic can yetel kin y ekobe hach lembanaccob U pacatobe
ti hach ciotziltan yilabal U yilahe ca hopi U nip pixantic Ca yumil ti Ds lae
tilic yalic than lae Be yn yumile yn hahal diose hahal ɔoc lukan yn miyatze
hahal ɔooc lukan U uchucile

(P. 13)

and He blessed the body of a handsome male person, a young man really handsome, the stature of the image lacked skin. It has a head, ears, eyes, mouth, hands, feet; there it lay in the holy presence of our holy father. He was not yet baptized,[164] he could not yet see, he could not yet move. When the forming well of this figure was finished, the breath of life was blown into it by our lord God. Then he came to life, but he could not yet even see. Then our lord God spoke saying, "Ephphatha,[165] see," and then the really handsome, eternal wise man saw. Then his . . . began to emerge; then the hair of his head began to emerge; and then he began to be covered in skin. Then he moved himself and saliva was put on his mouth by our lord God and his mouth opened. Thus he began to speak, thanking God his birth-giver,[166] raising his gaze heavenward as he sees the heavens and the sun and the stars, they are really a wonder to be seen. When he saw them, he began to thank our lord God saying these words, "O my lord, my true God, my truly perfect sage, truly perfect is the power

ucile yn yumile U ah sihsahule Manbahlen cachij ca ta paticunnahen ca ta
Uocsahen ti uinicil cha kax than yn cah ti tulacal hi bahun sihan taMenel uay
yokol Cabe hach Mactziltac yilabal yetel pactabal ti hunhul ca nip pixan ca
yax yum ti ADan ca ɔoci u sihsabal tuMen ca yumil ti Dios hach ah Miatzili
Ca hoᵽi U cicithantabal tuMen ca yumil ti Dios tilic u yalabal u xicincij u
yalabal ylto aDane cu yalabal tohcin a uol tech cuchi lae he tulacal babalob
lae tin sinsahe atialob hek^{lay}laobi balcheob xiknalob yetel y xacnalob y cayob
yanob ti kaknabe y chichiob yanob ti ykob heuac ca pat u kabaob hunhuntul
tiob ca utzac a payicob a Ueteltun Caix Utzac U kahtal ta uol u kabaob tumenel Ua bin yn pat U kabaobe bin tubuc tech lay u chun licil yn kubic ta
kab a ɔa U kabaob lae ɔocan tun yalabal lay than ti lae ca paṯi tumen ca yumil
ti Dios ca bini tu yahaulil U cilich Gloria ca hoᵽi U homolcinticcob sihsabil
balche yicnal ADan lae ti hunbanhanohij tutan ADan nuctac y Mehentac tulacal ca hoᵽi U patic U kabaob he bix

(p. 14)

of my lord the birth-giver. Before, I was nothing, then you formed me, you placed me in a human body. I am marveling at all of the many things that have been born because of you here on earth, it is a really incredible thing to be seen and viewed forever," thus praised our first father, Adam. When his (Adam's) creation from nothing had been completed by our lord God, he was a very wise man. Then he began to be blessed by our lord God as he was admonished and told, "See here, Adam," he was told, "Console yourself. All these things that I have created are yours: the creatures of the air and the four-footed animals and the fishes in the ocean and the birds on the winds, but you declare the names of each one to them so that you call them to you, and so that you will remember their names, because if I create their names you will forget. Because of this I entrust them to your hands to give them their names." This concluded the words that were said to him. Then he was left by our lord God when He (God) went to His kingdom, His holy glory. Then the created animals began to gather together around Adam. When they had gathered before Adam, all the large and small, then he began to create their names

he bix u nah maile hunhuntul tiobe ɔoccan tun U patal U kabaob tuMen
aDan lae

U yoxpel u pecτzil ca yax yum ti aDan y̱ yax na ti eva lay tulacal bal yutz
cinahob ychil lay kin lae Uchic U kubul sihsabil balchetiob U canan-
teob Bay alabci tiob tuMen ca yumil ti diose Ah tepale ca u tuchitahob xan
ca binob ɔocan tun lukkulob yicnanale ca hopi tucul ca yax yum ti ADan
tilic yalic Bla bix ualoh cu than adan Macx bin yn lakinte Uaye bin laylhin
lae ca u heah U yalakob tu Caten ca hopi yalic tu pucsikal yani xan Uet cul-
cinte yn lakinte uaye lic ca ɔocci U lah pacticob ychil tulacale cayx yilah [mi]
nan yet Uaan Minan yet p̱issan Ca u tuchitahob tu caten tulacal caix binob
ca ylab tumen ca yumil ti Dios U tucul lay aDan lae ca yalah ca yumil ti Ds
Mail Uchac U cu tal tu hunanal hach tibil ca yanac u lak cu than Ca yumil
ti dios Ca tun ɔabi ɔeɔec Uenel tumen Ca yumil ti Dios Uenel tun [n] [u167] cah
Ca kuchi

(P. 15)
that suited each one of them. This finished the creation of names by Adam.

The third part of the news of our first father, Adam, and first mother, Eve; all these things were well made within this day. Having been committed to caring for the created animals, as was commanded regarding them by our lord God Ruler, he sent them away also. When they went, finally finished leaving him, then our first father, Adam, began to think saying, "Well, how will it be?" Adam said. "Who will I accompany here; who will be the most esteemed to me among these?" Then he opened to the domesticated animals once again, he begins to say in his heart, as is usual, "Is my partner I will settle with here?" He finished surveying them and among them all he saw there was none standing erect like him, there was not a companion for him.[168] Then he sent them away again, all of them, and when they went, then his mind was seen by our lord God. "This Adam," said our lord God, "it is not possible for him to be alone; it would be a very good thing for there to be another," thus spoke our lord God. Then our lord God caused a little more sleep (upon Adam); when he was finally sleeping

ca yumil ti dios yinal Matan uyube ca hoksabi thunɔist[169] u ɔic u chalatil tumen ca yumil ti Dios Ma yubah cu checunttabi yinal tu xax ti Uenel U caah chelicbal tun U bacel U chalatic lae ca cicithantabi tumen ca yᵘmil ti Ds lay baac lae hun suthi u pec y u cuxtal huntul chupla hach cichpaM yet pisan angelesob he bix u pactabal Kankan oɾo U tzotzel U pole caix ɔabi u pixan ychil U uinicil lae cay[x] cuxlahij cuxan tun ca Ahsabi aDan ci yalabal ylab Mac yan ta xax lae cu yalabal tumen ca yumil ti Dios cayx U uncah Adam yume helay lae yn chalatiil yn baceli xan helelae uiria U kaba suhuy lae cu than ADan ti ca yumil ti Dios ɔoccaᵃn tun ᵘ cah kuchul tulacal lae ca hopi U cicithantabalob tuMen ca yumil ti Dios aDan yetel eva tanMuk yalabal tiobe tin sihsiheex lae yn sihsah uinicilexe a uohelMaex ten tin sihsahex ti Minan a yumex yetel a Naex he cenx tulacal yn ualmahthanile yn kat yn culcinteex a cici ɔocbesex yetel a cici tacuntex tulacal yn ualmah-

(P. 16)

our lord God arrived next to him without him hearing it. Then our lord God took out one rib from his (Adam's) left side without him feeling it. Then the bone, the rib was left with him by his side as he was sleeping lying down. Then it was blessed by our lord God, this bone; in an instant it moved and a woman came to life, she is really beautiful like the angels, the hair of her head is just like gold to be seen. And then her soul was placed inside her body, and she lived. When she was finally living, Adam was awakened. "Delight in hearing, seeing the person there at your side," thus was said by our lord God. And then Adam answered, "Lord, this here is of my rib, of my bone also. Now Virago is the name of this virgin," so spoke Adam to our lord God. The outcome of all this finally completed, Adam and Eve began to be blessed by our lord God while it is said to them, "You are my creations, you are my created humans, you know that by me you are my creation, you have no father and no mother; all of those commandments of mine I ask, I establish for you, [if] you keep and guard well all my

(P. 17)

Mahthanile bin yn hach yacunt tech y bin yn uilabeex yetel a kaMycex[170] Utz
yetel tibil Uay yokol cabe

Bayix ti caan xan Matan U yantal Numyaa uichilex Bay bin a kaMycex
Utz yetel tibil ua bin a ɔoc lukeseex yn ualMahthanile he tulacal balche-
cheobo xacnalob yetel xiknalob tin sihsah uay yokol cabe hach suc teex Ua U
yaMaeechobi xan tuMen hecen Macal Mac a uolahex a hantantex ychilobe
ca a pay tu kabaob bin tacobi xan Ca a yeeye MaCal Mac a katex a hantantex tuMen hach u yaMaechobi xan yetel u yaMaechobi[171] xan Bayxan aMal
oxpel Kin bin tal a yxiM a hantex likul ti caan yoklal Ma a Meyahex ten ten
bin yn tan ol tex yetel a hanlex y xane he ciMylex Matan U yantal ā uoko-
leex ti hunlukul Bayix ti yal A mehene xan bin sihic tutan kin cu tale binix
cuxlacex bahun U bakalbab Bay ā uoloah Ma yleexe Ua bin tukuc ā uoleex ti
cuxtal Uay yokol cabe bin yn chaex ta cucutileex yetel ta pixanex ti yahaulil
yn cicich Gloria ti caane Bayxane Ua a Uollahhex ca paltal tu catene bin yn
palcuntex tu caten lay tulacal cin ualic tex lae c ca a cici tacunte Ua bin a po-
chex yn UalMahthanile

(P. 17)

commandments, I will really love you and you will be seen by me and you will receive good and virtuous things here on earth.

As it is in heaven, you will have no misery inside you [here]. Thus you will receive good and virtuous things if you will keep perfectly my commandments. All these four-footed and flying creatures I created here on earth are very tame for you, and they love you also so that whichever of any of them you desire to eat, when you call their names they will come also, when you choose whichever of them you want to eat, because they truly love you. Likewise, every three days your corn, your food will come from heaven because you do not labor. I will take care of you and your food, and also you will never die, you will exist forever, and likewise for your children that will be born to you from this day forward, and you all will live however long as you desire, you cannot see it. If you are troubled by living here on earth, I will take you with your bodies and your souls to the kingdom of my delightful glory in heaven. Likewise, if you desire to be young again, I will rejuvenate you again. All this I say to you if you are obedient. If you disobey my commandments,

tulacal lic yn tzolic texe hun suttili bin yn lobol thanticex y̱ yn tohliccex Uay
ychil U ci otzilil yn pakal parayso lae hun suttila bin a uilab ã bayilex yetel
u hach yabal NuMyal yetel lix otzilil xan cu than Ca yumil ti dios ti ADan
yetel ti eva cuchi he than ɔab U tacunteobe Ma u yanal than cuchij lay Ma U
Makkikcob yetel u talicob U uich u yax cheil cab U cheel grasia cici thanan
tuMen ca yuMil ti Dios ah tepal U cheel cilich grasia yetel cuxtal yetel toh
olal Ma a talicex Ma a Makicex u uich xan yokbal hach talanil Ma u nhMa[172]
ã talicex yleex yn sihsah uinicilexe hahal than yn cah tex helel lae bin yn nu-
pintex yetel he tulacal yn sihsah balcheilobe bin U nupintechob tulacalob U
noh laili xan yn yaM alMehenex texe hach canal silla ɔaan tiob U lobil Angelesobe tu p̱atahob ti cane ãtialex licil yn sihsicex cu than Ca yumil ti Dios
tiob: [173]tzeCan joul tean[174] u he chitabal[175] ti aDan y̱ ti eva = lay silla lae =
hun suthi u chabal lep̱ olal Cisinob yicnal SihSabil uinicob lae Ca hop̱i U
MultumutiCob: ua bic U nah U LuKsicob y u tabsicob = lay than ALab tiobe
tumenel Ca yumil ti Dios = Ca tun hop̱i Catun

(P. 18)

all that I declare to you now, in that moment I will curse you and cast you out of here from this my beautiful garden paradise; in that moment you will see your disposition (nakedness) and really an abundance of torments and misery also," thus said our lord God to Adam and Eve in those days. Here is the word given to them to keep; there was no other order back then: that they should not eat nor touch the fruit of the first tree of the world, the tree of grace blessed by our lord God, Ruler, the tree of holy grace and life and health.[176]

"Do not touch nor eat of the fruit because it is very solemn, you are not worthy to touch it. See, you are my created humans, I am swearing this to you today, I will oppose you, and all these, all my creations, will oppose you. Most importantly, you are my first children, for you are the truly eminent seats given to the wicked angels that left them in heaven; they are yours, for which reason I created you," thus speaks our lord God to them. . . . there the seats were laid out for Adam and Eve, immediately the devils are taken in anger with these created humans. Then they began to conspire among themselves what would be a good way to remove and deceive them regarding this deal spoken to them by our lord God. So then they began

[In the left-hand margin running onto the top margin is written in darker, more recent ink: como a las 3 1/2 de la mañana Sabado Sr Dlefino Mo alma-neser el dia 5 ~~Dicimbre~~ Disciembre falliecio 5 de Disiembre de 1925]

u multanbaob = tu Audiensia = tilic yalcob tu batanbaob bix u nah ta thanix = bax bin ment. helelae = lay ua bin naCact cu . . . Chil Sillaob tzaantoon cu-chie ma u nahmaobii = bix u kab Luksic tiob ᵗᵃ thanex = Ma ua tibil ta thanex Ca hokol huntul tabsic = y u tial luksic tay thanob = tulacal = Seb chibtab-tic yoklal Ma uhach paktic U tial Samal Ua Cabeh helay tu sebale = hokok huntul toon hach Noh u Mayatz[177] u tial U Luksob ti keban[178] = Ca maac U binob ti Caan = y u ɔoc luksicob lay than Alab tiobe = tumenel Ca yumil ti D.ˢ lay bay helelae = patanob tumen Ca yumil ti D.ˢ = ma mac yanij tu sebal cin binel ten Cen Cisin Zerpiente yolkal tene hach noh yn mayatz = Chup-lalob cin binel yn tabes yoklal = ma chich u yoli = tumen he xiblale Chiich u yol yoklal ah mayatzil xan Cu thanob = Ca ɔoCi u multhanob = tu Audien-siaob ychil Metnal Caix homol bini lay huntul Cisin Serpiente: U kaba lae

---

Teet parayso terenal: tilic u chaic u uich chuplal y u kohbilan yan u xik yan u kab Canal u uinicil = tal u cah ti can tu thane Serpiente u kaba = Ca naci = tu yax Cheil Cab = Ca hopi u bakiic Uba yax che lae: lay uethan ma u talicob CuChie = tian[179] Eua:

(P. 19)

[In the left-hand margin running onto the top margin is written in Spanish: At about 3:30 Saturday morning, Señor Dlefino Mo, at dawn the 5th of December, died, December 5, 1925.]

to gather in an audiencia (court) while they spoke among themselves, "What way seems good to you? What will be done now if these ascend to the chairs, seats, given to us formerly? How can their hands be removed from them (the chairs) in your opinion? Perhaps, in your opinion, it is not a good thing that one leaves to deceive and remove from them, end, the words, all that pertains to what was promised? Now quickly one of us leaves, really great is his wisdom so that they (Adam and Eve) fall into sin, so that they will not go to heaven and fulfill the word spoken to them by our lord God. This to be done now as they are abandoned by our lord God; no one is there. I will go immediately, I who am the devil serpent because really great is my wisdom. I will go to the women because their will[180] is not strong, but regarding the man, his will is strong for he is a wise man also," thus they spoke.[181] Then they finished deliberating in their audiencia in hell, and then quickly he went, that one devil serpent, this is his name.

To earthly paradise he went to take the fruit to the woman, and its form[182] has wings, hands, its body is a snake, its speech was almost like a snake; its name is serpent. Then it climbed up into the first tree of the world; then it began to wind itself around the first tree there that they were forbidden not to touch in those days. Eve

naɔaan Chi Ca u nacsah u paCat Eua Canale Ca yilah = Ca hach haki yol tumenel = Caix Cilbanahi u pucsikal Chuplale = Ca yalah Cisin ti ma u kakal
a uol ten maa chaic SahaCil ten xan he tene Uay Sihene ā UiChilexe ten yax
Sibil uaye Cu than Cisin = Ca u nuCah Eua tus a Cah ten Ma tech Uil Cech
Uaye = Minan yn chilbal bay lae = Ma uay yanenie Cu than Serpiente Ca tun
u Cantah u than = ti Eua tilic yalic tie = yn kati yn uohelte = Ua bic u than
Dios tex tu kab che yn yanil lae = Ca a ualex Uuye lay yn than = Uohelte ma
a muclic ten = Cu than Cisin ti Eua = Ca a ualabtech Mabal u yanal lae halili
U uethah ma Makiic U uich che = yoklal talan bin tu than yoklal u cheil grasia = Cuxtal toh olal lay tun uethan = Ua bin makee bin u tohlacon . . . Uay
tu ciotzilil pakale = Ma a tablex U nucilibe = Bax[183] cibah Ca tu tohlahon
ti Cane Uchie Manbal U nac U makac ma u pec a uol tumen Manbal bin u
ment tex = Cabin Ɔococ xan = Eua makex bin o CoCex A mayatzil = hach
hahbal cin u alic tech = U nohlail xan bin kuchuch A PaCatex ti hun xaman y
hun chikin cu than Cu than Serpiente ti Eua = hach may Ualo tus a Cah ten
= Cu than Eua = Bla bin a uila Ua tus yn Cah tech = Ca U yuxah Serpiente
hunpel tu uich U Cheil Grasia Caix U makaah

(p. 20)

was close to its mouth when Eve lifted her gaze high and she saw it. She was really frightened because of it and the woman was disturbed.

Then the devil said to [her], "Do not let your heart be frightened because of me, do not have fear of me also. Me, I was born here among you, I was the first born here," thus speaks the devil.

Then Eve responded, "You are lying. I do not see you here (among the other animals)."

"My lineage is not of these; I am not from here," thus speaks the serpent. Then he gave his speech to Eve in which he says to her, "I want to know what God said to you about this tree branch where I am, that you speak, listen to this my speech, understand, do not hide this from me," thus spoke the devil to Eve.

"Then you (I)[184] say to you nothing else. Truly He prohibited not to eat of the fruit of the tree because of its mystery, He says, because the tree of grace, life, and health is thus forbidden, if we eat of it He will cast us out of here from the beautiful garden."

"Do not be fooled by His response. Thus He did when He cast us from heaven back then, nothing bad will happen from eating it, do not be unsettled because of it, He will do nothing to you. And when it is finished, Eve, your eating it, you will enter into wisdom. I really speak the truth to you, the reach of your vision will be the greatest from the north to the west (everywhere)," thus speaks the serpent to Eve.

"Truly perhaps you are deceiving me," thus speaks Eve.

"Well, you will see if I am deceiving you." Then the serpent picked a fruit from the tree of grace and ate it

serpiente taklic U uich Eua = ꝺoCan tun U makiic tan coch lae Ca u ꝺaah
ti Eua tan Coch xani = ylae bax yanil ti U makal tin makah tan Coch xani =
Mak tun helelae = Ma bahun U Cah bin U ment lob tech = Ua yabale le tun
be Cu than cisin ti Eua lae Ca hach Sahachi u pucsikal cuchie pecanix yol
Cuchi tumenel Ma tux u chaic than tumen patan tumen ADan cuChi tun
u ximbal tu U Canaⁿ pakal CuChi = Ca pecnah yol tic U hayab tan U tu-
cla xan tan u pec yol: y tu U Lubul ti bay U Uinicile yan ti bal[ca] Capel yol
xani = U cibah Eua lae Manbal U cante helea yn maki bin heuac tan u pec
U pucsikal Cuchi hun suthi U makiic Ca u pitlukkah = U ꝺoocsic yolah u
pucsikal = U tabsahanil tumen Cisine = Ca uli ADan = ꝺac Cuna hanili ti
ADan tumen Euae = ꝺoCan tun U tabsah Ca u pulah Uba = hach cilmac yol
Ca u pulah ᵘᵇᵃ Canal = Likul Canal alCab bin cil tu Cuchil ti metnal = hach
ciotzil kamic ti metnal = Noh tziCanix Ca kuchi tumen UChic U ꝺoySic =
yax uinic U no holCan lae

Ti ꝺocan tun U makiic Eua lay U uich pakal lae Ca hopi u hach yabal
Sahacil ti Cilbanac tulaCal U uinicil = Ca hopi u lubul u muk = y u po-
sal Ca hopi U Lukul u matan

(P. 21)

in the presence of Eve. When he finished eating half of this (fruit), he gave half to Eve also. "See how it is meant to be eaten? I ate half also. Eat it now, nothing bad is going to happen to you; if a lot (does happen), then it does," thus speaks the devil to Eve.

Then she really had fear in her heart at that time, she was unsure back then because she could take council from nowhere since being left by Adam back then, since he went walking in it (the garden), he was caring for the garden back then. Then she was unsure, she yawned, she is thinking also, she is deliberating, and such is the fall of mankind that are on the earth, they are indecisive also. Eve did nothing, she said, "Now, I will eat it," however she was doubting in her heart back then. Instantly she eats it, then quickly swallowed it. She fulfilled the desire of her heart; she was fooled by the devil. Then Adam arrived, the cursed food was given to Adam by Eve. When the fraud was complete, he (the devil) hurled himself down, really happy; then he hurled himself down high, from high (in the tree) and ran happy to his place in hell; really happily he was received in hell. He was greatly honored when he arrived because he succeeded in conquering the first man, this great warrior.[185]

Then when Eve finished eating this fruit of the garden, all mankind began to really, greatly fear and tremble, they began to be frail and pale, they began to leave the gift of

grasia U bucma Caix ChaCanhi U Suttal = Ca hopi yokol ti hach okom yol
ti hach ya u pucSikal Ca tali aDan lake yn uet Canan pakale = bax ta Cibah
bax Ca hach oktic = hach pochech xan = cu than ADan = Ca tu yalah Eua =
Be yn UiChame Sipen taksaben tumen Cisin tin makah U uich che = Uethan
tumen Cilich yume ma talice Cu than Eua = Ca Yalah tie = be chuplalae =
hach yan tin Uol ley bal Ca mentic lae = Cu yalabal tumen aDan heuac yn
yamaech = bal bin C utzcint helelae = Cu than ADan = Ca yalah Euae: Manbal u yanal Sipen Sipon Catulil Cu than Eua = be chuplale = bin yn mak lob
heuace yn Uohel matan u manel tin koch = binix kalac xani Ca u chaah ADan
= Ca u makah Ca u lukah Cuchi = Maix bini y̱ Maix u chuchi u manel tu
kochi Cakapi lay u ChiCul yan t koch = Con xiblalone = heix chuplale ma
chiCan yoklal u pitluktah = Mantaɔhix tu Cal xan

Ti ɔocan tun U Sipilob: tu Catulilob Cat tali Ca yumil ti Dios = yicnalob
oxtenhi u thanal ADan tumen Ca yumil ti D.ˢ = Matan U ⁿᵘCub tumen U
Sublacilob = ̱pucenpucob yalan Che habin SahaCob[186]

grace they wore. And then her shame appeared, then much anguish and pain began to enter in her heart. Then the companion, Adam, arrived.

"I am forbidden to care for the garden. What did you do? Why do you really cry, are really dishonored?" thus spoke Adam.

Then Eve said, "Oh my husband! I sinned, I was tricked by the devil, I ate the fruit of the tree forbidden by the holy father not to touch," thus spoke Eve.

Then he said to her, "Oh woman! Truly it exists in my soul this thing we did," thus it was said by Adam, "But I love you. How will we make it good now?" thus spoke Adam.

Then Eve said, "There is no other thing. I sin, both of us sin," thus spoke Eve.

"Oh woman! I will eat this evil but I know it will not pass through my throat, it will be blocked also."

Then Adam took it, ate, and swallowed it, and it did not go nor was it possible for it to pass through his throat, it was stuck. This is the sign that exists in the throats of us men, but the woman does not have the sign because she quickly swallowed it and it passed down also.

Then when they had completed their error,[187] the both of them, then our lord God arrived in their company. Three times Adam was called by our lord God[188]; they never responded because they were embarrassed, they were crouched down, afraid, underneath a Habin (Dogwood) tree,[189]

(P. 23)

bay uil minan tac u nokob ma u chac u ChaCanhal yicnal u yumile ^{ca tun thani} tumē ^{ca yumil} DSe ADan = ADan: ADan: ci yalabal tumen Ca yumil ^{ti Dios} = yn cilich yumee: tin nucah a than oxten a than: Cen tumen yn SahaCil yoklal ti Kamil a than Cen= Ca tin taCah ynba yalan Che = Cu than a ADan = hoken uaye ci yalabal tumen Ca yumil ti Dios = talel yn Cah yn Cilich yumee = Cu than Ca tali Ca u chaah hun lap u Leche = u nacab tu subtalob = y tu CuCu- tilob = y Eua Ca alabi tumen Ca yumil ti D.ˢ = tiob ADan bax lay lae = bax tamen tan bay loe = Cex lay grasia U Chic yn ƆaCeChe CuChie Cu yalabal tumen Ca yumil ti Dˢ = yn Cilich yumee = helay chuplal tu layti lubSahen ti Sipil Cu than ADan : Caten chuple = bax tumen ta lubSah a uicham ti Sipil yn cilich yume Cisin tu tabSahen Cu than Eua: bay tun bin U pulu pultic u batanbaob = y yokol cisin he Ceyabah Ca yumil ti D.ˢ: bay lae Ca hopi U keyah thantabalob = tu yail Keyah tumen Ca yumil ti D.ˢ = tilic yalabal ti chuplale he teChe ma bikin bin a uilab Utz y chibalob = tumen tech lubes ti Sipil ADan = lay U Chun lae: y yabal numya:

for as they did not have clothes, it was impossible for them to appear in the presence of the lord, so then it was said by our lord God, "Adam, Adam, Adam," so it was said by our lord God.

"My holy father, I [did not][190] answer your call the three times you spoke to me because of my fear of the strength of your voice to me, so I hid myself below the tree," thus spoke Adam.

"Go out from there," so it was said by our lord God.

"I am coming my holy father," thus he spoke. Then he (Adam) arrived. Then he took a handful of rough cloth, he placed it on their shameful parts and on their bodies, including Eve.

Then it was said by our lord God to them, "Adam why are you like this, I gave you grace and little sense back then," thus it was said by our lord God.

"My holy father, I fell into error because of this woman here," thus spoke Adam.

Again to the woman [God said], "Why did you cause your husband to fall into error?"

"My holy father, the devil beguiled me," thus spoke Eve.

Thus they made excuses among themselves and concerning the devil, but our lord God reprimanded like this. Then He began to tell them off; with harshness they were admonished by our lord God while it was said to the woman, "But as for you, you will never see goodness and descendants because you caused Adam to fall into error. For this reason, with great suffering

bin a Ualinte U Chun Cabal Cah lae y a uoltzilil y u kinam ti yan a Cimil
tiix yan a Cuxtal xani = bay tech xan xiblale ma utz bin a Culahbalexi ychil
u hach yabal numya: helan helantac = he in SihSah babalilobe: tin kubah ta
kabex Cuchie bin U nupin techob bin puɔlahCob techob = ti ma a Caxan-
ticob y a ualicobe = lay than bin u ƆoCesobe hetun texe ma a uoltahex a
ƆoCesex yn ualmahthanil yn CulCinah a tacuntex CuChie lay U Chun lae
= lukenex Uaye: xenex hetub a uolahex a mentex U yayatulul a siplexe = bay
lukicob ychil pakal parayso terenal lae: Ca binob yalan Che tu yam kaxob =
Ca hopi U mentic U penitensiaob Catal u xulel[191] U kinil U Cuxtalob = Uay
yokol cabe = Amen Jesus

(P. 24)

you will give birth, this principal duty, and your affliction and the pain that exists in your death and life also. Like you, man also is no good, you will sit among really great suffering different from these my creations that I placed in your hands back then, they will oppose you, will flee from you. You cannot find them and command them; they will obey these words, but you did not desire to fulfill my commandment I established for you to keep back then. For this reason, you are cast out of here. Go wherever you desire, do penance for your error."

Thus they were removed from the garden, this terrestrial paradise. Then they went to a desert in between the forests, then began the work of their penance until the final day of their lives here on earth.[192] Amen Jesus.

2

Genealogies, Parables, and the Final Judgment

AUH YN YEHUATL: YN PAUL: YN ONTLACHIX:
Y MICTLAN: CENCA MOMAUHTI: CENCA: CHOCAC:
ÇAN ACHITONCA: YN IPA MOQUETZ: YN TLEXOCHTLI:
CENCA YUHQUI MA: CENPOHUALXIHUITL: YN
IPAN QUIMA HUEL QUĪTLACAYTAC: YN DIAPLOSME
YN TLATLACATECOLLO YN INTETEPOZCAL: YNIC
TECHCOCOTONA: TEPOZAPACO: CONTLALLIA
YN TONACAYO: CENMICAC AYC TECEHUIA:
YN TLAHUELLILOQUE

AND PAUL SAW THINGS IN HELL; HE WAS VERY
FRIGHTENED AND WEPT; HE STOOD ON THE HOT
COALS FOR ONLY A SHORT TIME, BUT IT SEEMED TO
HIM LIKE TWENTY YEARS. HE SAW THE SEMBLANCE
OF THE DEVILS AND DEMONS WITH THEIR IRON
TONGS WITH WHICH THEY CUT US UP; THEY PLACE
OUR BODIES IN METAL TUBS; THE EVIL ONES NEVER
GIVE US RELIEF IN ALL ETERNITY.
—Schøyen Collection, MS 1692,
"Nahuatl Bible"

IN THE BIBLE, the book of Acts recounts that as the disciples stood watching the resurrected Jesus ascend into heaven, two angels appeared and said, "Men of Galilee, why are you standing there looking at the sky? This Jesus who has been taken up from you into heaven will return in the same way as you have seen him going into heaven."[1] Since that moment, Christians have been anticipating the return of Christ and his ushering in of a new age of Christianity. For Christians, the Second Coming of Christ is a monumental event marking the end of the existing dispensation, and the beginning of another. In the process of this ending and beginning, Christ judges mankind to determine their state in the new order. How this occurs, and what good works and sins distinguish the saved from the damned, dominated the theme of many a sermon from the early ages of Christianity to the early modern native-language texts of New Spain to the present.

In certain respects, the worldview of the Maya was not too dissimilar from that of early modern Spanish colonizers. As made evident from the previous chapter, the Maya took interest in creative period beginnings. Yet they also noted the destructive endings to these periods with an eye toward the re-creation of the next age. The precontact Dresden Codex and colonial Chumayel, Tizimin, and Pérez all reference a previous ending of a world age marked by a flood and the beginning of the next age.[2] In truth, it should not be surprising, then, that many colonial Maya texts, including the Teabo Manuscript, contain Maya-Christian redactions of the Final Judgment and the Second Coming of Christ with its role in beginning a new age of Christianity.

This chapter examines the section of the Teabo Manuscript (pp. 24–33) that immediately follows the Genesis Commentary and that details the genealogy of Christ and a treatise on the Final Judgment as inspired by Matthew 25. Regarding the latter, this chapter also explores texts within the Tusik and Chumayel to reveal cognate and thematically similar texts. In the end, the analysis provides further details into those aspects of Christianity that Mayas chose to absorb and preserve in their communal texts and examines how they creatively incorporated eschatological doctrine into their preexisting worldview.

The Genealogy of Christ

Immediately following the Genesis Commentary, the Teabo Manuscript continues explaining that Adam and Eve lived 4,050 years on earth. (Indeed, the genealogy may be seen as a continuation of the commentary.) After establishing the mortal state of man as a result of Adam and Eve's expulsion from earthly paradise, the text then outlines the lineage of Christ through Abraham as found in Matthew 1:1–16. The Gospel of Matthew was directed to the Jews, and the work places specific emphasis on proving Christ's divinity to that nation. Such an audience would be familiar with the lineage of Abraham and King David and the Messianic prophecies of the Old Testament. Thus, it is not surprising that the Gospel connects Christ to both throughout.

We can only speculate as to why the Teabo Manuscript includes the lineage of Christ—no other Maya work that I am aware of contains this text. But its inclusion seems logical when discussing temporal ages in the world-views of both Europeans and the Maya. Most reportorios included a chronology and discussion about the ages of the world. Because God created the world in six periods or days and rested on the seventh, medieval theologians believed that the world's past, present, and future likewise fit into six periods or ages, with the seventh following the Final Judgment and ushering in a period of peace and rest. According to Rodrigo Zamorano's 1594 *Cronología y reportorio*, some viewed the world's six ages as follows:

> [Theologians] consider the first age being since the beginning of the world until the universal flood. The second age was from the flood until the birth of Abraham. The third age since the birth of Abraham until the beginning of the reign of King David and others take it to the construction of the Temple of Solomon. The fourth since the end of the third until the destruction of the temple and the transmigration of Babylon. The fifth since the transmigration until the birth of our redeemer, Jesus Christ. The sixth since this birth until the end of this era, age, and time of the Final Judgment. And because in the creation of the world, God ended his work on the seventh day, the seventh age will be everything that follows after the Final Judgment that will be calm and peaceful.[3]

Thus, when discussing the Final Judgment of the sixth age, it would only make sense to begin with the commencement of that age, in this case the birth of Christ; it is possible that the Maya author(s) were following this pattern.[4] Moreover, the season of Advent typically includes sermons on both Christ's first coming (his birth) and his pending Second Coming.

Regardless of the motive, the Maya's appreciation for genealogy and lineage certainly did not begin with their European colonizers. The precontact hieroglyphic inscriptions found throughout Yucatan bespeak a strong tradition of preserving and recording noble lineages. This tradition carried into the colonial period, when, as Matthew Restall demonstrates (1997), one's chibal, or lineage, "formed a partial basis for identity, economic organization, and sociopolitical faction within each cah."[5] The marriage patterns illustrated in Maya testaments from Ixil clearly illustrate the importance of maintaining and preserving one's noble lineage through unions with similar chibalob.[6] Lineage also played an important role among Maya nobles who wrote numerous petitions to colonial officials to form connections with ancestors who assisted Spaniards in their efforts to conquer, convert, and colonize.[7] Even texts such as the *Popol Vuh* and its naming of K'iche' lords down to the colonial period demonstrate the importance of preserving genealogies.[8] And a genealogical diagram—perhaps the only other extant example outside the "Xiu Family Tree"—of Pedro Chan and Juana May's respective families further illustrates the importance of such, at least to some, in the colonial period (see figure 2.1).[9]

Although theological authors, including St. John of Damascus, included a discussion of the genealogy of Christ, the genealogy in the Teabo Manuscript is remarkably similar to that found in Matthew.[10] Indeed, there are only two discrepancies, and both occur within the first three lines of the text. In the first, the manuscript states "Abraham begat Jacob" instead of "Abraham begat Isaac; and Isaac begat Jacob," omitting mention of Isaac altogether. The second concerns the next line, where instead of the biblical "Jacob begat Judas and his brethren; and Judas begat Phares and Zara of Thamar," the manuscript reads "Jacob begat 'Jodam' and Judas and his descendants, Phares and Zara of Thamar."[11] The primary deviation concerns the mention of Jodam—an unidentifiable figure in relation to Christ's genealogy but likely a reference to Onan, one of Judah's sons, whose wife, Tamar, will eventually provide Judah with twins, Phares and Zara.[12]

This is not the only case where the admittedly difficult and relatively unknown biblical names proved a challenge for the Maya author of the genealogy. Such names appear phonetically written throughout the lineage, with the conflation of names and places occurring frequently. For example, the previously mentioned Zara of Thamar (Latin, *Zaram de Thamar*) appears as "Saromon detanan," Booz of Rachab (Latin, *Booz de Rachab*) as "baosdarad," and Obed of Ruth (Latin, *Obed ex Ruth*) as "obeter xuth." Such errors would have been avoided had the author been consulting the Bible or a Spanish priest. Furthermore, the Maya were extremely familiar with the Latin and Spanish preposition "de" that would have appeared in the Vulgate or a corresponding Spanish text. But somehow the preposition was lost in the name altogether, almost as if the Maya author was hearing the Latin name Booz de Rachab spoken and recorded such as "baosdarad," or simply had no idea Rachab was Booz's mother and included it in the name.

This then provides further insight into the copying of these texts. The

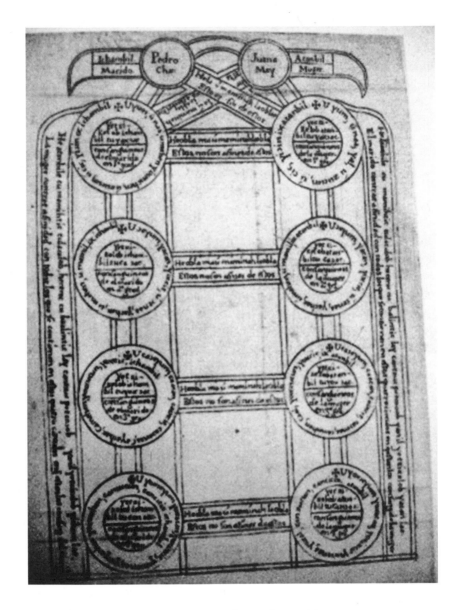

FIGURE 2.1. Genealogical Text of Pedro Chan and Juana May

misspelling of the names in the genealogy of Christ offers a few possibilities. The manuscript could have been authored as someone dictated the text. Indeed, Bricker and Miram made a similar suggestion when examining the spelling of a certain scribe that helped compose the Kaua:

> [T]he spelling of Spanish words is so bizarre that we wonder whether he recorded the words phonetically as the text was being dictated to him, instead of copying it himself from a written version. How else can the spelling of *se fundó* as *Segundo, no sin grande* as *nos ignorante . . . ya* as *lla*, and *hazen* as *acen . . .* be explained? These are the kinds of errors we would expect from someone who was not a native speaker of Spanish.[13]

The thoughtful layout and overall composition of the text offers another possibility, at least for the surviving version of the manuscript. Similar to the errors found in the Genesis Commentary's redaction of the Ptolemaic universe, it is possible that the Maya author of either the original or some copy along the way penned the lineage of Christ without direct reference to its original, perhaps as the lineage was dictated to him by a priest or some other person. Subsequent copyists, if any, would simply transcribe the names' erroneous spellings. This is not unreasonable, after all. Most of the names in the lineage would give the most ardent Christian reason to pause. For the Maya author, they were simply foreign and abstract names that derived from a long-ago age of Christianity.

Treatise on the Parable of the Sheep and Goats

The next section of the Teabo Manuscript (pp. 27–32) introduces the pending eschatological discussion (addressed in the next chapter) with its redaction of the parable of the sheep and goats that Christ gave to his disciples as recorded in Matthew 25:31–46. The parable was well known among ecclesiastics and theologians for its apocalyptic content and frequently appears referenced in works concerning the Final Judgment. In the biblical parable, Christ sits on his throne of glory while the wicked and righteous are separated before him "as a shepherd separates the sheep from the goats." The righteous gather on the right hand of Christ destined for eternal glory, while the wicked are on his left and intended for "eternal fire prepared for the devil and his angels."[14] According to the parable, works of charity, or the lack thereof, separated the righteous from the wicked, the sheep from the goats.

This Doomsday parable served as thematic fodder for a section of the Chumayel.[15] Here the section follows the biblical account while augmenting it with other biblical figures and names. For example, the righteous are told they will share the glory of Elisha, Methuselah, and Enoch who have seats in heaven (again we see the emphasis on seats). Although thematically similar, the passage differs from that found in the Teabo Manuscript. The manuscript employs the parable as a springboard to launch itself into a protracted discussion of the sins committed by the damned and the pains of hell. Although the Maya text fails to directly cite the biblical passage, its correlation is clear from its division of the righteous and wicked on the right and left hands of God.[16] That said, the Teabo Manuscript takes much liberty in altering and expanding the parable to suit its needs. Recall that the biblical parable uses charitable acts to distinguish the righteous from the wicked. Although the Maya text defines the righteous along such lines, the wicked are primarily those who did not believe and who did not "abandon [their] whoring and [their] concubinage."[17]

Regarding one's faith, the term employed for "to believe" is *ocsah ti ol*. As William Hanks demonstrates, this phrase is the product of reducción and employs the Maya verb *oc*, "to enter," with a causative suffix, the preposition *ti*, and *ol*, "heart," to mean "to cause to enter into the heart." The use of the root *oc*, "enter," appears frequently throughout the discourse of conversion, as it signified "an entering into a new reality."[18] To describe those who failed to enter into the new Christian life, the phrase simply employed the negative *ma* or a similar variant. Regarding sexual deviance, colonial Catholicism exerted much effort in defining and controlling the sexual desires of the natives, and such has always been the proverbial thorn in the side of the Church. As a sin, the topic occupies more space than any other in ecclesiastical texts. For example, in an 1803 manuscript Maya confessional manual designed for a Franciscan friar, more than half of the questions directed to the Maya penitent concerned issues of sexual morality.[19] No doubt the Maya trained in the schools of the friars received personally much instruction on what ecclesiastics defined to be sexual deviance; its appearance here as the deciding factor between salvation and damnation, then, is not surprising.

The Maya text is far from subtle in its description of the penalties accorded to condemned adulterers. Among other lines, we read, "For their torment, their bodies and flesh are peeled; very miserable things also happen to them so that they scream and moan from their great suffering in hell."[20] The text is full of dialogue from the sinners recounting their misery and wailings and heinous descriptions of the tortures reminiscent of the images produced by Albrecht Dürer or Jacob Isaacsz van Swanenburgh, a mentor of Rembrandt (see figures 2.2 and 2.3). The millennial Franciscan friars were well versed in such images and descriptions of hell and used many in their evan-

FIGURE 2.2. Jacob Isaacsz van Swanenburgh (1571–1638), *The Harrowing of Hell*

gelization of the natives. Not surprisingly, treatises on hell and its torments commonly occupy the pages of various native-language religious texts — and even moralistic plays — intended to instruct the natives of New Spain.[21] Moreover, images and paintings of apocalyptic doom adorn various churches and chapels throughout central Mexico and Yucatan.[22] Such European images and descriptions of hell and its torments certainly influenced those found in the Teabo Manuscript. Although the Maya believed in an underworld of sorts, *metnal*, it represented the location of the dead; metnal was not a pleasant place, but it also lacked the torments of the Christian hell prescribed to the wicked. At the time of the Spanish arrival, Christianity was expert in the use of graphic imagery to encourage religious devotion, and here we see its employment for and by Maya Christians.

After describing the horrors of hell, the Maya text returns to the biblical parable. The manuscript affirms that the charitable works of the righteous toward the servants of God also served God himself, or as the Bible would have it, "Whatever you did for one of these least brothers of mine, you did for me."[23] The righteous then ascend to heaven, single file, while playing trumpets and *chirimías*[24] "of great beauty." Here, the condemnation of the wicked follows the biblical account in that they failed to perform charitable works and thus were sent to the fires of hell. The section then ends with an "Amen."

Interestingly, within this section and Christ's dialogue with the sinners, Christ refers to his *hach keban*, or true/legitimate sin—a theological impossibility. Although uncertain, it is possible that within the eschatological context of the text Christ's "keban" refers to his impending judgment and destruction that will be released upon the wicked on his return. Here we see the fluidity of keban in its original form. It is doubtful that the Maya concept of keban equaled that of the Christian concept of sin, although the authors of Maya reducido paired keban with the concept from the beginning.[25] Similar to the Nahuatl word of choice for sin, *tlatlacolli*, the Maya understanding of keban seems to have included "fault" and "error" and myriad other definitions of a negative connotation, particularly when combined with verb roots, adjectives, and nouns ranging from *keban thanil*, "betrayal," to *keban uol*, "to be sad."[26] Yet even given the fluidity of keban, it is strange to see the stand-alone word used in conjunction with Christ in a religious text. Indeed, for the sinless Christ to refer to his sin—even if only in reference to the Final Judgment and destruction—is quite unorthodox, and although "keban" surely related successfully the misery and "badness" of that day (so often described in the scriptures as terrible), it is unlikely an ecclesiastic would have let such a correlation pass and again points to the native authorship of the text.

FIGURE 2.3.
Albrecht Dürer,
The Last Judgment, 1510

The next section (pp. 32–33), set apart by its Latin heading, continues the narrative of the previous section, and thus I place them together. However, the two sections do appear individually in other texts. In fact, this second part of the narrative also appears in the Tusik.[27] The Chilam Balam version of the passage is similar, although not an exact replica, with deviations in orthography and word choice. Moreover, the Tusik manuscript is oftentimes illegible, thus leading to gaps and holes in the text. The Tusik also couches the passage among apocalyptic themes as it immediately follows a discussion of the Final Judgment and its rendition of *The Fifteen Signs before Doomsday*. Regardless, it serves as yet another example of a cognate apocalyptic text and further testifies to the significance of such to the colonial Maya.

The section in the Teabo Manuscript begins with the Latin phrase *aa qua perduCat aD uitam eternam*, or generally, "bring us to everlasting life." This appears to be an attempt at the phrase *perducat nos ad vitam aeternam*, which is the priest's response to the Confiteor, or at the end of the three invocations at the Penitential Rite. The Maya text in this section begins with a drop cap and recounts the events and conversations relating to divided families where some are saved and others are damned, with sexual morality again playing the decisive role. Amongst the laments of such separation, blame is also found. Damned children not only curse their parents for their bad examples, but also for their lack of chastisement and correction. As a result the children "begin to fight among themselves and tear the bodies of their mothers and fathers" while devils torment them.[28]

The apocalyptic text further reflects Maya rhetoric and ideology. Speaking to the condemned, the text says:

> *xenex tukil metnal xenex ti hunlukul cici olal helelae: yanil kux cob y hunkul kak = Ma tupbin ti anix U hach yabal cisinob numsicex ti ya tilic a bucinticex kak y U ɔ^{al}bal ti a bakeex =*[29]
>
> (Go now to the corner of hell, leave forever the joy of today to where there is gnashing of teeth and eternal fire that does not extinguish and there are really great devils to afflict you while you are clothed with fire and your flesh fries.)

This line provides various observations. The Bible references the "four corners" of the earth on a few occasions, but always as a metaphor for "everywhere."[30] The Maya also reference a four-cornered terrestrial plane associated with the cardinal points, each with its own color: white north, yellow south, red east, and black west. The corners, or *tu'uk*, play an essential role in the quincunx organization of the cosmos, with a central space oftentimes occupied by a world tree; the corners also frequently appear in creation myths.[31] Moreover, the importance of the four directional corners continued throughout the colonial period, appearing in various documents including primordial titles and, more frequently, land sale documents or testaments with border markers or stone mounds to delineate the borders of a plot of land.[32] For example, in Francisco Itza's 1748 testament from Ixil he describes the location of his bequeathed land by describing the plots of land surrounding his in all four directions.[33] And Marcos Chan of Ebtun stated in 1696 regarding his land that "its stone mounds are at its four corners."[34] Today Maya shamans and farmers continue the tradition by praying to all four cardinal directions or corners, "tukil," of a cornfield prior to planting.

The use of corners appears in the line above as the wicked are sent to the "corner of hell," and this phrase again appears at the conclusion of this section. Although the Tusik contains a cognate passage, it does not employ this phrase. It is possible that the Teabo Manuscript uses the phrase *tukil metnal* to give space and location to metnal as possessing its own corner or tu'uk. The direction west and its color black is typically associated with the Maya underworld, as that is where the sun descended.[35] Although the Teabo Manuscript fails to assign a specific cardinal direction to metnal, it does take care to give it a corner in the cosmos.

Such subtle nuances join the frequent use of parallel constructions throughout the discourse to add a distinct Maya element to the text. Regarding constructions, an especially vivid example concerns the punishment of the wicked, whose bodies burn with fire: "bay u Yelel U hobon Cheil hobon Chee u balma kake" (as burns a hollow tree trunk, a hollow tree trunk that contains fire).[36]

Once again, the texts represented in the Teabo Manuscript resonate well within both a Christian and Maya worldview. The genealogy of Christ leading to his birth found prominence in the Gospel of Matthew and marks a common thematic topic in the season of Advent, when eschatological material frequently appeared. Moreover, the parable of the sheep and the goats likewise serves as an appropriate introduction to the upcoming discussion on the Final Judgment—a topic of immense popularity among medieval and early modern Christians.

Importantly, the Maya chose to record and preserve such treatises due in no small part to their correlation with a preexisting Maya worldview. For centuries both before and after the conquest, the Maya maintained (and in some cases created) lineage records to serve their purposes. Indeed, the Maya word for noble, *almehen*, has the implicit meaning of "the child of a man and woman of importance"; they are the *hijo de algo* or *hidalgo* in the Spanish sense.[37] The importance of the lineage of Christ, then, would sit well among the Maya, or at least it did at Teabo.

However, the genealogy of Christ and the subsequent parable of the sheep and goats are not mere facsimiles of biblical text or even European commentaries. Both, but especially the parable, contain characteristics that betray their authors as Maya. The metaphors, syntax, and orality of the text transform the European discourse into one better suited to appeal to a Maya audience. Like genealogies, apocalyptic material resonated well among the Maya as both the first and second comings of Christ serve as symbolic period beginning and endings to both Christians and Mayas—the significance of which will be discussed in the next chapter.

Genealogy of Christ, Parables, and the Final Judgment, pp. 24–33

(P. 24)

quatro mil y SinCuenta años Cuxanob Uay yokol cabe = heix ca tohlabieobe parayso terenal lae yoxpel u kinil Ca tohlabiob tumen Ca yumil ti D.ˢ Capel kin yanob ti parayso terenal lae Bay xul U kinilob lae nohcinabac Ca yumil ti D.ˢ = ti yahaulil Cilich glaria ti minan U xul maix U lah U chibalob Ca yumil ti Jesu Christo = U he ah Dauid

(P. 24)

4,050 years[38] they lived here on the earth, but then they were exiled from this early paradise; this third day was when they were banished by our lord God; the second day they existed in this earthly paradise as their last days. Our lord God glorifies Himself in the kingdom of holy glory without end nor conclusion. The descendants of our lord Jesus Christ, He that is of David:[39]

(P. 25)

+ + + +

Dauid . . . Mehente Abrahan

Abrahan . . . Mehente Jacob

Jacob . . . Mehente Jodam y Judas

U chibalob pares y Saromon detanan

pares . . . Mehente Aesron

Aesron . . . Mehente Aran

Aran . . . Mehente Aminadad

Amindad . . . Mehente Nason

Nason . . . Mehente Salomon

Salomon . . . Mehente baosdarad

Baosdarad . . . Mehente obeter xuth

obeter xuth . . . Mehente Jose

Jose . . . Mehente dauid ahau

Dauid . . . Mehente Salomon

Salomon . . . Mehente Robaan

Robaan . . . Mehente Abias

Abias . . . Mehente ASa

ASa . . . Mehente yoSapat

(P. 25)

David begat Abraham.

Abraham begat Jacob.[40]

Jacob begat "Jodam" and Judas and his descendants, Phares and Zara of Thamar.

Phares begat Esrom.

Esrom begat Aram.

Aram begat Aminadab.

Aminadab begat Naasson.

Naasson begat Salmon.

Salmon begat Booz of Rachab.

Booz of Rachab begat Obed of Ruth.

Obed of Ruth begat Jesse.

Jesse begat King David.

David begat Salomon.

Salomon begat Roboam.

Roboam begat Abia.

Abia begat Asa.

Asa begat Josaphat.

(P. 26)

yoSapat . . . Mehente lloram

lloram . . . Mehente oSiam

oSiam . . . Mehente tzoatun

tzoatun . . . Mehente Achas

Achas . . . Mehente Esachias

Esahias . . . Mehente ManoSen

manosen . . . Mehente Aman

Aman . . . Mehente Jasiom

Jasiom . . . Mehente t̶hechoniam binib y̶ yi Ɔin babilonia

tu pach tzukici babiloniae lae

t̶hechoniam . . . Mehente Saloctiel

Saloctiel . . . Mehente Salaber

Salaber . . . Mehente Abiut

Abiur . . . Mehente Eliachim

Eliachim . . . Mehente ACoro

ACoro . . . Mehente Saboc

Saboc . . . Mehente AChim

AChim . . . Mehente Eliut

Eliut . . . Mehente Eliasal

Eliasal . . . Mehente Matam

Matam . . . Mehente Jacob

Jacob . . . Mehente Josef

y esposa Ca Cilich Colel Suhuy S.ᵗᵃ M.ᵃ lay Sihci Ca yumil ti

(P. 26)

Josaphat begat Joram.

Joram begat Ozias.

Ozias begat Joatham.

Joatham begat Achaz.

Achaz begat Ezekias.

Ezekias begat Manasses.

Manasses begat Amon.

Amon begat Josias.

Josias begat Jechonias who went with his brothers to Babylon. After they were separated to Babylon:

Jechonias begat Salathiel.

Salathiel begat Zorobabel.

Zorobabel begat Abiud.

Abiud begat Eliakim.

Eliakim begat Azor.

Azor begat Sadoc.

Sadoc begat Achim.

Achim begat Eliud.

Eliud begat Eleazar.

Eleazar begat Matthan.

Matthan begat Jacob.

Jacob begat Joseph.

His wife was our holy lady, virgin St. Mary of whom was born our lord

Jusu christo Yumbil lae Amen Jesus

Ta kinil Ca bin yale Ca yumil ti Jesuchristo ti u lobil uinicob = tu Kinil Ca bin Kuchuc = hun yuk xot kine Ca bini Ca bin hayac Cabe = ti u bantal u lobil uinicob = tu ɔice hetun Ah tibilbcobe tu noh Ca yumitl ti D.ˢ = bin banlaCob tilic yalic tiobe = U tibilil uinicob Conex Cicitħanbil tumen yn Cilich Yum Conex hunkul Cuxtal = Meyahan Atial tex hopic Ci balCahile a Uuyahexe Yu tħan = a uocSahex ta uolex hecex tulaCal U almahtħanile a uuyahex U tħan = yn palilob y̱ Sacerdoteob yn tuchitahob = ta yamaexe tzec ti cex⁴¹ a xicin a uocSahex ta uol u tħan xan hetun teex u u lobil Uinicexe lobob tħanbilex tumen yn cilich Yum xenex tun tu kakil metnal = yanil Cisinob a Ɔoc luksahex u tħan: maix a uoSahex ta uol yn tħan y̱ u tħan yn palilob = yanhix choch keban tex Cuchi maix hahcunahex a p̱atic a kebanex tilic yalabal tex Ca a pat a coilex y̱ a ueyanCilex baix a ƆiboltiCex atantzil y̱ ichamtzile hetexe cħuplalexe lolob tħanbilex tumen yn Cilich Yum tumen U chic a pocħicex

(P. 27)
Jesus Christ the Father. Amen, Jesus.

On the day when our lord Jesus Christ speaks to the wicked men, on the day when the universal and Final Judgment comes, when the earth will be destroyed, the wicked will gather on the left, but the righteous will gather on the right hand of our lord God while He says to the righteous, "Come you blessed of my holy father. Come, eternal life has been prepared for you since the beginning of the world. You heard the word; you believed in your hearts all the commandments. You heard the word of my servants and priests that I sent. You loved the sermons[42] in your ears, you believed in your hearts the word also. But for you wicked men, you spoke evil of my holy father. Go now to the fire of hell where there are devils, until the end you neglected the word, and you did not believe in your hearts my word and the word of my servants they had for you to confess[43] back then. Nor did you agree to abandon your sin when it was said for you to abandon your whoring and your concubinage, likewise you desired married women and married men. As for you, you women, you are damned by my holy father for having made light of

yn ualmahthanile tilic a ueyinticex ychamtzile UChic a lubul tu hach yabil
keban ti humpelili a cucutilex Chuplale = bayxan xiblalob xan = tex u lobil
xiblalexe thubul a uicilex Patal a uol ta Coilex = cici olal a cahex yokol cab
= tan a ueyintiCex atanbil y yichamtzil = hetex u lobil xiblale y chuplalexe:
Ɔoc a cici ciolalex yokol cab = xenex tukil metnal xenex ti hunlukul cici olal
helelae: yanil kux cob y hunkul kak = Ma tupbin ti anix U hach yabal cisinob numsicex ti ya tilic a bucinticex kak y U ɔᵃˡbal ti a bakeex = tex xiblalex
y tex chuplalex = tech xan chuplal tech ta hauSah yn than = Yn than lic⁴⁴ Ca
yumil ti D.ˢ y yn patci yn keban tech kascunte yn tanlic D.ˢ y yn hach keban
Coten tun yn chatoh tech Bayx tech xan u lobil chuplale Coten tun yn cha
thancech tech tabSahen yokol cab Cat Sat yn Uol y U hachiobil⁴⁵ Coil y yn
Keban = a uetel helelae lolob thanbilech tumen yn Cilich Yum tumen tech ta
nachCunahen ti Ca yumil ti D.ˢ = Ma ta uoltah a paten tamuk yn cici oltic
yn keban a uetel = Cat hopoc U tzitzilic U CuCutilob tu batanbaob: y tan
kuxic U coob = y tan U chibil tanbaob =

(P. 28)
my commandment when you committed adultery with married men, having
fallen into a great sin with just your female body. Likewise, men; to you
wicked men, bury your appetite, abandon your desire for your whoring, your
worldly pleasures. You who commit adultery with married women and married men, to you wicked men and women, your worldly pleasures are at an
end. Go now to the corner of hell, leave forever the joy of today to where
there is gnashing of teeth and eternal fire that does not extinguish and there
are really great devils to afflict you while you are clothed with fire and your
flesh fries,[46] you men and women. To you women also, you that broke my
commandment. I serve our lord God by letting go of my sin. You ruined it. I
serve God with my true sin, come now so that I can take vengeance on you.
And you also, you wicked women, come therefore so I can question you, you
who deceive me on earth. Then I lost my reason because of the very bad whoring and my sin with you. Now you are cursed by my holy father because you
moved me away from our lord God. You did not want to abandon me while
I enjoyed my sin with you."

Then they began to flay their bodies among themselves, and they are
gnashing their teeth and biting each other.

Ca tun hach NumSabacob ti ya tumen cisinob tu yabal kak tactac cheanob
y U barctail[47] kak: ti U Cucutilob y xiblalob y chuplalob = tu numyaob: tu
tzitzilic U CuCutilob y U bakelob: hach Numyatzil ix yokolob tan u tatah
auatob y yaCanob tumen U yabal Numyaa: ti metnal tantan yalicobe = be
kasen ox Numut kuen: bikin U xul yn Numya y yn U aCan y yn tatah auat
Uay ti metnale = yoklal yan tin Uol pakmahi yn mansic kin yoyokol Cab =
kasen ox numut kuen ci tun U thanob tamuk yelelob = y tu nek U Uichob
ti U xiCinob bay yelel U hobon Cheil hobon chee: U balma kak tulaCal U
Uinicilob ti hach tuucnac U CuCutilob y hach kastac U Uichoob yan taac U
xuluboob tu polobe: y hach Nuctac ychacob tu yocob y tu kabobe = ti hach
kastac U Uichobe = tu batanbaobe: tan ix U pactic U Uich tu batanbaobe =
tu hunalob = Ca tun yal Cisin tiobe: hetexe yn palilex a Ɔac[48] lukSahex yn
than yoklal ti cuxanex Cuchie ten a payabelex ti tzuc aChil ten alic a belex
ten a ɔiboltahex = ten alic a Sublactalex ley ca Sublachiexe = Ca mahi a Con-
fesarlex ti padre: ti mahi [a] lah Cantic a Kebanex ten chiichcun ta uolex Ca
mahi a patic a kebanex = y a ueyex Ca tun hopi U Chiichtal yelelob ychil U
kakil metnal = hetun helelae mamac Uchac U

(P. 29)

Then they are really tormented by devils in the great fire which they really stoked with the gluttonous fire on the bodies of men and women. For their torment, their bodies and flesh are peeled; very miserable things also happen to them so that they scream and moan from their great suffering in hell.

They repeatedly say, "Oh, I am ruined, I am miserable! When will it end, my suffering, my outcries from being beaten, and my screams here in hell? Because I have discerned that I wasted my time on earth. I am ruined, I am miserable," they say while they burn, and their pupils and ears burn as a hollow tree trunk, a hollow tree trunk that contains fire. All the people have really foul-smelling bodies and horrible eyes; they have horns on their heads and really big claws on their feet and hands and horrible faces; they are in the presence of themselves also, they see the faces of each other only.

Then the devil says to them, "You here are my servants. You fulfilled my commandments because of how you lived back then. I guided you into licentiousness, I showed you the way for me to be desired by you, I told you to be ashamed so that you were ashamed to confess to the priest, you did not recount all of your sins, you were strengthened by me, so that you ceased to abandon your sin and your concubine. So then it begins that they are hurried along to burn in the fire of hell, but now no one can

Luksicex tin kab = Maix bikin yn patcex xan y ma bikin u xul y numsicex
ti yaa: Uay ti metnale = ti tun U talob than ti U Uey chuplal y xiblal xane:
ma xulumte tun yokol y yalil U Uich bin yukub = ylto christianoe kaak bin
a uukube y a hante bay bin Ɔebal a cici olal Uay yokol Cabe = ti Cuxanech
tan yanil ti metnale

Bayxan he cu yalic Ca yumil ti D.ˢ = tutulaCal xiblalob = Sihnalob Uay
yokol cabe = Uaix lic a Ɔaic takin ti chuplale = ti a coile Ca manic u
kakil metnal U tial a pixan Uaix lic a kamic takin yoklal a CuCutil tech chu-
pulale Ca Conic a pixan ti Cisin y a CuCutil ti u hach yail kak ti metnal: ti
ma xulumte U numyail kak = yanil Lusifer ti ix tun U Satal hunƆit a tzotzel
y a bakel tulaCal a uiniCil bin Xic tu kakil metnal = Ca bin U mol uba tulacal Uinicob ti hunpel elia kan Josepat u kaba ti tun yalic Ca yumil ti D.ˢ =
ti huntul Angel he u kabae = U Angelile San Miguel = Uya u te tu Can tukil lay Chakan lae: tilic yalic yalic = Cimenexe liKenex Caput Cux lenex ta
CuCutilex y ta pixanex Conex ti xotol a kinex y a kamex yutzil a belex y U
lobil a belex he cabin ƆoCoc u than Angele hunSutili bin U nutzlam tu u
batanbabaCob = tu batanbaob = y u pixanob yokol yoChelob = ti bay Cuxanob u pixanob

(P. 30)

free you from my hand; never will I release you also, and never will your torment end here in hell, for the carnal sinners of the concubine women and men also, endless will be the crying and the tears will be drunk."

See, then, Christian, you will drink and eat fire, thus your joy here on earth will be small when you live your life in hell.

L ikewise, our lord God says to all men born here on the earth, "If you give gold to women, to your concubine, then you buy the fire of hell for your soul. If you receive gold for your body, you women, then you sell your soul to the devil and your body to the really severe fire of hell, to the endless fiery torment where Lucifer resides, and then the loss of each of your hairs and flesh, all of your body will go to the fire of hell." When all beings gather themselves as one, Elias said it is called Josaphat,[49] then our lord God says of an angel, the angel named St. Michael, "Listen from the four corners of these plains as he says, 'You dead ones, arise! Live again with your body and your soul. Come to be judged and you will receive goodness and evil according to your deeds.'" And when the words of the angel are finished, immediately they will reunite among themselves, among themselves and the souls together with their sustenance as living souls

y U CuCutilobe Ca tim tali Ca yumil ti D.ˢ = tu Noh UChucil y tu noh tepalil
y tu Uinicil = y tulaCal Angelesob = y tu[la]Cal pixanob yanob tu yahaualil
cilich Gloria = bin talacob tu pach Ca yumil ti Jesuchristo U chab u CuCutilobe = ti ma bikin U xul U CiCi olalob= tu lumilob y tu pixanob = ti bananob tulacal Ah kebanob ti lum: hetun Ah tibilbeobe: ti bananob tu tan Ca
yumil ti D.ˢ = tilic yalabal tiobe = tumen Ca yumil ti Diose hetexe yn SihSah
Uinicilexe a U uyahex yn than ta Ɔoocbesahex tulaCal yn Ualmahthanil yn
patah yokol Cabe Ca ƆoCi yn lohic balCahe = a U uyahex u than yn palilob yn SaSerdotesob = yanhiob yokol Cabe a uichelex heleltune Conex CiCi
thanbilex tumen yn cilich Yum a ɔochekSahex yn Ualmahthanil U kahen cuchi = a Ɔahex ha ten = Uiheni xan y U yalaben ixix ma bucen kalen ti mascab
= Cuchi okomhi a uolex Ca talex a thibenex = Ca tun nucab u than = tumen
Ah tibilbeob yn yn Cilich yume binkin hi Uilab a ukchahal y a uihchahal y
a kalal ti mascab y a uulaCabil Cat Kamheche = Ca tu yalah Ca yumil ti D.ˢ
= tiob yanhi yn Numyail Palil ti balCahe = a Ɔahex u yatzilob ten uchic a
menticex = Conex a kamex U hel lay ti u yahaulil Cilich Gloria ti minan U
xul Mix u lah = Ca tu yalah tu lobil Uinicob = hetexe A Pochohenex ti hunlukul = xenex teet tu kakil metnale yanil cisinobe = a Ɔoc lukSahex U than =
U kahen Cuchi ix ma bucen Cuchi = Maix a Ɔahex yn yatzil xani = xenex ti
hunlukul kak = ti metnal yanil cisinob a Ɔoc lukSahex u thane ti ma xulumte
ti a CuCutilex

(p. 31)

and bodies when our lord God comes quickly in His great power and great majesty and in person. And all the angels and all the souls residing in the kingdom of holy glory will come following our lord Jesus Christ to take the bodies to never ending happiness both temporal and in their souls for all the sinners are gathered on earth. But the righteous gather in front of our lord God while it is said to them by our lord God, "You here, I created your bodies; you heard my word; you fulfilled all my commandments I left on earth when I finished redeeming the world; you heard the words of my servants, my priests; they were among you on the earth. Now then, come you blessed of my holy father; you fulfilled my commandments. I was thirsty, you gave water to me; I was hungry also . . . and I was naked in jail, you were sad so you came and visited me." Then the response of the righteous, "My father, when did we see you thirsty and hungry and imprisoned in jail, and you were a stranger and we took you in?" Then our lord God said to them, "These were my suffering servants on earth, (when) you gave them compassion, you did it for me, back then. Come, receive that reward in the kingdom of holy glory where there is no end nor conclusion." Then He said to the wicked people, "You here, you scorners, you will go there to the fires of hell forever where there are devils; you will carry this out. I remember, back then, that I was naked, and you did not have compassion on me. Go now forever to the fires of hell where there are devils. You will carry this out endlessly on your body

y̱ ta pixanex = Ca tun u tzolah U Ah tibilbeob xiblalob y̱ chuplalob = ti hun-
tzol tan u kay angelesob = ti hach ciotzil y̱ u Paxob y̱ u tronpetasob y̱ u chere-
miasob = ti hach ciotzil U kayob tamuk U binelob ti cilich Gloria tu pach
Ca yumil ti D.ˢ = ti hach lembanac U Uichob y̱ u pixanob ma bikin U xul U
Cici thantalob tumenel Ca yumil ti D.ˢ = ti minan U xul Maix U lah U CiCi
olalob xan Amen
aa qua perduCat aD uitam eternam

H Etun U lobil Uinicobe ti u bantalob tu uich lume = tan u kuxilob y̱ u
Ya Olalob tan yilicob u nacal u tibilil uiniCob = tu Pach Ca yumil ti
D.ˢ tan Yalicob yn uichame yn u ale yn chuplile yn nae = yn Yumee toc Cen
ta pach ti Can = Ma xacin a uichamen = a chuplilen = a U alen chaen ta pach
ci u thanob = Ca tun alacbac tiob tumen u tibilil Uinicob yn chuplile = yn
uichame = ma uchac a talel tin pach ti Can = he tene tu yoltah Ca yumil ti
D.ˢ yn Pattic Cin keban yokol Cab hetun tech ma a Uuyah U tzec padre yokol
Cab ma a ɔocbesah u than Ca yumil ti D.ˢ = Maix ta patah a keban y̱ a lobil
y̱ a Coil ti anech yokol Cab Cuchi = helel tune xotan a kinex binel ti metnal = Ca tun hechahac lume = Ca tun tacbucob tan chumuc kak ti metnal =
ChinChin pol y̱ u lumil y̱ u pixanob = ti yalic ti u Na palibilobe y̱ u Yumobe
= tilic u lolob than tu U Yum y̱ u Naob = he teche nae lolob than taac = Ym
tin chuchahe a ɔa tene he teche yn Uilah a Coil y a Ueyancil Ca in Canah xan

(P. 32)

and your soul." Then the righteous men and women are arranged in a line before the singing angels of great beauty and they play trumpets and chirimías of great beauty. They sing while they go to holy glory with our lord God, their faces are really shining and their souls will never cease being blessed by our lord God. There is no end or termination of their happiness also. Amen. Aa qua perducat ad uitam eternam[50]

However, the wicked people are gathered on the face of the earth among the embittered and guilty, in front of them they see the ascension of the righteous behind our lord God. They say, "My husband, my child, my wife, my mother, my father, take me with you to heaven. Perhaps you are not my husband, my wife, my child to take me with you?" thus they spoke. Then, it was said to them by the righteous, "My wife, my husband, it is impossible for you to come with me to heaven. As for me, according to the desire of our lord God, I abandoned my sins on earth, but as for you, you did not listen to the sermons of the priest on earth, you did not carry out the commands of our lord God, nor did you abandon your sin, your evil, your adultery while you were on earth. Now, you are condemned to go to hell." Then the earth opens up, then they are placed in the middle of the fire in hell head first, into the earth and its souls. The children say to their mothers and fathers as they curse their fathers and mothers, "You mothers here are cursed, the breast that I nursed you gave to me. As for you, I saw your adultery and your concubinage so I learned also.

(P. 33)

he teche a uilah Yn coil y̱ UeYancil Yn Ƥatic Yn uicham y̱ Yn xinbal y̱ yn keban
= Maix a tzectahen = y̱ Maa ualah Yn xicin CuChi helelel tune = lolob t̶han
taac lay Ym ta Ɔaah y chuche Ca tun tun Yn c̶ha toh tech U lobil Yn Yume =
bay tech xan U lobil Nabil = baix tech xan U lobil xiblale = tech ta chunSah
yn Satal ti metnal Ca tun hoƥoc U chibal tanbaob y̱ U tzitzilsic u cucutilob
= U naob y̱ U Yumoob Caix talYal Cisnob numSicob ti Yaa = y̱ kaak tamuk
u Yelelob u Cucutilob = tumen kak bay u Yelel U hobon Cheil hobon Chee
u balma kake = y̱ U Yabal kux co = y̱ tatah auat ti minan u xin maix u lah U
tatah auatob tukil metnal

(P. 33)

As for you, you saw my adultery and my concubinage, I abandoned my husband and I wandered with my sin. And you did not chastise me nor admonish me back then. Now then cursed are those breasts that you gave them to nurse.[51] Now I will take revenge on you my wicked father, likewise you wicked mother also, likewise you wicked men also. Because of you I am lost in hell." Then they begin to fight among themselves and tear the bodies of their mothers and fathers, and then underneath the devils they are tormented with fire while they (the devils) burn their bodies with fire as burns a hollow tree trunk, a hollow tree trunk that contains fire, with much gnashing of teeth and screams with no end or termination; they scream from the corner of hell.

3

Doomsday and the Maya

IT WERE RIGHT FOR EACH CHRISTIAN,
ALTHOUGH HE WEEP EVERY CANONICAL HOUR,
TO FEAR THE ACCURSED SUNDAY
A WEEK BEFORE THE DAY OF DOOM.
—Saltair na Rann, tenth century[1]

AND THERE WILL BE SIGNS IN THE SUN, THE MOON,
AND THE STARS. . . . PEOPLE WILL DIE OF FRIGHT
IN ANTICIPATION OF WHAT IS COMING UPON THE
WORLD. . . . BUT WHEN THESE SIGNS BEGIN TO
HAPPEN, STAND ERECT AND RAISE YOUR HEADS
BECAUSE YOUR REDEMPTION IS AT HAND.
—Jesus Christ, c. AD 33[2]

WHAT THE CATERPILLAR CALLS THE END OF THE
WORLD, THE MASTER CALLS A BUTTERFLY.
—Richard Bach, AMERICAN NOVELIST

THE NEXT SECTION of the Teabo Manuscript (pp. 33–35) contains a Maya redaction of the popular European text *The Fifteen Signs before Doomsday* and various sermons that served as introductions and conclusions to the discourse on the signs. As mentioned in the previous chapter, the Second Coming of Christ plays a large role in Christianity. Concern for the signs that precede the event likewise plays a significant role. For many, it was logical to assume that Christ's return should be heralded by signs. Fray Juan Bautista's Nahua aide, don Antonio Valeriano, stated in their 1606 Nahuatl *Sermonario*, "As the first coming of Christ our redeemer to save us was preceded by many signs and events, so too at his second coming there will precede many and marvelous signs."[3] Over the centuries, many took to searching the scriptures to find clues that would indicate when such a return might occur and what events would take place. The result is a vast corpus of eschatological works that circulated throughout the Middle Ages and early modern period.

This chapter examines the impact of the popular medieval text *The Fifteen Signs before Doomsday* on native-language religious texts in colonial New Spain. In the process, this chapter employs the Teabo Manuscript and a variety of Nahuatl and Maya texts to expose in new ways the relationship of such redactions to European archetypes, native culture, and each other. Furthermore, the analysis explores the popularity of *The Fifteen Signs* and eschatological texts among Maya Christian copybooks and texts. Similar to Creation commentaries, Doomsday prophecies heralding a new age repeatedly appeared throughout the locally preserved native-language texts of the Maya, who, much like Richard Bach, saw the end as a beginning.

Old-World Origins of *The Fifteen Signs*

The importance of the Apocalypse on medieval Christianity cannot be overstated. As the eminent medieval historian Johannes Fried stated, "Throughout the middle ages the apocalyptic preaching of Jesus . . . was the fundamental element of Christianity."[4] A focus on the individual's fate in the next life assisted ecclesiastics and theologians in encouraging constant self-assessment and a Christian life. Apocalyptic preaching throughout medieval and early modern times experienced periods of immense popularity and even indifference largely due to social and political events. Christians afforded apocalyptic reactions to moments of famine, war, disease, political instability, and, especially, discovery. The question of whether or not a particular event fulfilled apocalyptic prophecy was ever present on the minds of Europeans as they searched their texts.

Various passages throughout the Old and New Testament elucidate the signs heralding the Second Coming, oftentimes using metaphors and imagery that invite diverse interpretations. Similar to Matthew 25 and its parable of the sheep and goats, Luke 21 records an eschatological discussion Christ had with his disciples on the Mount of Olives. When his followers inquired after the signs preceding Christ's return, Christ provided a list. Among other portents were earthquakes, solar and astronomical anomalies, raging seas, and grief among the nations of the world.[5] The book of Daniel and its cryptic prophecies of enormous statues and beasts also provided important eschatological fodder. Yet perhaps the most important text in Christian eschatology is the book of Revelation. This apocalyptic work provides the longest and most symbolic description of the final days before Christ's return, the events of his coming, and the preparation of the earth and its inhabitants for its Final Judgment. The book abounds with references to many-headed beasts, angels of death, and violent events.

Other apocryphal works likewise speak of the Apocalypse. The *Fourth Book of Ezra*, the *Second Apocalypse of John*, the *Apocalypse of Thomas*, the *Sibylline Oracles*, and, of course, the writings of Joachim of Fiore all relate signs that will usher in the Second Coming and the fate of the world in the last days.[6] As Christianity matured and progressed over time, the vague and highly symbolic signs found within such works gave rise to myriad interpretations and various texts that circulated widely throughout the Middle Ages. Indeed, the topic of the end of the world and the Final Judgment frequently appeared in the works of medieval ecclesiastics.[7]

Among such works is *The Fifteen Signs before Doomsday*. In his work examining the text, William Heist employs ninety-six versions of *The Fifteen Signs* found in a wide variety of texts—from poems to histories to the writings of Thomas Aquinas—to argue the tenth-century Irish origins of the text. Most medieval and early modern authors claimed its origins from St. Jerome (c. 347–420), who supposedly found a list of fifteen signs among the *Annales Hebraeorum*, or Annals of the Hebrews. Yet this was likely an attempt to lend credibility to a text that fell between the learned and popular interpretations of Christianity. However, Heist argues that the origin of *The Fifteen Signs* lies in two Irish apocrypha from the tenth century: *The Evernew Tongue*[8] and the *Saltair na Rann* "Psalter of Quatrains," the latter being primarily based on the fifth-century *Apocalypse of Thomas*. More recent studies have continued to uncover texts relating the fifteen signs. Martin McNamara illustrates how Ireland has composed texts with the signs for over a thousand years, ranging from 750 to 1817–1819.[9]

Whether or not *The Fifteen Signs* has Irish origins remains unclear. However, it is clear that its origins are of questionable orthodoxy. Possibly based on an earlier Greek original, the Latin *Apocalypse of Thomas* is an apocryphal work that lists eight signs occurring on the eight days heralding the return of Christ; in the fifth century it was condemned by the Gelasian decree.[10] Furthermore, Irish literature, particularly that of the ninth through the thirteenth centuries, was the product of Latin apocrypha and local legends.[11] Because of its isolation from the rest of Christendom, the Irish Church created and preserved aspects of primitive Christianity—particularly those associated with visions—otherwise discarded by Rome.[12] The widespread influence of *The Fifteen Signs* indicates that despite its unorthodox origins, it circulated widely throughout Western Europe. This has been the case of other unorthodox texts originating in Ireland, including the *Vision of St. Paul*, which eventually made its way into a sixteenth-century Nahuatl text.[13]

Regardless of its origins, the signs gradually found their way into the writings of the thirteenth-century Spanish cleric Gonzalo de Berceo, who would put the signs into his poem *De los signos que aparecerán antes del juicio*.[14] Later, the signs would be available in print in sixteenth-century Spain via Peter Comestor's twelfth-century *Historia scholastica*, Jacobus de Voragine's *The Golden Legend* (1260s), the supplement to the third part of Thomas Aquinas's thirteenth-century *Summa theologica* and his commentaries on the *Liber sententiarum* of Peter Lombard, and the *Flos sanctorum*, which provided a Spanish edition and translation of Jacobus's text by the sixteenth century.[15] Certain signs even found their way into the works of William Shakespeare, particularly *Hamlet* and *Julius Caesar*, as portents of doom.[16] Although each rendition of the signs drew inspiration from earlier models, they oftentimes altered the order and content of the signs themselves (see Tables 3.1–3.5). Although clearly drawing from a similar legend, either oral or written, each text is distinct and reflects the author's preferences and emphases. That said, general observations are possible among those texts most likely to have influenced New World authors.

Similar to the cognate texts of the Chilam Balams and Maya Christian copybooks, determining who copied from whom can be problematic. However, it is clear that Peter Damian's *De novissimis et Antichristo* served as a large, but not the sole, inspiration for Aquinas's signs in his *Summa*, with the main difference being in a switching of signs nine and ten. Moreover, Jacobus de Voragine's text is a conflation of the Damian and Comestor types,[17] and, as would be expected, the *Flos sanctorum* is a near verbatim copy of Jacobus's text. Ecclesiastics in New Spain were well aware of these works and other commentaries on the Apocalypse, and they appeared in both their libraries and their sermons.[18] Thus it is not surprising that *The Fifteen Signs* accompanied such individuals and their books across the Atlantic. In a way, the text

Table 3.1. *The Fifteen Signs* in Peter Damian's *De novissimis et Antichristo* (Eleventh Century)[19]

1. Sea will rise fifteen cubits and stand like a wall
2. Sea will sink and hardly be seen
3. All seas will return to their original state
4. Sea creatures will gather on the water and cry out; only God understands the sound
5. Birds will assemble in the fields, each after its kind; they will speak and cry together for fear of the Judge
6. Fiery streams will rise from the west and flow across the face of the firmament to the east
7. Planets and stars will have fiery tails
8. Earthquake; all living things are brought down to the ground
9. Stones will split into four parts; each part hits the other; only God understands the sound
10. Trees and plants have a bloody dew
11. Mountains and buildings turned to dust
12. Beasts will emerge from the woods, mountains, and fields and roar, but not eat or drink
13. Tombs will lie open from sunrise to sunset while the corpses arise
14. Men will leave their houses and places, run like madmen, not understanding nor speaking
15. Men will die that they may arise again with the dead

sharing seen in the European versions of *The Fifteen Signs* foreshadowed what would occur to the signs, and various other religious tracts, among the native-language texts of the New World.

New World Renditions of *The Fifteen Signs*

All ecclesiastics were steeped in the medieval apocalyptic mind-set and literature that dominated so much of Christianity, and all brought with them to the New World a belief in the Second Coming and Final Judgment. As such, Nahuatl and Maya discourses on such topics are commonly found throughout their religious texts.[20] The vast majority of these derive from either a discussion of the seventh article of faith pertaining to the humanity of Christ ("He will come again to judge the living and the dead"),[21] biblical exegeses on Luke 21 or Matthew 24–25 normally read during the first Sunday of Advent, or general sermons on eschatological topics, typically the torments of hell. These discourses and whatever biblical portents they contain should

Table 3.2. *The Fifteen Signs* **in Peter Comestor's** *Historia scholastica* **(Twelfth Century)**[22]

1. Sea will rise forty cubits and stand like a wall
2. Sea will sink and hardly be seen
3. Sea monsters will appear and cry out as far as heaven
4. Sea and water will burn
5. Trees and plants have a bloody dew
6. Buildings will fall
7. Stones will strike one another
8. Earthquake
9. Earth will be leveled
10. Men will come out of caves like madmen unable to speak to each other
11. Bones of the dead will rise and stand on the tombs
12. Stars will fall
13. Living will die that they may rise with the dead
14. Heavens and earth will burn
15. New heaven and new earth and all will rise

Table 3.3. *The Fifteen Signs* **in Jacobus de Voragine's** *The Golden Legend* **(1260s)**[23]

1. Sea will rise forty cubits and be like a wall
2. Sea will sink and hardly be seen
3. Sea animals will appear on the water and cry out as far as heaven, which only God will understand
4. Sea and water will burn
5. Trees and plants have a bloody dew; flying creatures will come together in the fields, each after its kind, and not eat or drink for fear of the Judge
6. Buildings will fall; fiery bolts of lightning appear from sunrise to sundown
7. Stones will hit each other and split into four parts
8. Earthquake; all living things are brought down to the ground
9. The land will be level and mountains and other things turned to dust
10. Men will leave their caves and be madmen without understanding and unable to speak
11. Bones will gather above their tombs; the tombs will open from sunrise to sunset
12. Stars will fall and spray out fire; all beasts will gather and cry out, but not eat
13. All will die that they may resurrect with the dead
14. New heaven and new earth
15. All will resurrect to be judged

Table 3.4. *The Fifteen Signs* in Thomas Aquinas's *Summa theologica* (Thirteenth Century)[24]

1. Sea will rise fifteen cubits
2. Sea will sink and hardly be seen
3. All seas will return to their original state
4. Sea animals will appear on the water and cry out to each other
5. Birds will come together in the fields, cry to each other, and not eat or drink
6. Rivers of fire will rise toward the Firmament, flowing from the west to the east
7. Planets and stars will have fiery tails
8. Earthquake; all living things are brought down to the ground
9. Trees and plants have a bloody dew
10. Stones will split into four parts; each part hits the other
11. Mountains and buildings are turned to dust
12. Beasts will emerge from the woods, mountains, and fields and roar, but not eat
13. All graves from east to west will open to allow the bodies to rise again
14. Men will leave their houses and places and run like madmen, neither understanding nor speaking
15. All will die and rise again with the previous dead

not be confused with those found in *The Fifteen Signs*, which, as previously indicated, has a different history and content that is not firmly grounded in established doctrine. That said, and as will be seen below, select signs could and did on occasion influence a general discussion of the Final Judgment.

Despite such general references, ecclesiastics knew of the signs themselves. Commenting on the 1650 earthquake that devastated Cuzco, Peru, the Franciscan chronicler fray Diego de Córdova Salinas claimed that the city witnessed a sign:

> One of the fifteen signs that Saint Jerome discovered in the Annals of the Hebrews that must precede the Final Judgment, and the last (sign), he says, will be an earthquake wherein the mountains will be like a spool, the mountain peaks will unhinge from their foundations, the cliffs and rocks will be like dry leaves carried in the air, and men will flee to the withered and dry fields out of dread and fear.[25]

Throughout my research, I have discovered multiple colonial renditions of *The Fifteen Signs* in native-language texts—some in Nahuatl, others in Yucatec Maya. In Nahuatl texts, the signs most commonly appear sporadically worked into a general eschatological discourse and are seldom listed or even appear in their entirety. In contrast, Maya texts most frequently mention the

Table 3.5. *The Fifteen Signs* in the *Flos sanctorum* (Fifteenth Century)[26]

1. Sea will rise forty cubits and be like a wall
2. Sea will sink and hardly be seen
3. Sea animals will appear on the water and cry out as far as heaven, which only God will understand
4. Sea and water [will burn]*
5. Trees and plants have a bloody dew; flying creatures will come together in the fields, each after its kind, and not eat or drink for fear of the Judge
6. Buildings will fall; flames of fire will rise from the west and flow across the face of the Firmament to the east
7. Stones will split into four parts; each part hits the other; only God understands the sound
8. Earthquake; all living things are brought down to the ground
9. The land will be level and mountains and other things turned to dust
10. Men will leave their caves and be madmen without understanding and unable to speak
11. Bones will gather above their tombs; the tombs will open from sunrise to sunset
12. Stars will fall and spray out fire; all beasts will gather and cry out, but not eat
13. All will die that they may resurrect with the dead
14. New heaven and new earth will burn
15. All will resurrect to be judged

* The line abruptly ends due to a printing error

signs as a list and only occasionally blend them into a broader apocalyptic treatise. To better understand the significance of *The Fifteen Signs* in the Teabo Manuscript, the following provides an examination of central Mexican and Yucatecan texts that contain the signs, their authors, and an analysis of the signs themselves to illustrate similarities and differences.

Nahuatl Texts

As mentioned, Nahuatl texts rarely present the signs individually as a list, and fray Juan Bautista Viseo provides the only exception of which I am aware. Bautista was a Franciscan who lectured at the Colegio de Santa Cruz in Tlatelolco. He learned Nahuatl at a young age and was proficient in his abilities. Among his many Nahuatl works is his 1606 *Sermonario*, a large sermonary that provided extensive and lengthy sermons to be delivered on the four Sundays of Advent and during the feast days of St. Andrew and the Immaculate Conception. Produced in the "Golden Age" of Nahuatl text production when early ecclesiastics and native assistants collaborated to create some of the finest literary examples available, the sermonary was a result of a massive collaborative project that involved, either directly or indirectly, eleven friars and eight Nahua assistants.[27]

Included in the second sermon for the first Sunday of Advent is a discussion of *The Fifteen Signs*.[28] The text states that although signs would indeed precede Christ's return, the scriptures do not contain the order of the signs, nor indicate if they will occur long before or immediately prior to the Final Judgment. Regardless, Bautista states, "Yece çan achi quezquitlamantli tetzahuitl nictecpancapohuaz in quimohohuilia S. Hieronymo, yhuan S. Buenaventura" (But I will list only a few omens as Saint Jerome and Saint Bonaventure list).[29] The text also relates that St. Jerome said that he had read these signs in the *Annales Hebraeorum*, but that Jerome failed to mention if the signs would occur in immediate succession, or be spread out over time. The *Sermonario* then lists the signs, giving each one additional commentary and discussion oftentimes supported from other scriptural passages.

The majority of Bautista's signs (see Table 3.6) closely follow those found in the *Flos sanctorum*. However, the first sign and its measurement of fifteen cubits is similar to that of Damian and Aquinas. Most if not all of these works would likely have been available to Bautista and his Nahua aides. That said, Bautista's text takes ample opportunity to elucidate on each sign and describe the overall hopelessness of sinners at the Final Judgment. One noticeable deviation is the mention of the stones breaking into eight, not four, pieces. Here, the text employs parallel constructions, so familiar to Nahua rhetoric,

Table 3.6. *The Fifteen Signs* in Bautista's 1606 *Sermonario*

1. Sea will rise fifteen cubits (*caxtolmolicpitl*)
2. Sea will fall and be barely visible
3. Sea creatures walk on the water and yell
4. All water will burn
5. Plants will sweat blood
6. Houses and buildings will fall to the ground
7. Stones will break into eight parts; the sound will scare sinners
8. Earthquakes
9. Earth will be leveled
10. Men will emerge terrified from their caves
11. Graves will open from the west to the east
12. Falling stars, comets
13. Mankind will die
14. Fire will burn the earth and heaven
15. All will resurrect; the earth will be made new; people will be judged

to emphasize how even these small stone pieces "nepanotl monetechchala-nizque, nepanotl motetextilizque, nepanotl motecizque mocuecuechtilizque: auh inin ca caquiztiz, cenca quimmauhtiz, quimiçahuiz, quinçotlacmictiz in tlahtlacohuanime, in tlapilchiuhque" (will knock each other, crush each other, grind each other, crumble each other, and this will make a sound that will frighten, startle, scare to death the sinners, the offenders).[30]

Although not listed individually, the signs likewise appear woven throughout the second sermon for the first Sunday of Advent in fray Juan de la Anunciación's 1577 *Sermonario*.[31] The Augustinian's *Sermonario* is the only published sermary to include discourses for the complete church calen-dar.[32] In general, each Sunday or feast day includes two sermons: one brief, the other more lengthy, thus allowing the priest to select which sermon was most appropriate for the knowledge and perceived attention span of his na-tive audience. The signs appear in the second sermon as part of a lengthier discussion on the Final Judgment detailing the glory that awaits the righteous and the torment of all sinners.

As mentioned, Anunciación does not list the signs, but employs them as part of the general narrative. Moreover, the text indicates that the signs de-rive from the Bible and fails to give any other sources:

> *Yehica yn axcan, yn ayamo mochiua: uel achtopa techmonemactilia, tech-machtopaylhuilia yn totecuiyo Iesu Christo yn ipan Sancto Euangelio, yn quenin tetzauhmachiotl ualyacattiaz, yn aic yuhque omochiuh tlalticpac, atle ynamic, uel temamauhti, uel tecuecuechmicti ym muchiuaz.*[33]

> (Wherefore now, before it [the Final Judgment] happens, first and foremost our lord Jesus Christ gives us, prophesizes to us in the Holy Gospel about the ominous signs that will come first; never has it oc-curred in such a way on earth, it is without equal, it will be very fright-ening, very scary.)

Not all the signs are mentioned—Anunciación employs nine—and the signs themselves are simplified and lack lengthy descriptions (see Table 3.7). The text also mentions a sign not included in the traditional fifteen, but frequently cited throughout the Bible as a portent before the Final Judgment: the sun turning black and the moon failing to shine.[34] In the end, Anunciación, and presumably his native assistants, appear unconcerned with listing all the signs or even distinguishing those from the Bible and those cited elsewhere. Instead, the apparent goal was to emphasize a few of the fearful and chaotic signs preceding the Final Judgment to encourage faithfulness now.

Horacio Carochi was a Jesuit most famously known for his 1645 *Arte*,

Table 3.7. *The Fifteen Signs* in Anunciación's 1577 *Sermonario*

—Sea will rise
—Sea will fall
—Fish will walk on the water
—The ocean will burn and boil
—Plants will sweat blood
—Houses will fall to the ground
—All mountains will collapse and be leveled
—Stars will fall from heaven
—People will emerge fearfully from their homes

Table 3.8. *The Fifteen Signs* in "de Judicio Finali"

—Sea will rise, flood; water will be blood
—Plant and trees will sweat blood
—Earthquakes
—Buildings will fall
—Mountains leveled
—Men will leave their houses; madmen, no understanding
—Beasts won't recognize each other
—Beasts will go into the cities, chase people, but no eating
—Fire will burn everything; all will die
—Trumpet to announce resurrection
—Righteous arise with shining bodies; evil with black, smelly bodies

which James Lockhart described as "the most influential grammar of Nahuatl ever published."[35] Divided between the Bancroft Library and the Biblioteca Nacional de México is an eclectic manuscript thought to be authored by Carochi and native assistants. The manuscript contains a wide variety of doctrinal material from the lives of saints to doctrinal treatises on the end of the world. Among this collection of topics is a Nahuatl text with the Latin title "de Judicio Finali" (on the Final Judgment) that includes *The Fifteen Signs* and was likely composed in the 1640s or 1650s.[36] Similar to Anunciación's work, the text weaves the signs together with other biblical portents in its eschatological discussion. The signs listed in this text fail to follow the order of any existing text and vary markedly from any New World rendition I have seen. To be sure, similarities exist, and many of the signs are included in the narrative. However, the text does omit the signs of the sea receding out of sight, the yelling of the sea creatures, the gathering of birds, and the fighting stones. It seems as though the author used *The Fifteen Signs* as a canvas on which to paint a work of narrative and description that occasionally included dialogue. For example, the typical sign of the burning of the earth appears thusly:

> *Auh iquac ilhuicacpa quiualmiualiz in tt° d. yn tletl ynic tlalli xotlaz ynic tlatlaz tlalticpactli nouian yuhquin tlequiauiz yuhquin tletzontli*[37] *tzitze-liuiz pixauiz nauhcampa ualeuaz in tletl ualicoyocatiaz ualcuecuetlacatiaz ualla chinotiaz, auh mocennepanoquiui ynic muchi quitlatizq yn cema-nauatl. yc cen miquizq in tpc tlaca, yuan yn mochintin yolque in manenenq . . . , mochtin quicentlatizq quimichinoz, yc tlamiz yc poliuiz yn cema-nauatl aocmo nemoaz aocmo yoliuaz, aocmo tlacatiuaz.*[38]

> (And when our lord God sends fire from heaven, then the land will catch fire, the earth will burn. Everywhere it will be like it is raining fire, like flames will be falling, sprinkling, from the four directions the fire will come roaring, making lots of noise, it will approach burning the fields. And they [the fires] will combine so that all the world will burn. Once and for all the people will die and all living things, the four-legged animals . . . all will be completely burned, it will scorch them. Thus the world will end, be destroyed; no longer will there be living, no longer will things exist, no longer will there be births.)

Such description betrays the style of Carochi and his native assistants and is indicative of a fading Nahuatl prose that would not survive into the eighteenth century.

The document betrays a high degree of creativity when working with the signs. Like the others, particularly Bautista's *Sermonario*, the Carochi text frequently draws upon metaphors and couplets characteristic of classical Nahuatl. For example, when speaking of the state of the resurrected bodies of the good and evil, the Carochi manuscript states,

> *ca in qualtin cenca chipauaq yezq pepetlacazq, yuhquin tonatiuh mocuepaz yn in tlalnacayo, ynic tlanextizq, auh in amo qualtin vel tliltiq vel pochectiq yezq vel catzauaq vel potonq. etc.*[39]

> ([T]he good ones are very clean, they will shimmer, their bodies will become like the sun so that they shine. But the bad ones are really black, they will be really smoky, really dirty, really smelly, etc.)

Interestingly, fray Bernardino de Sahagún in Book Ten of the *Florentine Codex* consistently describes the "bad" people as filthy, dirty, and malodorous. The description of the bodies of the wicked would have resonated well with a Nahua audience that viewed the excess of filth and foul odors with negative connotations.

Other examples exist of the signs influencing a discussion of the Final Judgment in various Nahuatl texts. For example, in a sermon discussing the seventh article of faith pertaining to the Godhead in the 1548 Dominican *Doctrina*, the text provides a general description of the events of the last days that includes burning oceans and rivers, the deaths of mankind, animals, and birds, and the destruction and flattening of all mountains and buildings.[40] On other occasions, *The Fifteen Signs* appear to influence Nahuatl discussions of the portents as recorded in Luke 21 and Matthew 24. Such occurred in Paredes's *Promptuario* to include the rising of the ocean and earthquakes that level mountains and houses,[41] and again in Bautista's 1604 work "Book of the Misery and Brevity of the Life of Man." Here in his discussion of the Final Judgment that describes how people "nentlamattinemizque, neneciuhtinemizque, quiteociuhtinemizque, camictinemizque in miquiztli, in ipampa cenca huey nemauhtiliztli" (will go about languished, panting, hungering and wishing for death because of the very great fear), he blends into his treatise various signs including how people lose their sense, hide in caves, the leveling of all homes and buildings, comets, and the rising of the ocean.[42] As with many others, the text does not appear overly concerned with distinguishing portents derived from *The Fifteen Signs* from those with biblical origins. In a way, both the Bible and *The Fifteen Signs*—and no doubt other apocalyptic writings—created a reservoir of portents from which authors of Nahuatl texts could draw and create their treatises.

Maya Texts

The Fifteen Signs appear listed in four Maya texts. The signs located in the Morley Manuscript and the Tusik have received some attention from both Whalen and Knowlton.[43] Yet I have discovered the signs in two additional texts: the Teabo Manuscript and the "Maya Sermons" copybook of an unknown provenance. Certainly each text contains its own version of the signs by omitting some phrases while adding others, listing the signs in a preferential order, and illustrating a localized orthography and prose. That said, similarities exist as well; a comparison of all four texts reveals these important similarities and differences.

The signs found within the Teabo Manuscript, Tusik, and the "Maya Sermons" text betray the most similarity. Yet the congruity between the Teabo Manuscript and the "Maya Sermons" text extends even further to include a preface of sorts intended to introduce the signs, something which the Morley

Manuscript and Tusik omit in general. Like Bautista's 1606 Nahuatl text, both Maya texts seemingly designed their cognate prefaces and the subsequent signs as a sermon for a Sunday in Advent, likely the first. The Teabo text erroneously cites the twenty-fifth chapter of St. Luke as its thematic source. Because St. Luke only contains twenty-four chapters, it is likely that the author(s) intended to cite the eschatological chapter of Matthew 25, or even Luke 21 as does the "Maya Sermons" text, although the content of the Teabo text alludes to Matthew 25 as the source. Either way, it is unlikely a priest would have made such a mistake, thus further betraying a Maya hand.

The "Maya Sermons" text states the importance of understanding "the book of his coming, of Final Judgment (Apocalypse)" and cites St. Bernard and St. John Chrysostom for their study of the signs regarding the sun, moon, and stars, labeling them as *ah kinob*.[44] As mentioned, the ah kin were Maya priests who served in various religious rituals among the precontact Maya, including those pertaining to astronomy.[45] The text then joins the Teabo Manuscript in citing St. Bernard and St. Jerome, also referring to them as ah kinob for their revealing of the fifteen signs that precede the coming of Christ. St. Jerome is known for his translation of the Bible into Latin—the Vulgate—and his commentaries. In Yucatan, he is often associated with *The Fifteen Signs*, and a fresco of his image, with the lion he reportedly healed according to texts such as *The Golden Legend* and *Flos sanctorum*, appears in a sacristy in Teabo's cathedral (see figure 3.1).[46] The two manuscripts are obviously cognate. Yet each exercises a degree of artistic license when creating the text, adding a shade of detail here while removing a line of description there. For example, the Teabo Manuscript continues the theme seen previously regarding the sheep and the goats recorded in Matthew 25 by inserting various comments referencing the chapter's content of charitable works allowing Christ to reward the righteous for such.

The order of the signs themselves within the Tusik, "Maya Sermons," and Teabo Manuscript; their content; and even particular phrases within them all illustrate a strong likeness (see Tables 3.9, 3.10, and 3.11). Sign for sign, the Tusik text is the longest, followed by the "Maya Sermons" and then the Teabo Manuscript, which perhaps is slightly terser. Moreover, for reasons unknown, the Teabo Manuscript includes only twelve of the fifteen signs.[47] That the Tusik and "Maya Sermons" texts contain similar versions of *The Fifteen Signs* is not wholly surprising, considering that the majority of the doctrinal content of the former is also found in the latter.[48] Significantly, all three texts use the phrase "through or because of a miracle" represented by *tumen mactzil* in the ninth sign and *yoklal mactzil* in the thirteenth sign. To be sure, every sign engaged the miraculous, from the rising of the sea, to fire

FIGURE 3.1. Fresco Portrait of St. Jerome, Teabo, 1650s (courtesy of Richard Perry)

Table 3.9. *The Fifteen Signs* **in the Tusik**

1. Sea will rise as a wall
2. Sea will sink
3. Sea will return to its place
4. Sea creatures gather on the sea and cry out
5. Birds and beasts will gather out of fear
6. Fire will come from the west and east
7. Comets, lightning, falling stars
8. Earthquake; beasts fall to the ground
9. Stones fight, break into four parts, unite again
10. Plants have bloody dew
11. Mountains, buildings, forests will fall
12. Animals will come together in the plains
13. Graves will open for a day
14. Men come out of the caves, speaking without understanding
15. Fire purifies the earth, Christ comes

Table 3.10. *The Fifteen Signs* in the "Maya Sermons" Text

1. Sea will rise as a wall
2. Sea descends out of sight
3. Sea will be flat, normal
4. Sea creatures gather and yell
5. Birds will gather out of fear
6. Fire comes from the west and the east
7. Comets, lightning, falling stars
8. Earthquake; beasts fall to the ground
9. Stones will fight; crack into four pieces; be made whole again
10. Bloody dew
11. Mountains, buildings, forests will fall
12. Animals will come together in the plains
13. Graves will open for a day
14. Men will hide in caves, then emerge speaking without understanding
15. Fire purifies the earth, Christ comes

Table 3.11. *The Fifteen Signs* in the Teabo Manuscript

1. Sea will rise as a wall
2. Sea descends out of sight
3. Sea will return to its place
4. Sea creatures gather and yell
5. Birds and beasts will gather out of fear
6. Fire comes from the west and the east
7. Comets, lightning, falling stars
8. Earthquake, all trees fall
9. Stones will fight, crack into four pieces, be made whole again
10. Blood from maize and trees
11. Mountains, buildings, forests will fall
12. All beasts are gathered to be judged

from heaven, to bleeding plants. However, the "mactzil" phrase accompanies those signs that involve a restoration of some kind. For example, the ninth sign states how all stones will fight each other, break into four parts, and then unite again "tumen mactzil" (through or because of a miracle). Furthermore, "yoklal mactzil" appears on the thirteenth day to explain the restoration of the bodies of men.[49] Although "tumen mactzil" appears in the Morley Manuscript, it does so in reference to the tenth sign and as the cause of men having great fear, thus in a different context from the other three Maya texts.

No other European source uses this phrase, so we may safely assume it is a colonial invention that the Teabo Manuscript, Tusik, and "Maya Sermons" text use similarly to describe a miraculous restoration. Its inclusion in specific locations among specific signs testifies to a similar knowledge of that narrative of *The Fifteen Signs* found among learned Maya in the communities from which these texts emerged. Whether shared among these locales through a written or oral account—or both—it is clear that these communities preserved a similar version of *The Fifteen Signs*. Interestingly, *The Fifteen Signs* continues to influence the Maya today, at least in Tusik. The Tusik is an 1875 copy of an older original made by Marcos Balam. While researching the Maya in Tusik from 1978 to 1980, Paul Sullivan discovered a handwritten copy of *The Fifteen Signs*. According to Sullivan, the more modern text was remarkably similar to the one in the Tusik.[50] Although the Maya owner of the text, San Itza—the town historian and shaman—could not read its words, he knew what it said because his father used to read it to him and he had memorized the text. Of the various texts San possesses, he considers this particular text, which he calls a "History of God," extremely important.

In her initial analysis of the Morley Manuscript, Gretchen Whalen noted that some of its content derived from Jacobus's *The Golden Legend*, and additional research of my own has uncovered further links with medieval texts.[51] Among its many religious topics is *The Fifteen Signs*. Standing apart from the other Maya texts, the Morley Manuscript provides a somewhat different redaction of the signs (see Table 3.12). The manuscript outlines the signs numerically and, as with the other Maya texts, attributes them to St. Jerome and "his book of holy writing." However, there are differences not seen in the Teabo, Tusik, or "Maya Sermons" texts, and some are quite divergent. Aside from the occasional sign being out of order, the seventh sign detailing the gathering of men and beasts to cry out unintelligibly reflects a creative invention. Likewise creative are signs twelve, thirteen, and fifteen. Bloody rain appears in sign twelve, and although none of the more common texts include the sign, it does appear in the *Apocalypse of Thomas* and the *Psalter* among others.

As with its medieval predecessors, the thirteenth sign in the Morley Manuscript indicates that all men will die. What is unique is its mention of shining crosses:

> On the thirteenth day there will be the call of a trumpet from heaven.
> The trumpet says, "He saved the world, our lord, when he died on the

holy cross." This day (the thirteenth day) the crosses that are in the forests and within the towns will shine and will light up as the light of the sun.[52]

Since its introduction to the colonial Maya, the Christian cross and its meaning has included both European and Maya elements. In Europe, medieval scholars often blended the Cross with the Tree of Life, which some reported to have produced the wood for the Cross itself. Indeed, many medieval and early modern ecclesiastics viewed the Tree of Life as a representation of Christ—a belief held by some Christian religions today.[53]

In Yucatan, the cross represented the organization of the cosmos as a quincunx with four directional corners and a center. Each space was associated with trees and the tree in the center, and, as we saw in the Genesis Commentary, the *yax che* (first or green tree) was of particular importance for its role as an *axis mundi* upholding and connecting the under, middle, and upper worlds. In colonial religious texts, this tree became associated with the Tree of Life, the Tree of Knowledge of Good and Evil, and the Cross. Perhaps the most vivid example of the Cross's role in Yucatan concerns the Caste War (1847–1901) and the Cruzob Maya who took direction from talking crosses.[54] More commonly and relevant to the sign listed here, throughout the colonial period numerous examples existed of crosses erected at the

Table 3.12. *The Fifteen Signs* in the Morley Manuscript

1. Sea will rise forty arm lengths (cubits); it will appear as a great mountain
2. Sea dries up
3. Sea creatures emerge and cry out, but only God understands
4. Trees and plants have a bloody dew; birds will come together and not eat or drink for fear of the Judge
5. Ocean will burn
6. Everything made will be brought down making a loud sound
7. Gathering of men and beasts who unintelligibly cry out
8. Large and small stones will hit together and break apart
9. Earthquake that levels nature and buildings
10. Men will come out, be as if drunk, unable to speak to each other and fearing
11. Bones will come forth and pile upon the tombs
12. Bloody rain; stars will fall; beasts will gather on the plains and cry out
13. Trumpet; shining crosses; all men die
14. Heaven and earth will burn; land leveled
15. Trumpet; all resurrect for judgment

four corners or entrances of colonial Maya towns, plots of land, and other important places like cenotes.

Finally, a trumpet introduces signs thirteen and fifteen. No other text includes this instrument, but it is surely inspired by the Bible. The trumpet is used frequently throughout the Bible to herald an announcement or event commonly associated with the Final Judgment. Perhaps most relevant here are the seven trumpets blown by seven angels to usher in apocalyptic events as recorded in Revelation 8–11. In the end, the Maya maestro composing the Morley Manuscript drew obvious inspiration from existing versions—oral or written or both—of *The Fifteen Signs* while also taking the liberty of familiarizing the content according to personal and cultural preferences. Interestingly, although Coronel would eventually employ sections of the Morley Manuscript for his Maya *Discursos* (1620), *The Fifteen Signs* fail to appear listed in his printed work. That said, a few signs, including the rising of the ocean and the unintelligible shouting of creatures, do appear in his discussion of the signs before the Final Judgment.[55]

Concluding Sermons

Following its treatment of the signs, the *Flos sanctorum* includes some closing remarks concerning the appearance of the Anti-Christ and the Final Judgment.[56] As a popular hagiography depicting the lives of the saints, the *Flos sanctorum* circulated widely in both Europe and New Spain, although the Inquisition banned certain versions.[57] As mentioned earlier, various Maya texts derived their content from its pages. In regard to the *Flos sanctorum*'s final passages following *The Fifteen Signs*, Maya texts occasionally will include a similar section, although I have not uncovered one close enough to be considered cognate. As noted, the Teabo Manuscript ends its discussion of *The Fifteen Signs* at the twelfth sign; the next page begins a new discourse, and thus the manuscript does not include such concluding apocalyptic remarks.

However, the Tusik and "Maya Sermons" texts both include such sermons, and they parallel each other.[58] The texts outline invocations to Christ petitioning for mercy and grace during the Second Coming and further descriptions of the forthcoming destruction. Interestingly, the last ten or so lines of these closing remarks found in the Tusik and "Maya Sermons" have a loose cognate with a passage found on page 29v of Coronel's 1620 *Discursos* in its section discussing "how God is our savior and glorifier." And the intriguing correlations with other texts continue. When the "Maya Sermons" and Tusik end their harmony, the Tusik continues with a commentary on Matthew 25 that parallels that found in the Teabo Manuscript.[59] For its part, the "Maya

Table 3.13. Maya Texts Containing *The Fifteen Signs* and Its Accompanying Discourses

Manuscript	Origin	Preface to the Signs	Fifteen Signs	Concluding Sermons
Teabo Manuscript	*Teabo*	X	X	
"Maya Sermons"	—	X	X	X
Tusik	*Tusik*		X	X
Discursos predicables	Juan Coronel			X
Morley Manuscript	—		X	

* Italicized texts are cognate

Sermons" text finishes its paragraph with six or so lines that closely follow the final six lines of the paragraph in Coronel's *Discursos*.[60]

The next paragraph of the "Maya Sermons" text relates the Final Judgment that takes place in the Valley of Jehoshaphat[61] near Jerusalem, where, according to Joel 3:2, all nations are gathered to be judged. In particular, the narrative lists those who will be judged, including popes, cardinals, and the rulers of the earth. This paragraph again runs cognate with other texts, particularly a later section of the *Discursos* discussion on how Christ will come to judge the living and the dead (see Table 3.13).[62] This discourse on the Final Judgment also is similar to the narrative found in the Nahuatl 1548 Dominican *Doctrina*.[63] At times, the lines are remarkably similar between both the Nahuatl and two Maya texts, suggesting a similar source, possibly a European text, or an oral discourse common to evangelization.

General Observations

As evidenced from the texts examined, *The Fifteen Signs* clearly played a role in the doctrinal instruction of both Nahuas and Mayas. Regarding European archetypes, none of the texts listing *The Fifteen Signs* follows with exactness the signs as outlined in a European text. The signs and their order in the Teabo Manuscript, Tusik, and "Maya Sermons" text loosely follow those found in the Damian and Aquinas texts. However, there are differences in both order and content that suggest a creative redaction including elements from other works such as the earth burning with a purifying fire. The Morley Manuscript and Nahuatl works of Bautista, Anunciación, and Carochi all loosely follow the models found in the works of Comestor and the *Flos sanctorum*. Thus, multiple European models and versions influenced the signs in central Mexico and Yucatan. Although Nahuatl and Maya redactions of *The Fifteen Signs* owe their origins to Europe, the Nahua and Maya authors that composed these texts included their own interpretations and renditions.

These native-language texts also betray the signs' particular popularity among the Maya, surviving in unofficial, Maya-authored copybooks and in the memories of contemporary Maya elders such as San Itza. The number of Maya religious texts available to scholars pales in comparison to those in Nahuatl. Yet even in these reduced numbers, *The Fifteen Signs* appears listed in four separate texts and influenced the primary colonial sermonary printed in Maya. This is striking when considering that extant Maya religious texts provide examples of only two confessional manuals and a handful of catechisms—texts that dominate the Nahuatl and European material. Put simply, when comparing the content of existing Maya religious texts, *The Fifteen Signs* appears to have been very popular. Texts detailing the Creation would be the best rival for those relating *The Fifteen Signs*.

The extent of cognate texts evident among the eschatological texts in Maya of *The Fifteen Signs* and its accompanying discourses is impressive (see Table 3.13). Indeed, it is remarkable that the signs and/or their accompanying discourses found their way into the locally authored and preserved Maya Christian copybooks and Chilam Balams of various communities, as well as in a friar's printed text. Again, because these texts were recopied and redacted numerous times throughout the colonial period and beyond, an attempt to discover which text influenced which would be fraught with uncertainty. That said, because Coronel's work appeared in 1620, we know that some of these texts were circulating by at least the early seventeenth century if not before. Coronel himself states that his *Discursos* is a compilation of "various papers, that with my labor I have collected and copied, that the old priests had written, amending some things that in this era are not used, and correcting that which was not correct."[64] Thus, because portions of the *Discursos* are an edited edition of older sermons, it is possible, and even likely, that some of its content, including the cognate portions mentioned here, originated in the sixteenth century.[65]

Regardless, when juxtaposing the cognate texts, their similarities, and their alterations, the question arises again regarding how these texts circulated. Compare the following manuscripts' rendition of the sign proclaiming the gathering of sea animals on the water to moan and wail in fear of the coming Judgment Day:

TEABO MANUSCRIPT:

4. *he tu Canpil U Kinil bin Yanac chiCul he tulacal u bal Kaknabobe lay cayobe = bin u mol ubaob yokol haob tan u tah auatob y Y acanob yokol haa yoKlal u sacibob ti xot Kin cu talel lae:*

(4. Here on the fourth day, this sign will occur: all sea creatures and fishes, will gather themselves on the waters and be crying loudly and moan on the water because they are afraid of this Judgment Day that comes.)

"MAYA SERMONS":

4. *He tu canpel u Kinil chicul [l]ae bin ya^na^Ce ; he tulacal u bal Kakna-bobe; yetel Cayobe = bin homolcin u baob yoKol haa = tamuk y auatob. y yacanob yokol haobe yoKlal Sahacilob licil u talel xot Kin lae*[66]

(4. Here on the fourth day, this sign will occur: all sea creatures and fishes will gather themselves together on the waters while they cry and moan on the water because they fear that which comes, this Judgment Day.)

TUSIK:

4. *Heix tu canpel u kinil lae, bin yanac u chicul lae, heix tulacal u bal kak-nabe, y cayobe bin u mol u baob yokol haob tanmuk yauatob y yacanob yokol haob yoklel sahcob tumenel u tal xot kin lae.*[67]

(4. And here on this fourth day, it will occur this sign: all the sea crea-tures and fishes will gather themselves on the waters while they cry and moan on the waters because they are afraid because this Judgment Day comes.)

MORLEY MANUSCRIPT:

3. *tu yoxppel U Kinil. binil hokebal yalil ba^lob KaKnab. tulacal y. U nuc-tacilob = y = U meheniltacilob. Cayob. ti tatah auat. U beelteob. tu hunali Dios. ohel*[68]

(3. On the third day, all sea creatures will emerge from the waters of the ocean, and the large and the small fishes, there they cry loudly cries of pain that God alone understands.)

Generally speaking, due to the simplicity of the sign itself, all four manu-scripts convey a similar meaning. Similar to Maya redactions of the Ten Com-mandments or the Articles of Faith, the terse and common formulae of the signs makes more likely their similar redaction into Maya.[69] However, ortho-graphic and stylistic preferences make each entry distinct, and the fourth sign in the Morley Manuscript obviously draws from a different oral or written source.

Furthermore, and similar to Maya sermons or doctrinal treatises on specific topics, such differences increase significantly when comparing lines taken from a cognate sermon or discourse found within the manuscripts, where there is more room for expansion or omission. Consider the two prefaces to the signs found in the Teabo Manuscript and the "Maya Sermons" text.

Teabo Manuscript

HE than lic a uuyiCex lae Uay helae Ɔiban tu kaytah cilich Nabil yglesia lae = Ɔiban tu tzolol ti cilich S.^{to} Euangelio tumen Euangelio Ɔiban tumen San luCas tu hotukal u peƆel U capitoloil U chun tzeec helelae lay u nah oces ti olex = Con ya uinicilexe lay u nah a Ɔab a xicinex ti than = Yn mahante bay ten a uetelex = he Ca bin Uluc U cilich al Suhuye tu noh tePalile y tulacal Angelesob = tu pache Ca tun Culac tu Sillail u noh tePalil U cilich Ɔayatzil lae = binix homol acbal cah tu tan binix U huƆub U baob nachil = tu hunalob bay licil U hun molcintic U canan taman ah Canan tamanobe =

bay ta uuYahexe oheltexe Yn Ya Uinicilexe = bin a chaex lay than = Cin tzolic lae lay DominiCa lae U ChuCan U Dominicail = aeruento lae = U Yulel Ca yumil ti Jesuchristo lae = Ca bin Kuchuc tu kinil Yulel U Ɔab hunkul cuxtal = y hunkul cimil lay xot kin u kaba lay ta uuyahex Same = bin Yanac ChiCulob ti kin y ti : U: y ti ekob lay Ɔiban tu Yunil miyatz = tumen San Bernado y San Jeronimo ah Kinob

Ylaex tan u Kaytic ta xicinex = bicil bin tac Ca yumil ti Juchristo = u xotob u Kin balCahe = bin Yanac Chi-Culob ti Yan beil hol hunpis Kin Chi-Cul bin yanac= bay licil Yalic Ca yumilan San Bernado = bay licil Yalic San Jeronimo xane

Amen Jesus y Maria

Teabo Manuscript

Here are the words which you hear here today that have been written in the preaching of the holy mother church; it has been written in the explanation of the holy gospel according to the gospel written by St. Luke in his twenty-fifth chapter, the theme of this sermon today, it is necessary that you believe. Our beloved people, it is necessary that you give your ears to the word for my sake as I am with you. When he comes, the holy child of the Virgin in his great majesty with all the angels behind him, then He will sit in his seat of great majesty, of holy mercy, and they will promptly be seated in front of him, and they will separate themselves (the righteous), alone, as the shepherds gather together in one place their guarded sheep.

As you heard, understood, my beloved people, you will receive these words I explain this Sunday, all the Sundays of Advent of the arrival of our lord Jesus Christ. When He comes, on the day of his arrival He will give everlasting life and eternal death—this is called the Final Judgment that you heard about earlier. There will be signs concerning the sun and moon and stars, thus it has been written in the book of wisdom by St. Bernard and St. Jerome, ah kinob.

You see, it is being preached in your ears how our lord Jesus Christ will come in the last days of this world here. There will be signs, on the preceding fifteen days there will be signs, so says our patron St. Bernard, so says St. Jerome also.

Amen. Jesus and Mary.

"Maya Sermons"

He thanoob lic a uuyicex ti uay helelae Ɔibanob tu tzolan Euangelio ti alabij ti missa: lay Kam tu Kay ca na ti Santa yglesia tu uuyexe tumen bay Ɔibatul tu tzolan euangelio tumen euangelista San Lucas hun tuc Kul u peɔel u capituloil; U chun tzec helelae lay ocan ti col con christianoon lae yn ya uinicilexe U nahix a chen cocbex yn than yn mahante; bay toon a uetelexe tuchi ca bin huluc yal Suhay tu noh tepale yetel tulacal ange^{le}sob tu pache tij tun u cultal yokol u xecili tepale binix humolacbal Cah tu taan: binix hu molcintebaob ti hunhun tulilob nachil Bay licil hunbacanic yalak tamam ah tamanale,

hebac bay ta uuyahex yn aalice u nahix a uoheltex cex yn ya uinicilexe; he lay domingo lae adbiento u tial yulel yumilbil; Ciocci: u Yunil u lebal: ti xot Kin; heuac bay tu uuyahex same bin yanac chiculoob ti Kin yt. ti U. yetel ti ekob; bayx Ɔibanil ti yunil miyatz tumen San Berbernado, yetel San Juan criyostomo; ah Kinob cuchi lae;

ylex u Kati he ti matac Jesue Christo u xotob u Kin balcahe, bin yanac Chiculoob ti payanbeil heuac hol = hunpis tu baob chiculoob bin yanac ti payanbeil ti ma hopoc ti matac u xotol u Kin balcahe bay ticil yalic San Bernardo; bayix licil yalic San Geronimo lae

"Maya Sermons"

Here are the words which you hear here today; they have been written in the explanation of the Gospel that was said in Mass. Receive this speech that you hear from of our Mother Holy Church as has been written in the explanation of the Gospel by St. Luke Evangelist in the twenty-first chapter, the theme of this sermon today, the belief of us Christians. My beloved people, it is necessary for you to listen carefully to my word for my sake as we are with you. When the child of the virgin comes in his great majesty with all the angels behind him, then He sits on his chair of majesty and they will quickly be seated in front of him, and they will gather themselves (the righteous) together in one place on the right, separated, as a shepherd gathers together his sheep.

But as you heard my saying, it is necessary that you believe, my beloved people, this here Sunday of Advent regarding the coming of the lord; it is important to know the book of his coming, of Final Judgment (book of Revelation). However, as you heard earlier, there will be signs concerning the sun and the moon and the stars, thus it has been written in the book of wisdom by St. Bernard and St. John Chrysostom, ak kinob back then.

You see what was inquired of Jesus Christ about the last days of this world here. There will be signs preceding it, but among them there will be fifteen signs preceding, when it has not begun, when it is not yet the last days of this world here, so says St. Bernard, and so says St. Jerome.

Regarding the themes, content, and layout of these two texts, the similarities are obvious and point to similar sources. However, the deviations between the two texts are greater and more frequent than those seen in the fourth sign. For example, the Teabo Manuscript erroneously cites Luke 25 as a source of its sermon; remember that Luke contains only twenty-four chapters and that two popular eschatological exegeses in the Bible are found in Luke 21 and Matthew 25. The sermon seems to have confused the two, thus producing "Luke 25." The "Maya Sermons" text contains the correct citation of Luke 21. Moreover, although both texts indicate their reading in the season of Advent, they differ in their books of reference for the portentous signs. The Teabo Manuscript cites a "book of wisdom by St. Bernard and St. Jerome, ah kinob," whereas the "Maya Sermons" text states the importance of understanding the book of Revelation and cites a "book of wisdom by St. Bernard and St. John Chrysostom, ak kinob."

Could such similarities and variations, in addition to those orthographic and stylistic variations so evident in the texts, have occurred if the signs and the sermon were circulated among various cahob solely via written text? Possibly, particularly if the archetypes originated from the Maya schools and, once disseminated to the various cahob, became altered over the centuries. Yet such characteristics could also derive as a combination of oral and written transmission. *The Fifteen Signs* themselves held in the memory of learned Maya would have distinct characteristics to be sure, but also would have the most likelihood of retaining a similar format due to the terse nature of each sign. Yet the lengthier passages—such as the sermon above—are more prone to alteration, forgetfulness, and augmentation in their delivery, thus allowing the increased degree of alteration observed. In the end, it is nearly impossible to know for certain how the text was conveyed and redacted. However, the Teabo Manuscript and other Maya Christian copybooks strongly suggest the existence of oral templates in addition to those written for various religious themes that the maestros and notaries of each cah made their own upon its recording and eventual retelling. Once again we see the impact of the sphere of reducción, with ecclesiastic and Maya-authored religious texts likely created in the schools and then branching out to circulate among the forbidden Maya-preserved Chilam Balams and Christian copybooks, where their various written and oral forms became altered over the centuries.

Table 3.13 further illustrates the importance of the Apocalypse to the Maya. Period beginnings and endings are topics well ingrained into Maya culture.[70] Regarding period endings, Whalen noted that "the recording of cataclysmic events within a structured temporal sequence characterizes indigenous Maya genres, both the katun counts, and stories of previous world endings like those in the Popol Vuh. Thus *The Fifteen Signs* provided new information in a form somewhat familiar to a Maya audience."[71] This can also be extended to include all the myriad apocalyptic texts found throughout Maya works, including the parable of the sheep and goats discussed in chapter 2.

Apocalyptic themes of destruction and renewal continued among the Maya throughout the nineteenth century, as clearly demonstrated by the Caste War. What began as a regional and political conflict soon blossomed into a racial war fueled by a native religion focused on the veneration of a talking cross at Chan Santa Cruz. The cross encouraged an uprising of its Maya followers, the Cruzob, to *end* the domination of the Whites and begin a *new age* for the Maya.[72] Although the Cruzob's millenarian goals came to a disappointing end in the early twentieth century, the Maya-Christian belief of a new age ushered in by calamitous events continues to exist among many Maya today.

Furthermore, we should also consider the influence of the eschatologically minded Franciscans on the Maya texts. Inspired by Joachim of Fiore—the prevailing prophet of the Apocalypse—and the Spiritual Franciscans, many of the early Franciscans brought with them to the New World a millenarian tradition that favored apocalyptic teaching. Even Columbus, who associated himself with the Joachimite tradition, was steeped in the tradition estimating that the world had only 155 years remaining.[73] Unlike in central Mexico, the Franciscans dominated the evangelization of Yucatan. It would not be unreasonable to assume that *The Fifteen Signs* regularly found its way into the teachings of the friars.

Finally, the discovery of *The Fifteen Signs* among Nahuatl and Maya texts calls further attention to the European sources of those texts. We can trace the evolution of *The Fifteen Signs* from its medieval origins in Ireland, to early modern Europe and Spain, across the Atlantic to central Mexico and Yucatan, where it was translated into Nahuatl and Maya, and even into the twentieth century, with Maya elders still preserving the legend. Yet this journey from medieval Europe to modern-day Yucatan does not come without its losses. Although *The Fifteen Signs* experienced popularity among Maya Christian copybooks and texts, knowledge of the signs seems to have fallen into the realm of oral history subject to the memory of those, like San Itza, who had once heard the signs recited.

At the conclusion of the twelfth and final sign included in the Teabo Manuscript, an unknown Maya author stated that on December 11, 1803, he finished "a book called Genesis in order for it to be read." Although penned in a different ink and, likely, at a different time than the signs, and although we cannot be sure, it is possible that the author considered *The Fifteen Signs* as the conclusion of what began as a commentary on Genesis beginning with the Creation, Christ and his lineage, his Second Coming and role as Judge in the last days, and finally the signs that would precede these last days and the end of the world and rebirth of another. In all, it makes for an all-inclusive narrative of the world from beginning to end, and this narrative, as the author states, was to be read and shared. The remaining texts that appear in the Teabo Manuscript lack any clear connections with the previous narrative and represent the occasional ad hoc nature of Maya Christian copybooks and their compilations.

The Fifteen Signs before Doomsday, pp. 33–35.

(P. 33)

ad qua nos perducat Amen Dominica: adbentuc
Cume Uenexit Eilius Dominica 25: Capitulo

HE than lic a uuyiCex lae Uay helae Ɔiban tu kaytah cilich Nabil yglesia lae = Ɔiban tu tzolol ti cilich S.ᵗᵒ Euangelio tumen Euangelio Ɔiban tumen San luCas tu hotukal u peƆel U capitoloil U chun tzeec helelae lay u nah oces ti olex = Con⁷⁴ ya uinicilexe lay u nah a Ɔab a xicinex ti than = Yn mahante bay ten a uetelex = he Ca bin Uluc U cilich al Suhuye tu noh tePalile y tulacal Angelesob = tu pache Ca tun Culac tu Sillail u noh tePalil U cilich Ɔayatzil lae = binix homol acbal cah tu tan binix U huƆub U baob nachil = tu hunalob bay licil U hun molcintic U canan taman ah Canan tamanobe = bay ta uuYahexe oheltexe Yn Ya Uinicilexe = bin a chaex lay than = Cin tzolic lae lay DominiCa lae U ChuCan U Dominicail = aeruento lae = U Yulel Ca yumil ti Jesuchristo lae = Ca bin Kuchuc tu kinil Yulel U Ɔab hunkul cuxtal = y hunkul cimil lay xot kin u kaba lay ta uuyahex Same = bin Yanac ChiCulob ti kin y ti : U: y ti ekob lay Ɔiban tu Yunil miyatz = tumen San Bernado y San Jeronimo ah Kinob

(P. 33)
ad qua nos perducat Amen Dominica: adbentuc
Cume Uenexit Eilius Dominica 25: Capitulo

Here are the words which you hear here today that have been written in the preaching of the holy mother church; it has been written in the explanation of the holy gospel according to the gospel written by St. Luke in his twenty-fifth chapter, the theme of this sermon today, it is necessary that you believe. Our beloved people, it is necessary that you give your ears to the word for my sake as I am with you. When He comes, the holy child of the Virgin in His great majesty with all the angels behind Him, then He will sit in His seat of great majesty, of holy mercy, and they will promptly be seated in front of Him, and they will separate themselves (the righteous), alone, as the shepherds gather together in one place their guarded sheep.

As you heard, understood, my beloved people, you will receive these words I explain this Sunday, all the Sundays[75] of Advent of the arrival of our lord Jesus Christ. When He comes, on the day of His arrival He will give everlasting life and eternal death — this is called the Final Judgment that you heard about earlier. There will be signs concerning the sun and moon and stars, thus it has been written in the book of wisdom by St. Bernard and St. Jerome, ah kinob.

(P. 34)

Ylaex tan u Kaytic ta xicinex = bicil bin tac Ca yumil ti Juchristo = u xotob
u Kin balCahe = bin Yanac ChiCulob ti Yan beil hol hunpis Kin ChiCul bin
yanac= bay licil Yalic Ca yumilan San Bernado = bay licil Yalic San Jeronimo
xane

    Amen Jesus y Maria

1.[76]

H Eu yax chun u Kinil bin yanac ChiCul bin Yanac KaKnab = u hohochil
u Cucutil YoKol uitz Canaltacobe : maixtan u huɔububa tu cuchil bay
bin nacbal hunac peKe

2. he tu capel u Kinil lae bin Yanac ChiCul bin emec tu cuchil hahal tam bin
embal maix uchuc Ylabal tu chi u KaKnabil ——————

3. heix tu yoxpel u Kine bin yanac ChiCul bin Kuchuc tu caten ti bay Yanile
talen Kinac lae ——————

4. he tu Canpil U Kinil bin Yanac chiCul he tulacal u bal Kaknabobe lay
cayobe = bin u mol ubaob yokol haob tan u tah auatob y̱ Y acanob yokol haa
yoKlal u sacibob ti xot Kin cu talel lae: ——————

5. he tu hopel u Kinil lae bin Yanac ChiCul bin u mol uba tulacal chichob
y̱ tulacal balCheob bin hun molacob tumen u sahacil ti oKo ti xot Kin Cu
tale ——————

6. he tu uacpel u Kinile u bin yanac chicul bin hoKoc Kak ti chiKin licil u
thubul Kine = y̱ licil u hoKol ti laKine bin hoKoc Kak xani = ——————

7. he tu uucpel U Kinile bin yanac chicul bin yanac Yabal cumetasob y̱ tan u
lenbaob ti chachac

(P. 34)

You see, it is being preached in your ears how our lord Jesus Christ will come in the last days of this world here. There will be signs, on the preceding fifteen days there will be signs, so says our patron St. Bernard, so says St. Jerome also.

Amen. Jesus and Mary.

1. Here is the first initial day, there will be a sign, it will be the sea; the crevices, the body of the mountain, the high ones, they will not divide its (the sea's) place; it will rise as a great wall.

2. Here on this second day there will be a sign, it (the sea) will descend to a truly deep place; it is going to be descending; nor is it possible to see the seashore.

3. And here on the third day there will be a sign: it (the sea) will arrive again, like the coming of the day.

4. Here on the fourth day, there will be a sign: all sea creatures, those fishes, will gather on the waters and be crying loudly and moan on the water because they fear the Judgment Day that comes.

5. Here on this fifth day, there will be a sign: all birds will gather and all creatures will gather as one because of fear, they cry because of the Judgment Day that comes.

6. Here on the sixth day, there will be a sign: fire will come forth from the west where the sun sets; and where it emerges from the east, fire will also come forth.

7. Here on the seventh day, there will be a sign: there will be a large amount of comets and lightning will be striking,

(p. 35)

bay lubul u cahobe = eKobe Ylabale tal ti can lae ———

8. he tu uaxacpel u Kinele bin Yanac chichul bin yanac chac YKal = he tulacal cheobe mixtan u uatalob y u cutalob bin u lubucob tu uich lum ———

9. he tu boloni pis u Kinile bin Yanac chicul he tuniChobe tulacale bin u pisuba tan u nuptanbaob tu hunalob bay nucob y mehentacob = binix hetlahcob ti cancanbuhob = he tu catene bin tulisacob tumen mactzil tu caten ———

10. he tu lahun pis u Kinile bin Yanac chiCul tulacal xiuobeobe y cheobe bin emlahac KiiK YoKolob ti bay Yemel Kiik ti bal Yaae ———

11. he tu buluc pis u Kinile bin Yanac chiCul he tulacal uitzob y mulobe y nocACobe = paKbil tumen uinicobe y Kaxob Canal tacob bin lubucob tu uich lum ———

12. he tulah capis u Kinile bin Yanac chiCul bin U mol Uba tuCal balcheob ti xotol u Kinob = tan yoKolob tulacal tumen U Sahacilob = ti xot Kin lae ———

dia 11 de Desienbre de 1803 años caa ti ɔoci yn canbal hoksic hunpel libro Gensis u kaba u tial txocol Ca u sates ten yn yum Max bin y ylic ua yan Kasite ten u . . .

likewise, stars fall to the earth, they will be seen coming from the sky.

8. Here on the eighth day there will be a sign: there will be an earthquake, and all trees[77] will not be able to stand up and that which stands will fall on the face of the earth.

9. Here on the ninth day there will be a sign: all the stones will fight, they will be rubbing together alone, the large with the small ones, and they will crack open and divide into four parts; then for a second time they will become whole by a miracle, again.

10. Here on the tenth day there will be a sign: blood will fall from all the plants and trees just as blood falls from wounded things.

11. Here on the eleventh day there will be a sign: all the mountains and hills and the great buildings of men and high forests will fall on the face of the earth.

12. Here on the twelfth day there will be a sign: all beasts will be gathered for their judgment; all of them will be crying because of their fear of this Judgment Day.

The 11th of December 1803, when I finished learning to bring forth a book called Genesis in order for it to be read. That he forgives me, my lord who will see if there are errors, I the . . .[78]

Mary, Christ, and the Pope

"PEÇA À MÃE, QUE O FILHO ATENDE"
(ASK THE MOTHER, THAT THE CHILD ATTENDS)
—BRAZILIAN EXPRESSION

THE EXPRESSION ABOVE is found commonly attached to images of Mary that decorate the homes of many in Brazil. The role of Mary as intercessor and advocate likewise appears in the Teabo Manuscript. The pages immediately following *The Fifteen Signs* (pp. 36–37) appear as a first-person plea to both Mary and Christ for their divine assistance in attaining salvation. It is possible that this text was meant as a concluding sermon to *The Fifteen Signs*. However, due both to the different content of the sermon found in the Teabo Manuscript when compared to other concluding discourses on the signs, and to the different orthography and pen of the text, I have chosen to discuss it separately. Medicinal remedies, discussed in the next chapter, separate this text from a text on indulgences (pp. 40–41), which, although included in this chapter, is a separate text altogether. Like the first text, the indulgence text appears on a separate page, and both are in the same hand, which differs from that of the previous section.

The author(s) and compiler(s) of the Teabo Manuscript intentionally included both the plea to Mary and Christ and the indulgence text. This chapter explores their inclusion by specifically examining the role of Mary and indulgences among the Maya. Moreover, this chapter attempts to further understand these discourses by comparing them with others of a similar nature found throughout Nahuatl and Maya texts. In the end, these seemingly random additions to the Teabo Manuscript serve to shed additional light on those aspects of Christianity that the Maya of Teabo chose to record and preserve in their copybooks.

Mary and the Maya

In Catholicism, Mary holds an especially important role. Born without the stain of Adam's original sin in what is known as the Immaculate Conception, she lived a sinless life that included birthing and mothering the Almighty God. When Mary completed her mission on earth, her body and spirit rose into heaven in glory, known as the Assumption. As the Brazilian expression indicates, Mary plays an important role as intermediary between mankind and God. The God of Spanish Catholics was loving, but was also a being whose wrath and condemnation should be feared. Such Catholics similarly afforded Mary qualities more commonly associated with females such as patience, understanding, and forgiveness; as the mother of God, she was the prime candidate to serve as an intermediary—a role she fills to this day.[1]

Long before the arrival of Spaniards in the New World, then, Mary played a large role in the local religion of Spain. Yet her accessibility as the mortal mother of God extended beyond that of emotional compassion and understanding to include physical protection. Like St. James the Moor-slayer, Mary protected Spanish Christians in their fight against Muslims during the *Reconquista*, and the success and acceleration of the Christian takeover of Spain only increased her popularity.[2] As early as the twelfth century, Marian images and shrines began to dominate the region's religious landscape and won the greatest number of devotees. This devotion only increased throughout the sixteenth century and held strong during the Baroque period even as the votive devotion to Christ increased.[3]

From the beginning of Spanish contact among the natives of New Spain, Mary figured prominently among the early conquistadors and ecclesiastics alike. Columbus frequently employed her name when naming newly discovered islands.[4] Hernán Cortés displayed her image on his standard, and he reportedly left Marian images in native temples on his march inland to the Aztec capital of Tenochtitlan.[5] Sixteenth-century Franciscan chroniclers record the popularity of Mary among the natives and recount various miracles she facilitated. Mendieta recalls one early occasion among the natives Columbus encountered. During a storm, four natives took shelter in a cave. One began to invoke the name of Mary for protection against the lightning; the others ridiculed him for the effort. As a result, lightning killed the three naysayers without harming the devotee.[6] In another instance, a native noblewoman of Xochipila was in her last extremity when Mary appeared and gave her a few tablespoons of divine medicine that allowed her an additional month of life.[7]

Mary likewise found her way to Yucatan. Cortés's 1519 expedition that would eventually lead him to Tenochtitlan began with his visit to the Maya in Cozumel. Fray Diego de Landa recounts how using a native interpreter, Cortés preached to the natives against their idols and encouraged them to honor the Cross and Mary and left images of both in their temples. Later, another sermon by Cortés on the subject reportedly left such an impression on the Maya that "they came out to the shore saying to the Spaniards who passed: 'María, María, Cortés, Cortés.'"[8]

The ecclesiastics that followed Cortés likewise emphasized Mary in their instruction. As Louise Burkhart persuasively demonstrates, Mary became a popular subject in Nahuatl religious texts.[9] Regarding Maya texts, although Mary occupies the subject of the various Marian prayers, such as the Hail Mary and Salve Regina (Hail, Holy Queen), found in Coronel and Beltrán's *doctrinas*, in general she fails to appear as the subject of sermons or other treatises in printed texts. An exception to this would be Coronel's discussion of her role as Christ's mother in his *Discursos*.[10] In Maya Christian copybooks, Mary similarly appears frequently in prayers, although specific sermons dedicated to her are rarer. This, I believe, is not a result of a lack of knowledge of Mary, but simply reflects the lack of existing religious texts in Maya from which to sample.

The Franciscan order, which dominated Spain as well as the Yucatan, emphasizes an emulation of Christ and his teachings.[11] As early as the Marian sermons of St. Anthony of Padua, Mary and Christ both played large roles in the teachings of the order. Thus regardless of the paucity of extant written discourses in Maya dedicated to Mary, the Maya were well aware of her importance in Catholicism. The bishop of Yucatan, fray Francisco de Toral, instructed that Maya children learn the prayers in a particular order, waiting to receive the subsequent prayer until the first had been learned. First, the Maya learned the Our Father, then the Hail Mary, then the Creed, and finally the Salve Regina.[12] Significantly, two of the four basic prayers concerned Mary. Moreover, Mary and her life were the focus of various feast days that the natives were required to observe, including the feasts of Our Lady, Assumption, Nativity, Purification, and Annunciation.[13]

Perhaps the most obvious role of Mary in Yucatan was as the region's patroness as Our Lady of Izamal. Cogolludo records that in his efforts to convert the Maya, Landa installed an image of Mary constructed in Guatemala and brought to Izamal in the 1550s. The account relates various miracles associated with the image—the majority of which correspond closely to those wrought by saint images in Spain and with the cult of the saints more generally—including a 1648 pilgrimage by the Virgin to Merida to rid the city of plague.[14] In addition, Mary came to dominate the names of female baptized infants, churches, and various religious institutions; she served as the patron saint to *cofradías* (religious brotherhoods) and Maya communities.[15] Among Nahuatl and Maya testaments, her name was frequently invoked by the dying, and although the Nahuas generally possessed and bequeathed many more household images of Mary, her image also appears commonly among those few Maya testators who did make such bequests.[16] Today, Mary maintains her dominance of the New World in the form of Our Lady of Guadalupe, patroness of the Americas.[17]

An integral part of Marian devotion includes breviary anthems and texts dedicated to her. The Catholic Church requires its clergy to recite the Liturgy of the Hours, or the Breviary, daily. Included in the Breviary are various Marian texts and four Marian prayers that could be sung: *Alma Redemptoris Mater, Ave Regina Caelorum, Regina Caeli,* and *Salve Regina.* Moreover, possibly the most popular book owned in the Middle Ages by the laity was the book of hours, and Mary figured prominently in this work. Indeed, these devotional books almost always had at their core a devotional text known as the Little Office of the Blessed Virgin Mary that included scriptures, psalms, antiphons (sung prayers), responsories, and other readings centered on Mary.[18]

Similar orations of petition and praise to the mother of Christ found their way into both Nahuatl and Maya religious texts. Nahuatl catechisms, sermonaries, and doctrinas of various lengths contribute to a sizable corpus of Marian texts. Many instruct the reader on the role of Mary in Catholicism, while others offer a wide variety of prayers. Certainly many Nahuatl prayers were standard translations of the Hail Mary or *Salve*. Yet others represented verbose expositions of such prayers that created elaborate, poetic invocations which emphasized the humility of the petitioner and the glory of Mary.[19]

The Maya prayers to Mary in the Teabo Manuscript resemble those poetic expositions found in Nahuatl texts. Certainly the inclusion of an invocation to Mary and Christ—although the former appears more prominently than the latter—in the Teabo Manuscript provides an important addition to the Marian material in Maya; others include a prayer to Mary found in the Kaua and the extensive folios dedicated to her in the "Maya Sermons" text.[20] Yet the prayers in the Teabo Manuscript and the Kaua are most similar in that they resemble both those petitions found in Nahuatl texts, and those devotional anthems and invocations so often seen throughout European books of hours or the Little Office and various writings of theologians and Church fathers.

Significant among the latter is St. John of Damascus, who was instrumental in introducing the concept of Mary as a divine intercessor and wrote several important works on the Assumption.[21] Although no direct translation is evident, the invocation of Mary in the Teabo Manuscript resembles various passages of the Damascene's sermons. Such resemblance is limited, however, as the text in the Teabo Manuscript rotates the recipient of its pleas between Mary and Christ in uneven intervals. As such, the text and its eclectic and creative format is unparalleled, at least to my knowledge, by any specific European text.

The passage contains both Maya and European elements. Parallel constructions exist to give the text an altogether Maya character. For example, consider the passage, "hach otzilen cen ah tan kebanen Manbalen" (truly I am miserable, I am a great sinner, I am nothing). Another passage pleads for Christ to "Ca peɔucen tu kab ah chibalob y ah Cayballob ti yn pixane heklay cisinobe" (withdraw me from the hands of the wild animals and fishermen of my soul, which are the devils). The comparison of wild animals to devils also appears in an illustrative story found in the Morley Manuscript and Coronel's *Discursos*. The story is an example of the medieval genre of exempla that used contemporary examples to teach Christian concepts. Here, the devil in the form of an *ah chibal*, or wild animal, attacks a sinner only to be cast away by the fervent prayers of priests.[22] As early as the Classic Period, evidence suggests that the Maya believed in co-essences. These were animals or natural phenomena that shared the consciousness of their human counterparts. While the Maya owner is awake, his co-essence remains dormant; when asleep, the co-essence roams and, with certain personalities, could take the form of a wild animal to cause injury or death to its victims.[23] During his fieldwork, Sullivan noted the persistence of this belief surrounding the late wife of San Itza. Some believed her death resulted from being killed "while in the form of a black dog, the guise she habitually assumed for nightly sexual assaults against a certain young man in the neighboring village."[24] Thus, the relationship between a ferocious wild animal and the evil spirit of the devil resonated well with Maya culture.

However, although the passage includes the creativity of a Maya author, it draws upon various European themes. In one instance, various Old World epithets appear in the text as Christ is described as "u sasilil balCahhe" (the light of the world) and Mary as "u xaman ekil KakNabe" (the North Star of the sea). The first epithet references Christ's self-proclamation as the light of the world found in John 8:12 and frequently employed throughout European religious texts.[25] The second references the constant nature of the North Star to describe Mary's ability to be a constant guide to Christ and salvation.[26] The epithet appeared regularly throughout medieval and early modern times and is employed in one of the four Marian antiphons, *Alma Redemptoris Mater*. Indeed, in many ways the passage in the Teabo Manuscript is an expansive redaction of this antiphon, which reads as follows:

> Loving Mother of the Redeemer,
> gate of heaven, star of the sea
> assist your people who have fallen yet strive to rise again.
> To the wonderment of nature you bore your Creator,
> yet remained a virgin after as before.
> You who received Gabriel's joyful greeting
> have pity on us poor sinners.

Clearly the Maya petition to Mary and Christ included in the Teabo Manuscript does not replicate the antiphon, although the genre or some other unknown text could have served as inspiration.[27] In the end, the passage is a creative piece that weaves both Maya and European elements together to form a text worthy of preservation in the copybook.

Indulgences among the Maya

In the Kaua, its Marian prayer immediately follows the Genesis Commentary and is itself followed by a section Bricker and Miram term as "Papal Instructions for Avoiding Purgatory."[28] Interestingly, the Teabo Manuscript follows a similar, although not exact, rubric. Following the prayer to Mary and Christ is a blank page and then a series of medicinal remedies recorded much later in the twentieth century (discussed in the next chapter). The following page (40) begins a new text that loosely corresponds thematically with the Kaua's "Papal Instructions for Avoiding Purgatory" text. Comparing the two texts exposes immediately similar passages and lines. However, the majority of the passages in the two texts differ and generally fail to provide a line-for-line match.

The passage in the Teabo Manuscript begins by citing those popes known for their support of indulgences; the popes mentioned are the same as those appearing in the Kaua. The text then speaks of the acts one must perform to earn an indulgence. According to Catholic doctrine, divine justice requires both an eternal and temporal punishment for sin. Although confession removes the eternal punishment from the penitent, the temporal consequences must occur either in this life or in purgatory. Indulgences draw upon the *thesaurus ecclesiae* (treasury of satisfactions) that Christ and the saints created with their overly abundant good works and bestow them upon worthy individuals to remit the temporal punishment of sin. Medieval crusaders were among the first to receive such indulgences, but soon everyday individuals would have access to such benefits.[29]

In the Spanish crusade of the Reconquista to restore Iberia to Christianity from its Muslim conquerors, papal indulgences granted to the crusaders flourished. Later, the early modern *bula de la cruzada* became the most popular way for average Spaniards to engage in the effort. Such bulls, called *buletas*, appeared as printed broadsheet summaries of the indulgence and were distributed by the thousands. Those willing to pay the relatively cheap price in alms could obtain such a document. Patrick O'Banion's work illustrates how many such recipients "often saved them for years after they had expired" and even "hung them on the walls of their homes [or] . . . were buried with their copy."[30]

Various versions of the *cruzada* existed, but the most popular was the *bula de vivos*. This bull came in two forms. The *bula común* was most common and typically available for the relatively cheap price of two *reales*. The other was for the elites and for an increased price offered the same benefits.[31] The success and popularity of the bula de vivos was impressive and allowed the bull to cross the Atlantic. The Yucatecan synod of 1722 ordered priests to "explain the valor and importance of the indulgences of the Church, especially those of the cruzada, and what they [parishioners] should do for their part to have them."[32] In an effort to protect the natives from extortion, the Spanish government prohibited the sale of indulgences in native towns early on. This, however, did not reflect reality, and agents of the Santa Cruzada offered indulgences in native towns, sometimes announcing the sale with great pomp and circumstance that could include bands of trumpeters and other musical instruments. The curate of Chunhuhub stated that the Maya willingly and eagerly entered into contracts to obtain the bulls, although the coerced sale of indulgences occurred as well.[33] From the late sixteenth to the early seventeenth century, Pedro Sánchez de Aguilar—who would also conduct numerous investigations into the idolatries of the Maya—served as commissary of the Santa Cruzada, which was licensed to preach the benefits of such bulls and sell them in native towns. Aguilar and his commissaries were wildly successful, selling thousands upon thousands of bulls throughout the province.[34]

Thus, indulgences reached even the most remote of Maya communities in New Spain, including Teabo. Reports exist that suggest the Maya sometimes treated the bulls as sacred objects and even offered them sacrifices.[35] Moreover, the lasting importance of such documents among the Maya is evident in their preservation. For example, in the Maya Christian copybook relating the Passion (GGMM no. 66) is a printed broadsheet of such an indulgence issued for the years 1798 and 1799 and available for two reales. An indulgence also appears in the copybook relating a Maya Arte de bien morir (GGMM no. 70a). And the hieroglyphic text of the Madrid Codex contains a section where, as John Chuchiak convincingly argues, a rare handwritten bull of the Santa Cruzada was used as a "patch."[36] Similar to Spanish owners of such indulgences, the Maya owners apparently desired to save these bulls and place them within their copybooks and other significant texts to enhance their spiritual value.[37]

The Maya text offers various possible methods of receiving "u satal keban" (the loss of sin), or an indulgence, presumably after one has purchased a bull. Most involve praying the Hail Mary and Our Father five times in reference to the five wounds of Christ. Yet another concerns the possession and veneration of a *Santo pis*. This term also appears in the Kaua, and Bricker and Miram translate it as "holy yardstick," no doubt due to the definition of pis as "a measure" of sorts, while admitting that a Marian belt could also be meant.[38] Because pis also carries the meaning of "hem," I choose to translate it as such, and later in a section of the Teabo text not appearing in the Kaua is a promise that "maac bin U tac^{sic uichil} U noke matan U tabal tu tumuc ol cisino" (whoever will look intently at the cloth never will be trapped in the temptation of the devil).[39] Other stated benefits derived from its veneration included prevention from sudden death—in which presumably the victim would not have a chance to confess before dying—mortal sin, offense, or even being struck by lightning, the latter perhaps resonating the strongest with Maya culture, as lightning was a distinguishing characteristic of the rain god Chac.[40] What exactly "Santo pis" references is uncertain, although possibilities include a piece of the holy robe of Christ that the Roman soldiers removed from him prior to his crucifixion, or some other portable yet venerable article of clothing as the text also mentions the transport of this holy hem to other cahob, similar to a procession of a saint.[41] In regard to Christ, the Gospel of Luke records the miraculous healing of a sick woman who merely touched the hem of his cloak, or the holy hem.[42]

Both the prayer to Mary and Christ and the text on indulgences are brief and highly influenced by Christian themes. Yet both provide important insights into the contents of Maya Christian copybooks and the colonial religious landscape. The subject matter of the texts illustrates the dissemination of knowledge regarding Mary, Christ, and even the popes and their support of indulgences. Indeed, all such subjects appear frequently in the "Maya Sermons" copybook, particularly in regard to Marian texts. Certainly the Teabo texts betray Maya elements. However, the themes, figures, and general contents of the discourses reflect a European concern for the remission of one's sins so as to enter the next life prepared. The two texts in the Teabo Manuscript and those two similar texts in the Kaua all undoubtedly originated from a similar source of unknown origin—perhaps from one of the many European archetypes available, or a local creation in one of the Yucatecan schools. Regardless of their origin, these texts circulated among the Maya communities to be recorded, altered, rewritten, modified, and preserved in books such as the Teabo Manuscript.

Prayers to Mary and Christ, and an Indulgence Text, pp. 36–37, 40–41.

(P. 36)⁴³

. . . U Kubentic Uba uinic ti Ca cilich colel Suhuy Santa Maria yetel ti Cah lochil hesu christo AMen Jesus Be yn cilich Colel suhuy Maria okotba yn Cah tech tumen Cab lahci yn Cilich yuon ta suy nak Be u xaman ekil KakNabe okte aba uoklol tu tan a cilich Al yn uah lochil ti Jesuchristo Be u sasilil bal-Cahhe tichkakte yn pucsikal Ca sasilac yn naat ti yn cuxulic uay ykol Cabe yetel yn pustic U lumil yn pixan be kazen uay yalan A cilich canil Cilih s̄s̄m̄ā trinidad okes A uich ten ca a ɔab ten a cilich grasia yn ɔabesic U tanlah . . . A cilich Al yn uah lohil tie Jesuchristoe be yn cilich colel suhuy Maria ye a kab yokol yn pol ca yn . . . cunte yn cunte⁴⁴ yn uich yalan U tepail Al yn ua lo-chil ti Jesup̄/x/topto be yn yumile DSe okes a uich ten Ca peɔucen tu kab ah chibalob y ah Cayballob ti yn pixane heklay cisinobe be yn cilich Colel Suhuy Maria chincunah yn Cah tech yalan a tepalil hach otzilen cen ah tan kebanen Manbalen Cen sihanen Uay yokol Cabe . . . cen Uay yalan A cilil canil otoch tacunten yalan A lich boy ca Utzac U . . . ti Kabe Uay yo okol Cabe be kasen

(P. 36)

. . . dedicate him/herself as a person of our holy lady virgin, St. Mary and to our redeemer, Jesus Christ, amen Jesus. Oh, my holy lady virgin Mary, I am beseeching you through joined hands my holy . . . in your virgin womb. Oh North Star of the sea, plea for me before your holy child, my redeemer Jesus Christ. Oh, light of the world, illuminate my heart so my understanding is enlightened as I live here on earth and I remove the dirt from my soul. Oh, I am ruined here below your holy heaven, holy most Holy Trinity have compassion on me that you give to me your holy grace, I give service . . . your holy child my redeemer, Jesus Christ. Oh, my holy lady virgin Mary, place your hand on my head so I hide my face under the royal child, my redeemer, Jesus Christ. Oh, my lord God, have compassion on me, withdraw me from the hands of the wild animals and fishermen of my soul, which are the devils. Oh, my holy lady virgin Mary, I am humbling myself before you, under your reign, truly I am miserable, I am a great sinner, I am nothing, I was born here on earth . . . here below your holy heavenly home, I hide under your protection so that . . . here on earth. Oh, I am ruined,

(p. 37)[45]

cen ah Mahan cuhilen Ma a uilic yn lubul yn cilich colel suhuy Maria otzilen
cen Ah tan kebanen be u sasili balcahe a kab yn yanil tumen yn keban A kab
yn uih a uicnal y A paactic cen be yn cilich colel Ala yn uol tech bin A uokes
a uich ten anten tu tan cilich Al yn U ah lohil ti Jesusp̄to be yn yumile Diose
Uᶜhuc tumen tusinile ti culan naK tu noh DS. yumilbile Cat tuchitabech Uay
yoKol Cabe Ca a sates U keban ᵃh kebannob al lohaabol Ah otzilob a hosah-
hob ti MasCab kalannilobe bayx a uanticen cen ah tan kebannen ekmayil yn
cah tuMen yn keban Nunᵘya yn cah tin Mahan Naten . . . Mahan Cuchilen
ma nach yn nat cen ah tu . . . . . y naat be yn cilich yumile Diose Matan yn
tacunte a cilich AlMahtḣanil cech yumil Dios An . . . chichcunte yn Muk
ocaan tin uol bin cin cen ocaanix tin Uol bin cuxlac cen ta cilich kab ti manan
U xul Mayx U lah AMen Jesus y Maria

. . .cicih. . .[46]

---

lay u pis yooc

(P. 37)

I am a borrower of divinity, do not see me fall[47] my holy lady virgin Mary. I am miserable, I am a great sinner. Oh light of the world, I am in your hand because of my sin, I hunger for you and repay me. Oh my holy lady, I have confidence in you to have mercy on me, help me in front of the holy child, my redeemer Jesus Christ.

Oh, my lord God almighty,[48] seated on the throne of the great God the Father, when you were sent here on earth, you forgave the sins of sinners, you redeemed the miserable, you liberated those in prison, the drunks. Likewise you helped me, I, a great sinner, I am blind because of my sin, I am amazed at my borrowed understanding . . . my limited understanding . . . my knowledge. Oh, my holy lord God, I never kept your holy commandment you, lord God . . . I strongly believe, I will believe it, I will live in your holy hand where there is no conclusion nor end. Amen, Jesus and Mary.

. . .

This is the measurement of his foot.[49]

He papa yum Cab ynosensio U kaba U . . . ua mac uinicil Bin tazic uba y icnal
U cilich pasion U cilich uinicil Ca yum ti Jesus x̄pto tu yabal ti tzicul . . . yabal
than tal uinic payal he te tanmuk u kulic C ah lohil ti Jesus hristo oxten Ca
paya chitic c hun petz kin bin mente lachun Ca bak U yantal satal kebanni ᵗⁱ
chistiyano U seb chitahix papa clemente y papa Bonifacio yetel papa gregorio
yetel papa Benedicto yetel papa Joans he ti huhuntul ca santo yumob loe . . .
chatahob lae ti ua mac uiniccil bin kultic U cilich uinicil Ca yumil ti Jesus
christo bin U nahte hokal hab U noh satsabal U keban Ua bin U payal chite
hopeɔ Ave maria hopeɔ pater noster tamuk u ziic tu hopel u tzicul U cintanil
C ah lohil ti Jesup̄to Ua mac yanile Santo pis tan U kultic tan U payal chitic
C ah lohil ti Jesup̄to oxten U payal chitic ychil hunpel kin matan U chetun
cimil mayxtan U cimil Ma u choch U keban Maⁱˣtan U macal U pa lubbul
ychil Ah ualbil Keban matan U macal u pacat tu uich matan u cocintabal
tumen paak pach maixtan u haɔal tumen chaac uaix maac uinicil bin u bines
Santo pis tu yanal Cah tan U katic U lakobie lic U nahaltic U noh satsabal U
keban tumen Ca yumil ti Dios Uayx maac bin U tac^{sic uichil} U noke matan U
tabal tu tumuc ol cisino Bayx chetun cimil

(p. 40)[51]

The pope, father of the world whose name is Innocent[52] . . . anyone who will bring themselves unto the holy passion of the holy body of our lord Jesus Christ, with great reverence . . . great humility the person cries to him there while worshiping our redeemer who is Jesus Christ; when three times we pray in one day it will make 600 indulgences for the Christian it is promised. Pope Clement and Pope Boniface and Pope Gregory and Pope Benedict and Pope John,[53] each one of these our holy fathers received. . . . so that whichever person who will worship the holy body of our lord Jesus Christ will merit 100 years of great (plenary) indulgence[54] if he will pray[55] five Hail Marys, five Our Fathers while he gives of the five in honor of the wounds of our redeemer, Jesus Christ. Anyone having a holy hem[56] for worshiping prays to our redeemer Jesus Christ, three times he prays in one day, he will not die suddenly,[57] nor die without confessing his sin, nor will the person fall into mortal sin, never will the person see it with his eyes, he is not offended by false testimony, nor is he struck by lightning; or if any person will take the holy hem to another town to where his fellows are desiring, he earns a great (plenary) indulgence through our lord God; or whoever will look intently at the cloth never will be trapped in the temptation of that devil and die suddenly.

(P. 41)

... bal bin u kate ti Ca yumil ti Dios tu tucul U ɔocol U payal chitic hopeɔ
Abe maria yetel hopeɔ pater noster binix ɔabac tu cebal tumen Ca yumil ti
Ds U sasahil U keban tan U chayic U cilih Nunya U yaya tul yn te U keban
ma samac cimic y hit ah ualbil keban licix U yanhal U nahaltic U palilob Ua
bin U payal chiteob hopeɔ Abe maria yetel hopeɔ pater noster tan U kultic-
cob c ah lohil ti Jesus christo yanix okolal tiob xan binix Antabac tumen Ca
yumil ti Dios yabix U tibil Mactzi yetel grasia yan U nahte huntul christiano
Ua bin U payal chite y U yabal U ya olal tu pucsikal tan U payal chitic Ca
tun yal bay lae Amen Jesus

(P. 41)

. . . will he desire from our lord God in his thoughts. He finishes praying five Ave Marias and five Our Fathers and the forgiveness of sin will be given quickly by our lord God; he is taking the holy misery of penance of my sins that will never die and . . . mortal sin since there exists the merit of the servants if they will pray five Hail Marys and five Our Fathers, they are worshiping our redeemer Jesus Christ, they have faith also and will be helped by our lord God. A Christian has as merit many good miracles and grace if he will pray and call, with remorse in his heart he is praying, so then he says it like this. Amen Jesus.

5

Records of Death and Healing

THE DOCUMENT OF MY FINAL WORDS IN MY
TESTAMENT WILL BE SEEN, INSOMUCH AS I WHOM
AM IGNASIO PECH, THE SON OF PEDRO PECH
THE CHILD OF LORENSA YAM.
—LAST WILL AND TESTAMENT OF
IGNASIO PECH, 1748[1]

THURSDAY, APRIL 2, 1874, AT ONE IN THE
AFTERNOON ELARIO NA DIED. HE DIED
SUDDENLY BECAUSE OF PAIN.
—CHILAM BALAM OF NA[2]

H-MENS KNOW HOW TO ESTABLISH SOMETHING
LIKE A CHEMICAL CONNECTION WITH THE PLANTS.
. . . THE H-MEN, WHAT HE DOES IS HE ASKS THE
PLANT TO CURE YOU. . . . A PLANT IS CONNECTED
TO THE SAME FLOW OF LIFE AS WE ARE.
—DON ALDO, H-MEN[3]

REGARDING THE HERBS AND PLANTS
THAT THE INDIANS USE TO CURE, THERE ARE
MANY VERY BENEFICIAL ROOTS AND HERBS,
THERE ARE A GREAT NUMBER THAT GIVE
GOOD HEALTH TO THE NATIVES.
— *RELACIONES GEOGRÁPHICAS*[4]

VARIOUS ENTRIES ARE WRITTEN on the pastedowns and initial and final blank pages of my personal copy of scriptures I received when I was eight years old. These entries include important religious events that occurred to myself and my children, including dates of baptisms, blessings, and other ordinances. Such records seemed appropriate to include in a work of personal importance to me and one that is carefully preserved. And although "official" records of such events exist, these notes provide personal as well as immediate and easy access to these significant moments.

The various notes found throughout the pages of Maya manuscript works, including Christian copybooks, suggest that they thought along similar lines. The death record quoted above derives from the final pages of the Na, and although an "official" death record was made and now exists in the Archivo Histórico del Arzobispado de Yucatán in Merida, it would seem that one of the compilers of the Na, José Secundino Na, desired a personal record of the death.[5] Similar entries exist in various Books of Chilam Balam and Maya Christian copybooks to betray further the common practice of recording significant events to the author/owner of the work.

Yet not all records speak of death; others celebrate life and its important religious milestones, including birth and marriage. Still others include medicinal remedies. Although extensive and lengthy lists of remedies and cures exist in various Chilam Balams, the few entries found in the final pages of the Teabo Manuscript more closely resemble its death record in that the remedies are personal notes placed in a book of significance for preservation and personal and easy access. Such remedies and death records provide important information on the personal preferences of the author and the activities within the cah. Yet perhaps most significant, the recording of deaths and medicinal remedies exposes further the dual nature of these works as being both communal and personal compositions.

Recording Death

In 1722, Bishop Juan Gómez de Parada held a synod in Yucatan where it was stated that every curate should maintain four books in which are recorded the baptisms, confirmations, marriages, and deaths that occur in his parish. The proceedings then provided a rubric for how such records should appear. Regarding death records, the prescribed entry is as follows:

> In such and such year of the Lord. In such and such [day] of the month of (name), he/she died with or without a testament (name of the deceased), Spaniard or Mestizo, native of (name of town), single, widower or husband to (name of spouse) native of (name of town). He was buried on the same day or on the following in the church of (name). He received, or not, the holy sacraments. And I (name) curate or deputy curate of the parish (name) took this account and signed it. Complete name and signature.[6]

In addition to the book recording all the deaths, the synod instructed ecclesiastics to encourage the proper recording of a last will and testament for the natives before their death. This was to assist in both a fair division of their property and the well-being of their soul.[7]

Ecclesiastics generally left such mundane record keeping in the charge of the town notary, and existing documents from various cahob suggest that Maya notaries adopted Spanish rubrics in various ways. Although some cahob maintained detailed testaments, others seemingly preferred a more simplified declaration of piety.[8] Regarding a separate book for the entries of deaths, none in Maya exist today to my knowledge from any cah, although that does not mean they did not exist. Instead, extant death entries typically appear in various cah-maintained manuscripts from cofradía records to Maya Christian copybooks.[9] And although marriage and cofradía records are not uncommon, death records dominate the existing corpus.[10] Perhaps this is because, unlike baptism, confirmation, or even marriage, recording the deaths of notables in the cah best aligned with precontact practices. That said, none of the notations follow with precision the rubric that the 1722 synod provided, although most incorporate some elements. This deviation is not unusual as the formulaic, prescribed preamble of the last wills and testaments penned by Maya or even Nahua notaries often displayed personal and local preferences.[11]

Death records appear throughout a variety of copybooks and Chilam Balams. The copybooks relating the Passion, an Arte de bien morir, and various prayers (GGMM nos. 66, 70a, 71, and 72 respectively) all contain death records inserted throughout their pages. The Chilam Balam of Na also records the deaths of notables in Teabo, and the Teabo Manuscript contributes one single recording of a death in the cah. This sole entry appears vertically along the inside margin of page 19 and runs horizontally along the top margin to read, "como a las 3 1/2 de la mañana Sabado Sr Dlefino Mo almaneser el dia 5 ~~Dicimbre~~ Disciembre falliecio 5 de Disiembre de 1925" (At about 3:30 Saturday morning, Señor Dlefino Mo, at dawn the 5th of December, died, December 5, 1925). The ink is much more recent than that in the main text and betrays a Maya hand.

Significantly, five copybooks exist which include death records from Teabo. This provides uncommon access to those names the maestros and notaries deemed sufficiently important to record. Table 5.1 illustrates the names and dates recorded in these books. These Teabo copybooks and their death records provide a rare opportunity to achieve some additional insights into colonial writing. First, nearly all the records date from the late nineteenth century. Surely earlier versions of such copybooks contained similar death records that were not included in their most recent editions, further illustrating that these works were ever changing and were not simple facsimiles of earlier versions. Perhaps the personal preferences and entries of a maestro or notary did not transfer to his successor.

Furthermore, select entries from various Teabo manuscripts continue to find relationship with the Na family and the compilers of the Chilam Balam of Na, José Secundino Na and his father, José María Na. For example, María Petrona Selestina, whose death in 1855 was recorded in the "Yucatec prayers" copybook, was the daughter of José María Na. Later, the 1860 death of his wife, Rogeria Dzul, appeared in a separate copybook, the Maya Arte de bien morir.

Moreover, similarities in handwriting, prose, and orthography among entries in different works betray that the authors of the death records varied in their choice of copybook. For example, the orthography and handwriting of the entries made in 1875 correspond across those found in the Na and the "Passion Text," thus suggesting a single author (see figure 5.1). Moreover, similar matches occur with the 1873 birth and death records found in the Na and the "Yucatec prayers" manuscripts (see figure 5.2). This submits that these maestros and/or notaries either possessed or had access to multiple copybooks. Some of these they had written themselves; others had come into their possession. Either way, and similar to the precontact *itz'aat* and h-men, Maya specialists in each cahob trained in religion and writing composed, maintained, and passed along these manuscripts.[12]

Table 5.1. Copybooks from Teabo and Their Death Records

Manuscript	Deceased	Date
Teabo Manuscript	Señor Dlefino Mo	12/5/1925
Chilam Balam of Na	Elario Na	4/2/1874
	María Viviana Yah	7/4/1875
	Camilo Ye	8/6/1875
	Pedro May Santos	8/15/1875
	María Ramos Coyi	11/7/1878
	Concepción Chulin	12/9/[1878]
	José Secundino Na	5/15/1885
	José Modesto Ek	1/20/1892
	Desideria Aké	9/25/1892
	Herculano Ek	1/4/1893
	María A. Chan	4/13/1893
	Matilde Chan	12/19/1893
	Teofilo Nah	1/23/1895
Passion Text, GGMM no. 66*	? Mutul	5/25/1811
	Nicolas Hau	?/29/1875
	Anastacio Ek	8/28/1875
	Margarita ?	8/29/1875
	Jose Blas Moo?	8/19/1875
	Marcelina Euan	8/21/[1875]
	Maria Victoriana Na	10/6/1875
Arte de bien morir, GGMM no. 70a*	Candelaria Chable	7/23/1860
	Rogeria Dzul	7/27/1860
	Basilio Naal	2/21/1872
	Maria Itza	3/16/1872
	Jose de los Santos Ek	4/2/1878?
	Juan Pech	3/23/1882
"Yucatec prayers," GGMM no. 71	Maria Petrona Celestina	2/4/1855
	Maria Pabla Ye	5/2/1873

*Various entries are unreadable, thus making the list incomplete

Certainly the entries in Table 5.1 do not reflect the entirety of deaths in Teabo during those years. Why then record some names and not others? Although we can only speculate, it is likely that the recorded names of the deceased had a notable connection to either the notary, cah, or both. Of the various chibalob represented in the entries, those appearing most frequently—Na, Ek, Chan, Mo—surely represent elite families in Teabo.[13] The Na chibal held enough prestige and education to author the Chilam Balam of Na, and the death of Dlefino Mo recorded in the Teabo Manuscript represents a chibal that would later hold the office of *presidente municipal* (mayor) of Teabo multiple times in the twentieth century. In the end, the choice of whose death to record further demonstrates the autonomy and agency of the authors and notaries of such copybooks.

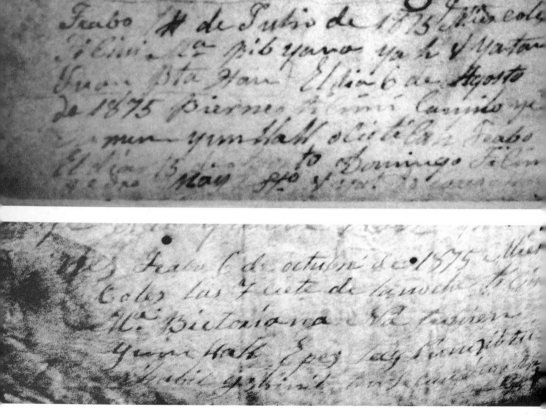

FIGURE 5.1. Examples of 1875 Entries from the Na and Passion Text (Princeton University Library)

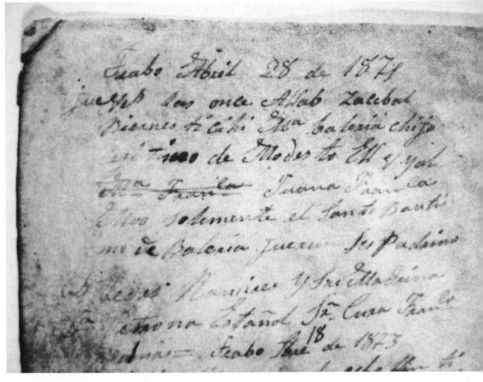

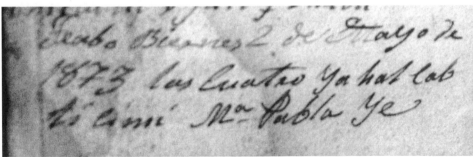

FIGURE 5.2. Examples of 1873 Entries from the Na and "Yucatec prayers"
(Princeton University Library)

Recording Healing

Bishop Gómez de Parada addressed a variety of concerns in his 1722 Yucatecan
synod that expanded far beyond the proper recording of events in a parish.
One such concern included the presence in Spanish parishes of "people who

use sorcery, incantations, spells . . . and are healers or that have writings of spells and superstitions or any other forbidden books."[14] Admittedly, Mayas did not monopolize the position of healer in colonial society.[15] However, they were included in the accusation. The Church viewed with suspicion, and even contempt, any cure obtained through means deemed "questionable" and that did not originate strictly from God and his authorized servants. Previously we saw how the Maya author of the Chilam Balam of Ixil neglected to name the author of its medicinal remedies, instead asserting as the source "El Cid Campeador."[16] Moreover, Maya and Nahuatl confessional manuals both typically included questions asking penitents if they engaged in such activities. An 1803 Maya confessional manual, for example, queries if the penitent ever cured someone using spells, and Molina's 1569 Nahuatl manual inquires, "Cuix quemmanian aca ticitl oticnotz, ynic . . . mitztlacuicuiliz, yn anoço mihchichinaz . . . ?" (Did you ever call on a healer to . . . draw noxious objects from you, or suck [things from] you?).[17]

The Maya employed medicinal remedies long before the colonial period. The Maya's calendars, gods, and religion all played a role in their medicinal practices. Landa, and later Cogolludo, describe various gods of medicine and their rites, including those associated to Ix Chel, Itzam Na, Cit Bolon Tun, and Ahau Chamahes.[18] Indeed, the divine and one's health intimately corresponded, as demonstrated by the Maya performing rituals to specific deities to prevent certain illnesses.[19] This is not all that dissimilar from the beliefs of sixteenth-century Spain that connected epidemics and disease with a disapproving deity and his saints.[20]

Local flora and fauna played an essential role in the medicines of the pre-contact Maya, and existing documentation testifies to the continued efficacy and role of such remedies in the lives of the colonial (and modern) Maya. In the sixteenth century, Spain's Philip II issued a questionnaire to local officials in an effort to better govern his overseas colonies. Question twenty-six of fifty inquired after "the fragrant herbs or plants with which the Indians cure, and the medicinal or poisonous virtues of them."[21] Although responses varied, a common one stated that "most of the Indians did not cure their illnesses if not with herbs and roots and they bleed those parts that hurt them."[22] The Maya medicinal and ritual texts that have survived today, known as the Ritual of the Bacabs and the Sotuta and Mena manuscripts, and the Books of Chilam Balam of Chan Kan, Na, Kaua, Ixil, and the Códice Pérez all contain medicinal remedies.

Spaniards also took an interest and recorded such remedies in various works. As Bricker and Miram noted in their study of the Kaua (2002), Spain learned from its Arabic past how to compose medicine books of remedies, and those found in the Kaua, although different in content, share a similar format to those created in Spain. Such a tradition crossed the Atlantic to produce various Spanish works on local medicinal practices. For example, Sahagún included myriad plants and remedies in books 10 and 11 of his *General History of the Things of New Spain* or *Florentine Codex*, and Nahuas at the College of Tlatelolco composed the sixteenth-century Badianus Manuscript, which lists various botanical plants and remedies. For Yucatan, various examples exist, including the *Libro del Judío, Manuscrito de padre Herrera, El libro de medicinas muy seguro*, and *Libro de medicinias*.[23] For their part, Maya texts and their inclusion of remedies among culturally and religiously significant compositions illustrate the continued connection between medicine and the divine. Moreover, and similar to doctrinal treatises, many of the mentioned texts contain cognate passages of remedies from other Maya texts, thus further exposing the circulation and sharing of the content of the works themselves.

Understanding the importance of medicinal remedies among the Maya and their connection with the divine helps explain their presence in the Teabo Manuscript. Like the death record of Dlefino Mo, these remedies were appended years after the writing of the main texts and most likely originated in the twentieth century. Yet their inclusion in this Maya Christian copybook maintained by religiously trained maestros and/or notaries who helped oversee the Catholic well-being of the cah exposes a double role for these individuals. They preserved and maintained not only the spiritual nature of the cah but also the physical nature—which of course was (and, for many, continues to be) connected in many ways. An example of this is found in the Teabo Manuscript's remedy for a snakebite and its employment of the leaves of the *sip che* (literally, "sin tree"), which remains common in curing rites today. According to David Bolles, sip che has uses other than as a medicinal remedy: "usually seven or nine sprigs of the plant are collected and used for such things as a brush to sweep away the evil winds or as decorative pieces around the altar but which function to keep away the evil winds."[24] Thus the plant contains both a physical and a spiritual benefit.

Today, as in precontact and colonial times, h-men and curers in many cahob—similar to the aforementioned historian and shaman of Tusik, San Itza—continue to preserve and engage both the religious and medical knowledge of the cah. They can be seen as "the present-day descendant of the Post-Classic curers and the ah kin, and perhaps the maestro cantor of the colonial period."[25] In her work examining contemporary h-men, Marianna Appel Kunow notes the importance of prayer in medicinal cures, recording the words of don Tomás: "Every person who cures with plants has their own *Milagros* (miracles); their own belief in which saints will help cure the sickness that person has, to discover which plant to give them."[26] Moreover, following their Spanish counterparts, many remedies in the Chan Kan conclude with the phrase *paybe Dios*, or "God willing."[27] In many ways, such remedies represent a fluid negotiation between the old and new, preexisting religious rituals and beliefs and Catholicism.

In general, the medicinal remedies in the Teabo Manuscript differ from those found in the Books of Chilam Balam in that they are brief twentieth-century annotations to the manuscript. In other words, they were an afterthought and not conceptualized as being a part of the original religious composition. Some share the same pages as religious discourses; others were written in the margins or even appear upside down. The remedies cover the ailments of *pasmos de las mujeres*—a term used to describe various abnormalities and irregularities of the menstrual cycle, usually as a result of eating or coming into contact with cold items, especially during menstruation or after childbirth[28]—rashes, snakebite, body pain, and erysipelas. All such ailments are not uncommon and appear in various forms throughout other manuscripts. Yet unlike the Kaua, Chan Kan, Tekax, or Na that contain large sections of similar passages, the remedies fail to have cognate versions in any other text. Indeed, the majority of inserts read as a recording of personal practice, not as a copy of an existing text. Oftentimes, the instructions that typically accompany remedies found in the Kaua, Ixil, Na, or even Chan Kan, for example, fail to appear in the Teabo Manuscript. Instead, many entries are simple laundry lists of items needed in a cure with the occasional brief note of instruction.

Despite such brevity, many of the plants used in the remedies here likewise serve similar purposes in other texts, suggesting a common usage that extends beyond a particular cah.[29] For example, in its list of ingredients to remedy snakebites, the Teabo Manuscript includes garlic and tobacco, two ingredients also found in similar remedies recorded in the Kaua and the Sotuta and Mena Manuscripts.[30] Moreover, and similar to other texts including the Kaua, certain remedies in the Teabo Manuscript are homeopathic, prescribing ingredients that reflect the ailment. For instance, the remedy for a snakebite, or *chibal can*, includes the plants *sac bacal can*, "white corncob snake," and *u xiu can*, "the snake's plant."[31]

Like other remedies throughout Maya texts, those in the Teabo Manuscript illustrate a conversation between a Maya and Spanish colonial world. Certain remedies include Spanish-introduced items such as the lemon, and the text itself is an oftentimes frustrating mixture of a phonetically spelled hybrid of Maya and Spanish. That said, the entries are another testament to the importance such remedies played and continue to play in the lives of the Yucatec Maya. Indeed, Maya medicinal books continue to circulate among the natives, including the father of h-men don Pedro, who "learned about plant medicine from a man who had a book on the subject, which contained a history of medicinal herbs" titled *Xiu* or "plant."[32]

Certainly the death record and medicinal remedies recorded in the Teabo Manuscript differ from the work's other contents. Maya authors penned these entries years after the primary text. Yet their inclusion allows for a further understanding of these Maya-preserved copybooks. Both death records and medicinal remedies played a role in early modern Spanish society. Such practices persisted in colonial Yucatan where the Maya continued to make these annotations in their own works, no doubt due to precontact parallels. Death records appear in Chilam Balams and other Maya manuscripts, indicating the religious training of their authors and notable deaths in the cah. It is doubtful that such a selective recording of deaths was ever intended for the eyes of ecclesiastics. More likely, the records reflect the personal notations of the author on the passing away of notable acquaintances, relatives, and notable figures in the cah. Furthermore, the similar entries found among various copybooks in Teabo suggest an author's ownership and/or access to the cah's important religious works.

The inclusion of medicinal remedies among the religious texts of the Teabo Manuscript illustrates the enduring importance of curing in Maya society and its connection to religious specialists. The Teabo Manuscript suggests that the keepers of religious and historical knowledge likewise maintained the physical well-being of the cah through a knowledge of the local healing practices.[33] Although employing similar ingredients and styles, including homeopathic healing, the remedies found in the manuscript lack cognate versions in other known Maya texts, including the Chilam Balams of Tekax and Na—both authored in Teabo. Perhaps if the Teabo Manuscript had been dedicated to medicinal remedies, such a correlation would appear. As it is, the entries appear to be personal notes of the owner/caretaker of the manuscript at the time. Regardless, their presence provides yet another example of how Maya culture continually made and remade religion to fit local demands and traditions; in this case, a religious copybook wherein the recipient could find information on the creation of the world, the genealogy of Christ, or a cure to a snakebite. All such knowledge, important to the cah and its residents as it has been since precontact times, would be found and preserved in the hands of specially trained Maya, not those of the Catholic priest.

Various Medical Addenda, pp. 39, 41–43

(P. 39)[34]

Teabo 8 de Enero de 1911

para curar pasmo de las mujeres

mangeull (manguey)

cascara de pixóy

ol kab (ho kab) su ojas

chal che

oregano

tres matas de cabaxan (cabal xan)

una mata de caballaxnic (cabal yax nic)

se sancocha con miel

---

para un abroto (aborto)

[de] un filomenno (fenómeno)

U raiz peregil (perejil)

sancochado

tambien

xcanbahuah (x-canbal hau) con miel

---

su fruto de Valzamito (balsamito) con Anis

---

habac na^{a}h con miel

(P. 39)
Teabo, January 8th, 1911
To cure chills or cramping of women
maguey
bark of pricklenut tree (*Guazuma ulmifolia* Lam.)
mayflower leaves (*Tabebuia pentaphylla* (L.) Hemsl.)
camphorweed (*Pluchea odorata* (L.) Cass.)
oregano (*Origanum vulgare* L.)
three sprigs of *cabal xan* (*Elytraria imbricata* (Vahl) Pers.)
one sprig of wild petunia (*Ruellia tuberosa* L.)
it is parboiled with honey

For an abortion of a phenomenon[35]
a root of parsley (*Petroselinum crispum* [Mill.] Fuss)
parboiled also
contrayerba (*Dorstenia contrajerva* L.) with honey
the fruit of balsamito (*Momordica charantia*) with anise (*Pimpinella anisum* L.)
serve stuffed[36] with honey

(P. 39 CONT., RIGHT HAND COLUMN)
para un abrotos un fenomeno
manguell = chalche (chal che)
cascara de pixoy
olkab (ho kab) su ojas
se sancocha con miel
que tengan 1/2 botella por todo

---

es lo mismo
rais helemuy (elemuy)
se sancocha con miel
que tengan 1/2 botella
por todo

---

es lo mismo cascara de
tamay se sancocha con miel

(P. 39 CONT., RIGHT HAND COLUMN)
For an abortion of a phenomenon
maguey, camphorweed (*Pluchea odorata* (L.) Cass.)
bark of pricklenut tree (*Guazuma ulmifolia* Lam.)
mayflower leaves (*Tabebuia pentaphylla* (L.) Hemsl.)
it is parboiled with honey
having 1/2 bottle for all

It is the same
root of *Guatteria Gaumeri*
it is parboiled with honey
having 1/2 bottle for all

It is the same
bark of the skyrocket tree (*Zuelania guidonia* (Swartz) Britt. & Millsp.)
it is parboiled with honey

(P. 41)

U chibal can U Ɔacal
x tancas che, u motz sac bacal can
9 pu[n]tas hu lee sip che
hierba y zapo[37] u xiu can
hu[n]pel boyo hajo hu[n]Wal Kutz
Wiix ɔabil hietel
chubil yetel le ɔacah .
nek hiah[38] nek limon
Wa coh . . . u chibal corrales can
hoyan bin corales hichil ·

(P. 41)

The remedy for a snake bite

prickly ash tree (*Zanthoxylum fagara* (L.) Sarg.), the root of the night-blooming cereus (*Cereus donkelaarii* Salm-Dyck.)

9 tips[39] of the leaf of the *sip che* (*Bunchosia glandulosa* (Cav.) DC.)

herb and rough skin [of the] *u xiu can* (*Stigmaphyllon ellipticum* (Kunth) Juss.)

1 garlic bulb (*Allium sativum* L.), 1 leaf of tobacco (*Nicotiana tabacum* L.),[40]

urine are given, and

it is cauterized with this medicine

seed of sapote (*Manilkara achras* [Mill.] Fosberg), seed of lemon (*Citrus limon*)

the pelican flower (*Aristolochia grandiflora*)[41] . . .

it will be poured inside the bite of the coral snake

(P. 42)

extrato de Maulita

para dolor que core todo el cuerpo

Erisipelel 22 de Mayo de 1910

Buscaras ojas de pimuta de

tubasco, y ojas de x kuxu can

ojas de agaucate

Junto molera y despues

cogeras horina para

des[h]aser el que tiene la

enferniandad uso extrema

(on the left hand side of the page is the following)

un puñio de sal agua un cantaro bien erbido

2 puñio de seniza de madera

para un remojo de piez

el que tiene dolor de cabeza

(at the bottom of the page written upside down is the following)

1__A

1/2

2 1/2 Z

(P. 42)

extract of Maulita

for pain that runs throughout the entire body

erysipelas, May 22, 1910

You will seek leaves of pimiento de tabasco (*Pimenta dioica* var. *tabasco* [Willd. ex Schltdl. & Cham.] Standl.)

and leaves of the rouge plant (*Rivina humilis* L.),

leaves of avocado (*Persea americana* Mill.)

Grind together and afterwards

you will take the urine to

undo he who has the

illness, use externally

(on the left hand side of the page is the following)

1 hand measure of salt water, 1 pitcher well boiled

2 hand measures of wood ashes

for a foot bath

for he who has a headache

(P. 43, WRITTEN UPSIDE DOWN)
una medicina para isipel
Lom tolooc – y chichibeé, y.
pech Ukkil – x ek u ne ak
y x kaNitz – debe restar en el –
debe Vañiase (bañarse) – chimay
en el mero puerta del gallinero
dejaras la ropa alli mismo
Volberas (volverás) a cogerlo en el dia sigiend (siguiente)
Eliccir para Colico,
(on the right-hand side of the page is the following)
18 de septimbre de 1909 empiezo tronar mi sendido

(P. 43, WRITTEN UPSIDE DOWN)
A remedy for erysipelas
persimmon herb (*Milleria quinqueflora* L.), and the common wireweed (*Sida acuta* Burm.),
and *pech ukil* (*Porophyllum punctatum* Mill. Blake), *x ek u ne ak* (black tail snake vine)[42]
and *x kanitz* (*Lacuma campechiana* Kunth), should remain in it
should bathe/soak, Campeche mimosa (*Acacia milleriana* Standley)
at the very entrance to the henhouse
you will leave the clothes right there
you will return to collect them the following day
Elixir for colic
(on the right-hand side of the page is the following)
September 18, 1909 I begin to lose my sense

Conclusion

AS ASSISTANTS TO THE PRIESTS . . . ARE TWO
RELIGIOUS OFFICIALS CALLED SECRETARIES
OR SCRIBES (*YUM X-CRIB*). THEY ARE THE ONLY
ONES WHO CAN READ OR WRITE IN THEIR OWN
LANGUAGE AND, THEREFORE, HANDLE OFFICIAL
CORRESPONDENCE. IN ADDITION *THEY ARE
RESPONSIBLE FOR CUSTODY OF THE "SACRED BOOKS," IN
WHICH ARE CATECHISMS, OLD ALMANACS, BIBLES, AND
FOLKLORIC ACCOUNTS WRITTEN AT VARIOUS PERIODS BY
THE INDIANS THEMSELVES.* IT WAS IN THE POSSESSION
OF ONE OF THESE SCRIBES THAT I DISCOVERED,
IN 1935, THE MANUSCRIPT OF AN OLD
BOOK OF CHILAM BALAM, KNOWN TODAY AS
"CHILAM BALAM DE TUSIK" (EMPHASIS MINE).
—ALFONSO VILLA ROJAS[1]

For many, a walk through modern-day Teabo might give the impression of a town conflicted between the old and the new. Homes constructed in the traditional Maya way sit across the street from convenience stores, *huipil*-donning women share the plaza with those wearing GAP T shirts, and outside the *palacio municipal* stands a basketball court. But perhaps instead of conflict, we should see negotiation—a working agreement between the old and the new, between what has always been and what is happening now. The Teabo Manuscript allows us to glimpse how such negotiations were made regarding religious worldviews during the colonial period and a bit beyond.

Works such as the Teabo Manuscript, other Maya Christian copybooks, and the Books of Chilam Balam are instrumental in our understanding of what the Maya chose to record concerning Christianity. Maya Christian copybooks, although technically forbidden compositions, illustrate those aspects of colonial religion that the Maya author and subsequent contributors and copyists deemed important enough to preserve. Certainly it is possible that ecclesiastics were aware of such locally preserved copybooks, but the authors and audience remained Maya. Put another way, Mayas composed and preserved these works and their contents over the centuries not for the Church, but for reasons that mattered to themselves and the cah.

So what did they write? The themes, topics, and individuals that appear throughout the Teabo Manuscript and other religious compositions of the Maya are those that resonate strongly with both European and Maya world-views. The popularity of and fascination with the creation and termination of the world corresponded well with the period beginnings and endings of the Maya calendar and the gods of their pantheon that both blessed and smote, created and destroyed. The Teabo Manuscript features prominent figures of the Christian worldview, including Adam, Eve, Lucifer, Christ, and Mary, all of whom play significant roles in the daily lives of individuals through their role in the creation, damnation, and salvation of mankind. Interestingly, it is those elements of Christianity that best correspond to a Maya worldview which survived the centuries to appear in the copybooks or in the oral accounts of contemporary Mayas.[2]

The Teabo Manuscript demonstrates that whether the teachings of Aquinas or indulgences, the Maya drank deeply from the font of European theology. Yet the Maya did not simply reproduce facsimile translations of the European worldview into their copybooks. Instead, orthodox Christian doctrine and preexisting Maya beliefs provided material from which the Maya could create an even better story, one that spoke to both cultures and responded to regional and local demands.[3] The occasional modification or alteration of a traditional Christian doctrine or tale should not be viewed as subversive on the part of the Maya. Certainly Christians today do not consider themselves as such when they exercise their agency to selectively choose which tenets of their faith to uphold and which to ignore or perhaps bend slightly. The Maya similarly exercised their agency to create and maintain a Maya Christian worldview by choosing which elements of Christianity to record and how they would appear. In the process, they continued a tradition of accommodation and negotiation long extant within Christianity, from its inception as a Jewish sect to its inclusion of Gentiles without requiring them to uphold Jewish law to the impact of barbarian society on its medieval practice to its early modern reshaping in the face of Protestantism.[4]

The similarities between such stories as the Genesis Commentary or *The Fifteen Signs* of the Teabo Manuscript among various colonial Maya works expose in new ways the presence of cognate religious texts. The frequent appearance of these discourses, albeit in various forms, suggests their common knowledge and popularity among the colonial Maya authors. With certain religious texts found within these Maya Christian copybooks, there was a template of sorts, perhaps oral, written, or both, common among authors, but each cah and author made it their own.

As mentioned, whether these template discourses circulated physically through written form or orally is uncertain. I have offered the possibility that such stories owe their origins to the schools Maya noble youths attended and then left to return to their own respective cahob, carrying with them their training and, perhaps, texts. This parallels William Hanks's concept of reducción and the dissemination of a Maya reducido throughout Yucatan. Like Maya reducido largely produced within the ecclesiastical sphere that eventually branched beyond reducción to become autochthonous and include versions of Christianity unsettling to religious officials, religious texts created within the schools could disseminate and become modified with elements important to the local cah. The similarities in the formulaic preambles of Maya testaments from various cahob provide an illustrative example. Despite local and stylistic preferences of the cah and notary, the religious preambles of Maya testaments from the cahob of Ixil, Cacalchen, Tekanto, and Ebtun all share fundamental formulae. For example, all generally begin with an invocation of the Trinity, declare the testator to be of sound mind, cite the name and cah of residence of the testator, and acknowledge the inevitability of death while requesting specific arrangements for burial and requiem masses.[5] Such formulae arose from Spanish antecedents taught to the Maya notary, who then adapted them to best fit local and cultural needs. In a very real way, they mirror a similar process that occurred with Maya religious texts including, possibly, the Genesis Commentary, *The Fifteen Signs*, and others listed in Table 6.1.

Despite the written antecedents of these texts from which their current versions emerged, the oral recitation and preservation of the Genesis Commentary and other cognate texts surely contributed to their preservation, dissemination, and alteration. The Maya, like the Nahua, had an uncommon ability to memorize long dictations because they were a culture of limited literacy who depended on such.[6] Thus such stories could likewise be the product of memorized oral history, or perhaps the result of someone reading a text while another copied it down only to be recopied later for reasons of preservation. Indeed, the oral transmission of such religious texts would explain the common misspellings and orthographic variations. Moreover, the Latin found in the Teabo Manuscript is badly corrupted and, like the biblical names in Christ's genealogy, spelled phonetically. This suggests the Maya author derived the passages from memory or an existing manuscript that likewise contained such errors as a result of spelling the words as they sound orally.

Table 6.1. Cognate Passages among Maya Religious Texts

Thematic Topic	*Locations of Cognate Versions*
Genesis Commentary	Teabo Manuscript; Morley Manuscript; Kaua; Chan Kan
Preface to *The Fifteen Signs*	Teabo Manuscript; "Maya Sermons"
The Fifteen Signs	Teabo Manuscript; Tusik; "Maya Sermons"
Concluding sermons to *The Fifteen Signs*	"Maya Sermons"; *Discursos predicables*; Tusik
Meaning of Mass	Kaua; "Passion Text"; Chan Kan
Exemplum	Tusik; "Maya Sermons"; Morley Manuscript; *Discursos predicables*
Parable of sheep and goats	Teabo Manuscript; Tusik

Regardless, no priest would have made these mistakes, and the Maya were clearly not aware of what the Latin meant. This, then, reflects a larger trend of an increasing loss of knowledge in regard to the contents of these copybooks until it reaches the contemporary situation reflected in individuals such as San Itza of Tusik, who can somewhat recall the content when read aloud, but lack the knowledge to read the text itself. Like the important Declaration of Independence whose contents and language most Americans are unaware of or fail to understand, the knowledge contained within Maya Christian copybooks eventually eroded with time, although the manuscripts themselves were preserved for their historical importance.

Moreover, the Teabo Manuscript sheds some much-needed light on the authors of Maya Christian copybooks and even the Chilam Balams. From the good fortune of the manuscript contributing to what is now a sizable collection of texts from Teabo, comparative analysis of such texts provides insights into their authors. Death records from Teabo appended to the back of the Arte de bien morir (GGMM no. 70a) containing the signature of Secundino Na illustrate his participation in various copybooks, including the Chilam Balam of Na. Orthographic analysis and comparisons of prose between the appended entries of various copybooks from Teabo likewise indicate that authors and notaries had access to multiple manuscripts, noting a death in one while later choosing another for a separate entry.

This, then, adds additional clarity to the image of the role of the religiously trained maestro or notary as he maintains various manuscripts, copybooks, and documents, rewriting some while adding entries to others, all the while serving as guardian of all things spiritual in the cah.

The Teabo Manuscript illustrates in both general and intimate ways the ability of the Maya to play a large role in determining for themselves what aspects of Christianity and colonial life would be preserved in their local manuscripts. The Teabo Manuscript and other similar texts were at the same time communal and personal compositions. The religious discourses recorded were certainly shared with the cah on specific occasions. Yet at the same time, the pages of the copybook included select records and medicinal recipes of significance to the author(s) and subsequent contributors. In this sense, the Teabo Manuscript is another product of a colonial Maya world that constantly negotiated the old and the new, the corporate and the individual, Christianity and the indigenous worldview.

Appendix

THE TEABO MANUSCRIPT

Chun pahal Ychh u pechil vayan
Saber bal cah tumen Cayumil ti Dios uch ti
uchayan batob yutz cinhob ychil vacpel kin
klahito bah yutz cintci y umetc Cayumil ti
y cayax Nate eVa Genesis 8 enexo de
año 1116 — 45

Diban tumen Cilich bolon ahmiyatz moyses t
yunil miyatz henesis Vhaba tilic yalic Vsihsa
caan y luume hohochil han ti Maix bal
yan yokol ti hunkul he uac he caan Mabax
yoklal bay licil Vcanticob Batomi yaho
Doctoresob tilic yalicob heuan lae licitac
nak vsoeol vsihsabal tumen Cayumil ti Dios
tu chupah vpictanil Angelesobi Vhach chic
m tacil sihsabilob yxmazulumte ix Cuxtal
kob tumen Cayumil ti Dios Ahtepal
tun vsihil angelesobe baylicil Vcantic
yunil miyatz consito Vhabae y Doctoresob bayx
licil Vcantic yetel yalic Caymilon san Juan Dama
seno vhabae hekl lay caan yan yn fineo Vkabae
yaxe chun Can y cute Caymil ti Dios ahtepal
y caan primexo moua Vhabae ti mayto Vyox
chun Can cusut y caan christaxino Vhabae

...ynyte ypana susil ch hochento cuchi catun Vsihsa

Dios sasil cahuy ch hochenie heix ch hochenil cu cuchie

cahaba fah ahbil henxesasil ilo Cayalah Kinil caix

Vach vsashal yetel Vthubul Bay tun soctukan hic

yt cutahic Vagax chun Kin lae helay sasil lae cuihan

Sasto thomas tuvi set muyalae lembamachis yuh ti

nath cayumil ti Dios heix muyalae layoci y vh cinab

o lun casocie tisabi y tical cinabi y Primero mouil

Vagax chun caan cu sid tiyalahe catun ylah cayumil

ti Dios hach cici socluttanile tulacal Vsihsah batile ca

tun yol tah Vcunt cint Vchun Vkinil heltay Do

mingoe tucases hij tun Vkinil Casgutçunah cayumil

ti Dios firmamento helay cää yan hebal y tali la

hebal tulacal hibahun Vsihsah balil tulacale lay

vunctus Caan esferas Vhabae heltay uohani

aytahun talt lic tulacal tae ————

[decorated initial] eix Vchebal Vhach lemb ay Vsotchi can

hal tulacalbal loe lay yan Vhach uilal

Cachel tic hibicil holanil tumen nelob vyah miy

a hiloh astrologosob hach Canal tae Vmiyahob

bay Vcah Rey Dn Alonso yan ticastillae Ah

miyat yalabal hecaanob lae buluc tasili ta

bacabon sesielos heix Vnohol yan hach Canale

lay ym fixeo lae Vbabalil Kak bolon pixanob

Santosob y Santaob yane tile lic Vpaelaon Pacte
xialobe bolon pixanobie heix Caton ympixeo tre
n chich esligmatin V'pec maix tan V cutgi tihun
hetun tahunte caane yanyalan ym pixeo tae lay
ameromanll Vparachian Caan Casiatic Vbae yotllan
lay cusut tumen hun tul Angel taba tuhunah tul
tikin Ahahiar tichi hina hun ol atinil ti'cantclaui
ouas V'kin zil yalabale ti'lic V'sut tob tupach laaki espe
uo V'Mabaobe heix caan loe minan chobi baix yikin
yalan xan maixbalyani lay bolontas Cane chiitaaine
V'Mabae hetun riaxeactos Caare firmamento V'Kaba
lay yani lob tak lic chot tibay ta lic
sipit Kabe helay loe tuwich lembanae V'sast
cat tob yani lobe   AMen Jesus

geiac hetun planetasob mati llanob ychil
chobi tiyalah tae yotllat hun hun kia caan
yani lob bay tc'il zolic coh tihunzol V'binelob y
yalic planetasob lae satiano tu Vuctas caan yan sa
Jiter tu'uctas caan yan maxte tuhotas caan yan
Sol tulantas caan yanllenias tuyoxtas caan ydn
mexcurris tucatas caan yan luena lay nas fd
okot lae tix yan tae Vcharyan Vsihsah ba balil

yumil t' Dios ɔieh natis Kaħe bay teɔ yalic itɔɔo
to gose caanob haɔantacob ti mobimientosob yoħtal
heil y nanaol ticob ti ebob ayti planetasob ti'tic Vhalam
ucob Asentiicosob consentucosob uħabaob ychil y
Romanseil tharul suubersob c' Vthan lae hek lay y
chil ymaya than lae efsielos Vħabaob xane bay u
cah es feaasob menentacobe ceenac vximbalobe bay
xuaón yolahtlobe Blaohel tahac y natabac helelae
ħibal tieyalic Kulemɔib usihsah Cayumil ti Dios lae

                        Amen

ucafel uhinil lay fimamento V cuchil yaanil
usihsah bahl Cayumil ti Dios tutan cheumac
haa Kaħnay ychlate heix haa lae chxistal uħabae
yaanmalabale ayoħtal bay hach yiyipnacil haa lay
chxistalno lae aroħtal hail cuchiy yoħtal bayitie Vya
labale ychil Kuemibobe cuchi bay uCah Vseafiente
moysen ɔua yalabale ayoħtal Baxail Cuchiy bay ucah
tiħich Suramento yan tial taale Vah uyalabale yoħtal ua
hil cuchi hexac hexya tuyalabal cici than yoħale lay
consiagravón Vħabae minan vhoc uahi blamaix tan V
minantal mac alic caibi Kulemɔib lae tixan timal
cah tieuac tes caan lae baynen yilabale bay bidaoe
bay plomoe V fixmaul V ba Camac acufot chcanhal

Capaitic hi ba yan tac tutane tiex yayax afactibile
tie yħic ɔoe tumenel bay yol cah mail Dios Vbel tic

yotiba caldic Vscutel Vtembac caan ym pixco yo
temba Vfacal Voilich Vinicil Cuзumil ti Jesuchristo y V
temba Vpacal Voilich Colel Suhuy Santa Maria y Vcha
yan Santob yetel Santoob crci than Vinicilobe bay
San Juan euangelista unicten tembancil ma Vchaydni
hetulacal siban ychil Kulem sibobe Vhach hah hach
tohil xan tulacal bay bail yabe Ahbolon pixan San
Agustin hecilich kulem sibobe Vnaat uinic bin kin
chuc cie maltu chan Vhach nacate yobtlal hach ha
h y hach tohixan bay bail yabe cob As tologosob
lic ufotchican cuni cob ti machan cenil y tensahsa
xaxxaarrxaaa sil tibay lae
H etin tucantas caan yan hotunae lay nv pule
Hohol lae bicyabe yah miya zil itanumi yetel
Vpac zil lae ty tukinil lunes lae hach hat cab
cuchi calubi lucifer ti hal ti caan hundai ti; timetn
al catohtabie y V chay en engelob y cotbesah Vtha
y etelobe bayix Vthan xan he Vkinil lunes lae Ma
yuzil kini tumen lai ti Vkinil sipci y yuz cintci
mauhilel lucifer y Vchayan Vlobol angelesob lubiob
tetupa che

Yu yoxpel v kinil chi pahi luume tumen Cayumil
ti Dios yol pixan tiha yokol cuchi Cauha sah vba
hii nachil Cauhucah vbahelay Hatt nab viia ba lae
Cab cinhij tumeume vchebal vhoktlahal xiuob yetel
cheob y vcha yan vyanal balob ho kiob yok kol
luume bay bic yanil tac helelae si si than bi tix
luune tumen Cayumil ti Dios huen suthix v pixchahal
luume tumen xiuob y cheob y xuiteob y cha hue tac
cob ti helan hetirix tatacal xane heuac minan v
chuuk tiob lae Yuyoxpel v kinil lae tu yuk cinah
Cayumil v Dios paraiso terenal

v Canpel v kinil tu yuk cinah Dios luuminaxia
he lay kin y ve lae cau tatt cu nah ti caan kin
y ve hetin lae luuminaxia Mayox vyalabal lay
oci lae v noho chil tich katt yoklal lay tich katt
tix yetel v sah cunic yoktal Cab lae heix ve luumina
xia menox v yaiabal yoklal voil tich katt yoklal
lay tich kin yetel sasil cunic ahab lae

Bay xan yuk cinah ehob Cayumil ti Dios ca
sahob tu uaxactas Can heix ve lay nax pul coktal
hetun kine tu canto caan yan tix yan hii vuhal
v cutalie yoklal ti yan hi yetel sahsab lay muiyal
hach lembanac occi tu unici Kin lae Catiac

Cati ac yan tu tan chumuc caan Vchibal Vyan...
Sasiltiob cuchie heuac Mayol tah cayumil ti Dis ah...
pel lay tux yansi hie yetel topitix cul ti xan...

ti cix yutie hun tul Doctor helin y Vo casihiob...
Muyalhaso Meyahops Vtlakil Vpacatsob heu...
tu Canpel Vkinil tun sih sab cob cuchi Cahops vle...
Mba vpacat Vtlakilob tix Vchaah Vlembaob yetet V...
Sasiltob ti hunpel Muyal yan sihsabi tumen Ca...
yumil ti Dis bay Vchic quuya y Maria axoc...
Cex Samee ti tun li Hid vsasitl tulacal ettali yetel...
_____ planetas ti Kin lae _____

Vhopel hi tun Vkinil Vsihsah Cayumil ti Dis ba...
cheob lay chichobe ychil haa hi tubsi hi cayobe ny...
cob yetel chichan tacobe heix cayob lae ti yanhobi...
chil haa CaeMiob Cabalil tuhach ta Mi haa cat...
3op ho kiob tixitknalob vchuc canob Caual tixik baix...
O than tabiob tuMen Cayumil ti Dios Vtial cayaba...
cob hach yan hiix v vulal vsihilob ychil hunnpel Ki...
lay chichobe y lay cayobe tumend he lay cay y ch...
chobe chach yanel Vbaob lae tixitknalilob y baob...
tic Cubanto V xiltobe _____

yocħel tu Vkinil öihsah Cayumil i Dios bal chacb
tunich lum y chuyenbalcheob ti bay uruh maile tu
pachi une yetel oacħi luschix uxul Cħu Meyah ca
yumil ti'Dios yotah Mente y yuz cintci vinio yl<x
ti huntul Meyol tah Cayumil ti'Dj Vnicil VMe
yah i tubabahiui Vnahe hel lay tuyanal bale heuac
yoltah Cayumil ti'Dios Onte pal ti Vuxul V Meyah y
oocVMeyah yoltuba tuhunale bacacix oocan y
oihsic tulacal Vbal Caane y luume yetel tulacal Vbal
caan yetel luume y tulacalbal tu oih sah cuchic heuac
Malihel l'Onde yoh Ma V chac li yol Cayumil ti'Dios
ohicou lae Va Melahi tusah Vtu M tic Ci'lich Santi
t:Me tinidad hun nab Dios tioxtul V personatil yu
:Alt:i Meheribil espiritu Santo bay bcil V cici pat can

D'KuleM oib lae

Amhij y o oltah Cayumil ti Dios VMente y
tupele ajax vinic Cayumil ti'Dios Cahoßi Vkaok
cuincob yetel Vmultunticob Ci'lich oxtul Personas
Santis ima tinidad Cathanahi Dios yunubil Dios
Mehenbil Dios es pixitu Santo ti li'ayalic tubatanba
ob CaVcuz cinte hun tul Vinic ti bay lacRohbilane
y tac Vinicile tial tic Cayob ayanob ti Kanab yetel

ħuchob

Chichob yan ti ykle yetel balcheob yan baach [...]
Cithan tabaob ylex tohtil bahun Vhaach nohil V
hiplic vinic Cayumil ti Dios ti be Vhaach Vnoh cun
dbal tumen o tich oxtul V personas Santissima Me tri
ridad ti be VMul tintacob Valic vnah V Mentic cob
yax vinic vay yokol cabe Vnohlay ti tan yli be Dios y
umbil Vho chob V Hohbilanob y yet pisan tic hahal
hach bay Vuinicil Cayumil ti Dios ti be [...]
vanan Vuinicil ti canal ti lic V pacat ti caan [...]
ol te binel yt nacalie heli lay Maya ahob [...]
yan Vsih sahob bali lob chibal V pacatob yokol [...]
uMe tulacale ti takan Vuichob te [...]
Vhanalobe hetun huntul Vuiniclae Mabay loe
Canal Vuaan y ti kan V pacat cha kax thantil
tumtab o V pixan yt pacat Meix V [...]
zozohel hali vuinicil yoktole Meix sab Vsih
sibal hal Vkuk Mel xane ti bay V namal ti V
chuyan Vsih sahilobe saah yoc ti vaan Vtalel y
Vyabal yah Miya hili ayetel V cux olal ca
than

than Santo thomas yu vpixanil sih nal ti Dios
vyumel ti Extanbaob y angelesob eryanlob he pix yu
nal Cayumil ti Dios e bay xan yan nix vciiu chach
vnohil sihnal ti Cayumil ti Dios xan he Cayumil ti
Dios Ohteyale yumbil tumen tulacal bal cah tusi
nil bay ti caan yetel ti luume yetel ti Metnal tu
lacal ti sihsah Cocan bhaabaix vinie lae uz cinab tu
Men Cayumil ti Dios lae Vyumil te sih sabilob lay
ti bahix maob Cuchij xan bay licil yalic San Juan
puinasente hach bay uyet pixan Dios Cuchie hach
Ontopal yetel Justilla v tohil ti chich olal yetel
hah ach yu tic Cu than San tomas he v sic sah
Cayux yam Dan lae lay sip ci tuMen v Kebane
lay Hinam tic vzicile lay tuMen Ma tan
vzicile tuMen sihsabil babalob helelae henac
hetun Vbaylan yetel Vkohhilan Cayumil ti Dios
yin ti cuchie Mabahun Sat Vini lae baca ix
Keban chahie bay bic tu hunali Dios ti yuchu
cile y tepail tioxtul vpeasonas bayx tu vinic lae
pin pehu v pixan ti yanix Vchucil ti Kah sah u
                                              Kul

ti Dios yunbil naail liHil ti Dios espiritusanto Bay
xan hebic tukunail Dios yan yotel yet has tuyukul ba
Cah tusinile Malub Minion Dios bayix Upixan winic
xane ti yan ti ix se cebal cah heli lay Cucutile tuba
cal yoklal yanil Metab MyNen Upixan yoklal lay
Cuxbe layix xiMbanilc layix pecsilic xane

Cafel upechil Sibanil licil li Cantabal yetel Uniniche
Sabal pat a Uuinicil Cayax yuM ti eDan tumen Caya
Myl ti Dios y Unicol sih sab ci cayax Naa hicie
Sibar yala han ti yunil MUyaiz Genesis Uhaba li
than tuchi cavoo Umul tun Cob citich sartiha W
sibanil ychil Citich Kulewoib lae Caemiob laix talob Amaya
texenax tuhach Sozilil Cuchi yet pixan Vuenba ya
Caan He lay yanil tuMenel Cayumil ti Dios
yabal Macsic tac tibahunbale ti ix yan tac V yenlal Vah
sah babalil tusinil Unoh lail Vyax chel Cab lae tah totem
Vuichan cal hun ppel hab hun hun pel Vyantal Vuich
than San Juan evangelista yoklal yilah et sabi ictu Men
hun tul engel heix tac cob paraysolae lah capis V tulumil
Vhod ti lenbanac ti sasac takin yetel Hankan takin y lah Ca
tul engel laan tac Cot tu tulu Mil Vhod cha Kux than

32

than tzil vy iloobal ti ix caton yalil hunpel oyab hach
ti li kul tuchtun voilla vhuncha cutic Dios Uhtepal yala
nyoc cayumil ti seruchaiste cuha kol sabyab lae hach
sahide than tzil yetel vcrozill vonchil vpakal cayumil
ti Dios te parayso teneraosih saitzy cayax yuM ti Dan lae
helel tun aul tic cex christiano vyanaMal vNu cul hu
sat vprimicil cayax yuM ti Dan tu Men cayumil ti

——— Dios lae ———

atun tzol heo tun chumuc parayso teneraa cilich
uni ma trinidad oxtul personas sob te tic vMultumticob
tan tumbul Dio yuMbil Dio Mehenbil Dio espirtu Santo
tuthanob Maiote uzcinte yetel cMente vinic tac hok
za venatil tial tic yetel vyuMil te yn sihsahbaba
va oo yoktcab ti luum yoktal laix conantic vpach
tial tic vyabal Kanche vyabal silla vsatahob yetelpa
tu Men Bizicbail vlobol ongelobe cu than cayumil
te six ti socan tun yalic thanoblae lae Cabinob citanil
upach parayso teneraa vchacb vhokesob vhach vzil vni
luum taMbl vhach Mabenil luum ti hunlukul lah
lasaptu vhoksah Dios yuzil luum lae Damasenov
haba hokoy luum tuMen cayumil ti Dios lae cala
v

cabil caix valu than tix vuinicil hauatil xiklal v cichcal
1 mil vinic tan celem hach cichic celem v Uohbilan chacac
huaan yan v pol yan v xicin yan v vich yan v chi yan
v hol yan v yoc u ch tan tiui tich tan cacibich yan ya
May te oloct haa y kel mayte pacat nic Mayte pa
cais ie can tun v cici pat tal v enhail lae caus cabi tu
yikil caxtal tumen cayumil ti Dios catun cuxtahi ma
y to pacat nac catun tu yalah Cayumil ti Dios thanlac
Epeta pacat nen caix pacat nahij ti hach cich celem ti
hunlukul Ah Miyal catun hopi v hokol v...
cahopi v hokol v zo zel v pol caix hopi v yol...
caupesah vba casabi tub tuchij tu cilen cay...
ti Dios ca he chahi uchi cahopi v than tu...
v pixan Cayumil ti Dios yah sihsahule ti bail noi...
v pacat canal tan Mauk vyilic can yetel tun y...
hach lembanac cob v pacatobe ti hach cicolil tan y...
bal vyitahe cahopi v nip pixan tic Cayumil ti Dios lae
ti lic yalic than lae Beyn yumile yn hahal Dios he...
hal sol lukan yn meyahe hahal soos lukan v...
ucile

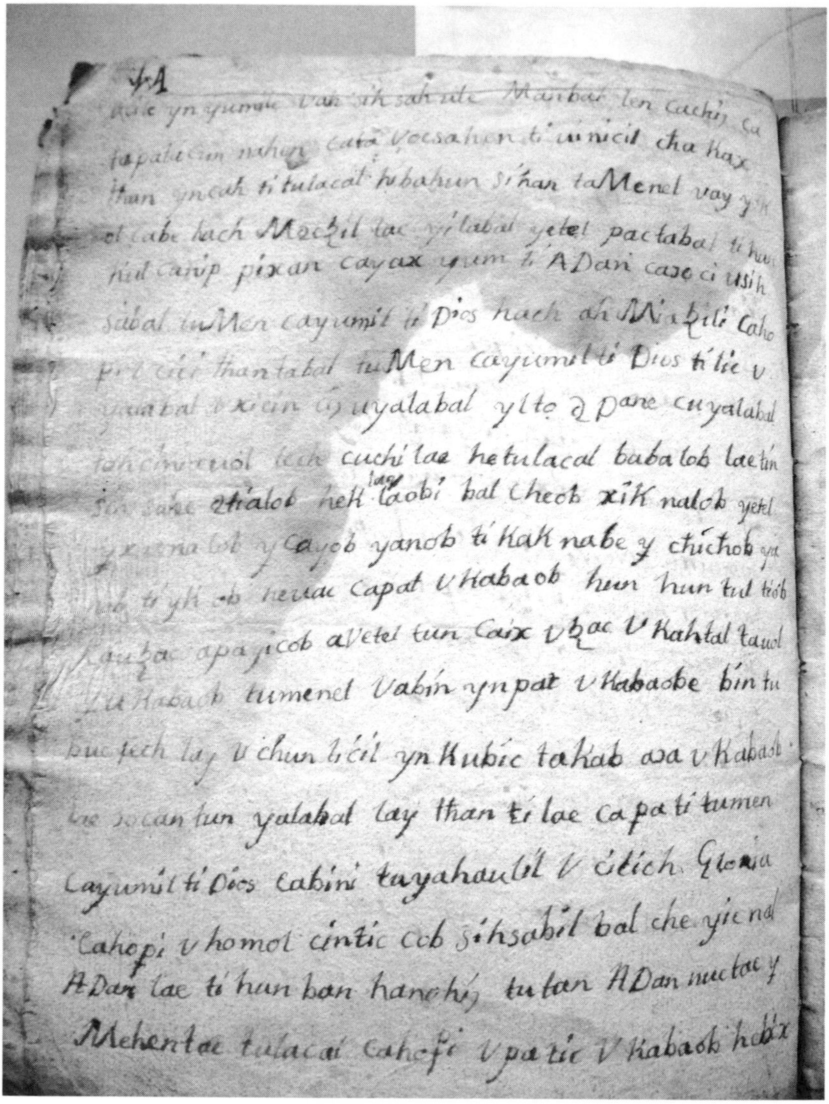

bebix unah maile henhun tu'tiobe sot can tun
ye tail Vhuba tuMen ɔDan loe

V yoxpel V pecħil cayax yum ti ɔDan y yax na te
eVa lay tulacal bal yukcinahob ychil lay Kin lae Vchie
Vhubul sihsabil bal che tiob V cinan teob Bayalab s tiob
tuMen Cayumil ti Diose Ahi pale cautuchi' talahob
ano Cabi nob oo Can tun luh Kulob yicnanab cahob
tu cul cayax yum ti ADan tilic yac Blaox un ok
cuthan ɔɔ₂n Macx bin ynla Kince Vaye bin
be cauhe oh Vyalak ɔo tu Caten cuhopi yati
sihal yani xan vet cul Cinte ynla Kin te Vaye
ooc ci Vlah pactic cob ychil tulacale cayx y tah
nan yet Vaan M'nan yetpis san Caduchi tahob
tu Caten tulacal Caix binob Cay lab tumen cayum
1 ti Dios Vu cul lay ɔDan loe Cayalah Cayumil ti Di
Mait Vchac Vcutal tuhunanal hach ti'bil Cayanac
Vlak cuthan Cayumil ti Dios Catun oabi oeoec Ven
el tumen Cayumil ti Dios Venel tun cah Cakuchi

cayumil ti Dios vinic Matan v yube ca hoti sabi thuu[l]
out vite e chalatal tumen cayumil ti Dios Ma yuba[l]
cache cunt tabi yinal luxax ti vend veach che[l]
uin v bacel v chalahit ca ca cici than tabi tumen
caymil ti D[io]s lay baae lae hun sihi upec y v cuxtal
hun til chupla hach cichpa[n] yet pisan angeles
tebix v paciabal Kan Kan oxo v Ro Rel v pole cay
sabi v pisan ychil v uinicil lae cay cuxtahij cuxa[n]
hin ca kh sab y[p]an ci yalabal y lah Mac yanta xa[n]
y... ci yalabal tumen cayumil ti Dios cay[x] vuncah
y...yume... ue lay lae yn chalatiil yn baceli xan

...ui... vinic v Haba suhuy lae cu than ADan ti ca
yumil a Dios oc can tun vcah Huchul tulacal lae ca
hopi v cici than tabalob tumen cayumil ti Dios ADan
yuil ella tan Mak yalabal ti obe tin sih si heex lae
yn sih sah uinic lexe a uo hel Maex ten tin sih sah
ex ti Minana yumex yetel a Naex hecen xta
lacal yn ual mah tha...ile yn kat yn cul cin to ex
a ci ci oc besex yetel a ci ci ta cun tex tulacal yn ual
mah

Mah thanile bin yn hach yacunt tech y bin yn u
tabeex yetel akaMy cex Vʒ yetel ti'bil Vay yohol cabe

Bay ix ti' caan xan Metan vyan tal NuM yacu
chi' tex Bay bin akaMy cex Vʒ yetel ti'bil Vabin
ʒoc tukescex ynual Mah thanile hetulacal bai ch
chedbo xacnaloob yetel xiH naloob tinohcah Vay yohol
cabe hach Sucteex Va vyaMae echobixan tuMen tolen
Maçal Mac ʒvolahex ʒhantantex y chilobe inafay tu
Kabaob bin tacobixan Caaye eye Maçal Mac akalex
ahan tan tex tuMen hach vyaMae chobixan yetel
Mae chobixan Bay xan aMal oxfil hin bin tota yx
M ahantex li'Hul ti'caan yohlal Maʒ aMaçahex ten ten
bin yntan ol tex yetel ʒhantex y xane heliM yle Maʒ
tan vyantal ʒvoholeex ti hunlukul Bay ix ti'yal aMe
henexan binsihic tu tan hin Cutale binix cux lacex ba
hun Vbakal baob Bay a volah Maytleexe vabin tuhu
avoleex ti' Cuxtal vay yohol cabe bin yn chaex tacu
cu ti'leex yetel ta pixanex tiʒyahaulil yn oich gloxia ti
caane Bay xane va avoltah hex capal tal tu catene bin
yn pal cun tex tucaten lay tulocal cin ualic tex lae
c Ca acici tucunte vabin afochex yn Val Mah thanile

78

hulacal tic yn holil texe hunsut lilic bin ynlobol than trex
y yn tohbe cex vay ychil vciofilil ynpahal parayso lae
heix sut ticla bin exi'lab abayilex yetel vhach yabal Nu
Myal yetel lixofilil xan cuthan cayumil ti Dios u Adan
yetel ti eva cuchi he than sab vtacunteobe Ma vyanal
than cuchis lay Ma v Makil kik cob yetel vtalicob viuch
yyax cheil cab vheel grasia cici thanan tuMen ca
yuMil ti Dios ahtepal vched olich grasia yetel cuxtal
yetel tiholal Ma atali cex Ma Makicex vuich xan yo
kool hach taiani l Ma unh Ma atali cex yleex yn
sihsah vinilil exe hahal than yn cah tex helel lde
bin yn nupinitex yetel he tulacal ynsih sah bal cheilobe
bin vnupin te chob tulacalob vnoh lailix xan ynyalil
al Mehenex texe hach canal silla xa an tiob vlobil
Angelesobe tupatahob ti cane abalex licil ynsihsicex
cuthan cayumil ti Dios tiob: helan poul team vhechitoobal
tiaoon y tic va= lay silla lae= hunsuthi v chabal ley
olal cisinob yicnal Sih Sabil vinicoblae cahopi v Multi
mutitob: vabil vnah v balkis cob y vtabis cob= lay than
A bas tiobe tumenel cayumil ti Dios - caxun hopi

5 de Diciembre de 1925

v multanbaob = v chi bienzia = ti lie zil zob tu batanbaob

bic vna tathanix = binbinxert belelae = lay vabin na caet

cpil zillaob zaanto on Cu chie maze nae maobii = bix v hlab

licki zetioolraue = vauatibil tathanix Caho hoe zumtul

zobri = y ziul liclizi toy thainab = tu facal = zeb chibtab

tie yol lal, maunhaob paaltie v toal tomal v a Cobch lulay

tu rebale = tho liott bi zatuel toor hach non v maya z ziul

v zuil zob ti Heban = gaena ac v binch ti Caan = y v zoluch

si Cob tay tain vti zob tiobe = tumenel layumil ti gs lae

bay hele lae = patanob tumen layumit ti gs = mansae goun

tuzekal tun binetun Cen Cizin zee pliem yol lal tue wale

noh yn maya z = Ctuep la lob ain binel yntabez yol ich na zlaich

v yoli = tumen hicib lale Chiich v yol yol lal ah maya zil

xan Cuthanob = Ca zo ti v muulthanob = tue Audinciaob

y chil Met nal Caix homol bini tay hun tul Cizin zeapi

ente: v Habalae ~ ~ ~ ~ ~ ~ ~ ~ ~

Feet para y zo torenel: ti lie v Chaie v zich Cheeplal

y v lioh bilan yan v zich yan v llab Conal v Vin

lit = talulah ti Can tuthane zexpiente v Haba = Cana

ei: tu zaze Cheil Cob = Ca hopi v baliie v ba yax che

lae: bay v ethan mautalicob zee chie = tian zua:

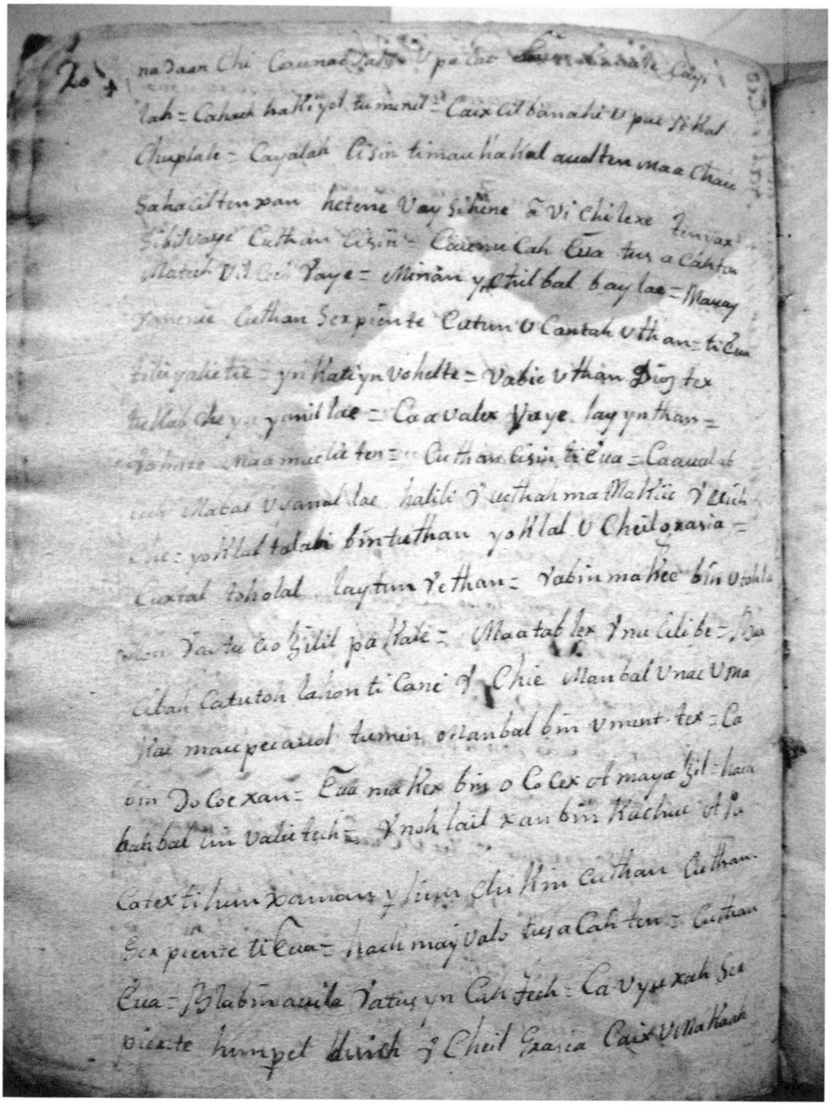

Serpiente tahka u uich ca ... Jocantun v mahkic tancoch...
tac cau raahti cua tancoch xani yta bax ynal ti v otahal
tun mahah tancoch conic Mahtunhelelac Mabatum
v Cah bin v ment lob te... Juyahale letunbe cuthan cin
ti cealac cahach sa hachi v pue si hal cuchic pe comix yok
cuchi tumenil matac v chaic than tumen patan tumen
a Dantache tanu ximbal te v cano pahal cutuc ca
pecnah yok tic v haynab tan vtulop an tanv puc yok ...
v tubul tibay v ini tile yantibal ca pel yok xani v...
bah cuatac Manbak v lante helea yn mahtibin her tic tan
v pu v puasi hal cuchi hunsut hi v mahkic caupic...
kah vdoot sic yotah v pue si hal vtab sahanil ...
Cuine Cauti a Dan Jac cunahanitile a Dan
tumen cuac Jocantun vtab sah Caupulah v ba
hach til mac yok Caupulah camal si hal camal...
Cab bin cit ta cuchil timet nal hach tic si til ...
timet nal Hoh si camix ca hachic tumen v chic v...
sic yax vini vrohol canlae ~ ~ ~ ~ ~

i Jocantun i mahkic cua lay i uich pahal tae caho
pihach yabal sahacil ti cil banae tula cal v uini cil caho
si v lubul v inuuh y v pahal cahopi v cuhal v matan

gracia ybuena Caix Chalanhi v Suctal = Cahopi yo
Hol tihaah oKomyet tihach yau pu Si Hal Catali a Don
laHe ynret Canan pakale = baxta li bah bax Cahach ok
tu = hach poihech xan = Cuthan A Dan = Cuti ya tah
Cua = Beyn ti Chame Si pen tah Sabon tumen Cisin
tin maHah v wih Che = Vethan tumen Cilich ymne ma
taice Cuthan Cua = Ca Jalah tie = be Chup la lae = hach
ma tin sol leybal Camen tu lae = Cu ya labal tumen a Dan
cua yn ya maech = bal bin C vz cint hete lae = Cuthan
A Dan = Cayalah Cuae = Manbal v yanal Si pen Si pon
Cata il Cuthan Cua = be Chup lale = b myn maH lob hewa
Ca yn vo hu matan v ma tunel tin Koch = bi nix kalae
xan Com Chaah A Dan = Caunma Hah Cau tu Hah
Cati = Max bini y Max v chuchi v Momel tu Ho Chi
Ca Hapi tay v Chu Cul yan t Koch = Con xib talone = hi
ix Chup lale ma chi Can yo H lal v pit luH tah = Mantas
hix tu lal xan ~ ~ ~ ~ ~ ~ ~ ~ ~ ~ ~ ~
i Jo Can tan v Si pilob = tu Catuli lob Cattali Cuyu
mil ti Dios = yicnalob oxten hi v thamal A Dan
tumen Cayumil ti D³ = Maxan v lub tumen v Sublu
Cilob = pu Cen pulob yalan Che hasin Cahalob

bay vil minan tac v nokob mac chac v Cha cambal 23
çunal vyumile cantey thani tumen cayumile
A Dan: ti Dios A Dan: A Dan ti ya
labal tumen Cayamil= yn Citich yumee= tin nucah
athan oxten athan len tumen yn Saka Cil yoklali
Kamil athan Coo= Catin ta Cah yn bal yalan Che=
Cathan a A Dan: hoklen vaye cuyala bal tumen
Cayamil ti Dios= talelyn Cah yn Citich yumee= Cuthan
Catali Cau thaah v keen lap v Se che= v malas ti
talob= y tu Ca Cu tilob= y Cua Caalabi tumen Cuya
mil ti Ds= tiob A Dan baxtay lae= baxtamen tansuy
loe= Caexlay grasia v chic yn Dale Che Cuchie Cuyalaba
tumen Cayumil ti Ds= yn Citich yumee= helay chuplal
lay ti lubo Sahen ti Si pil Cuthan A Dan: Caren chup
lee baxtumen talueb Sah au cham ti Si pil yn Citich yume
Casin Cu tab Sahen Cuthan Cua: bay tumbin v pucy pucthe
v batan baob= y yo Hol Casin he Ceyaban Cayumil ti
Ds: bay lae Cahopi v Keyah than ta balob= tu yail Keyah
tumen Cayumil ti Ds= ti he yalabal ti chup lae he
te Che ma bi Hin om auilab v y y chie balob= tumen tech
lubes ti Si pil A Dan= lay v chan lae y yabal num
ya=

bin a valinte v Chun Cabal Cah lae y auolilil y v
Rimam ti yan a cimil tiix yan a Cuxtal xani = bay tun
xan xibtale ma vz bin a Cutah ba lexi y chil v hach
yabal numya: he tun helan tae = hein Sch lah ba bali
lobe. tin Rlabah ta Haber Cuchie bin v ne pin te Chob
bin pustah Cob tachob = ti ma a Caxan ti Cob y auilic
be: bay than bin v Dolesobe he tun texe ma auoltahex
a Dolesex yn valmah thonил yn Cal Cinah ata cun tex
Cuchie bay v Chun lae: lu Henex v aye: xenex hebub
auolahex avuentex v ya yatulul ai plexe = bay lu Hicob
y chil pallal para y So terenal lae: Cabinob yalan Che
Cayam Rapab = Cahopi v mentic v poni tensiaob Ca
tal v xulel v Kinil v Cuxtalob = Vay yo Hol Case
Amen Jesus ~ ~ ~ ~ ~ ~ ~ ~
ya tro mil y Gin Cuenta año Cu xanob Vay Jo Hol
Cabe = heix Catoh labicobe: paxa y So terenal lae yor
vel v Kinil Catoh labiob tu men Cay umil ti D. Ca
pel Kin yanob ti para y So terenal lae Bay xel v
Kinilob lae noh Cina bae Cay umil ti D. ti ya hae
lil Cilich glaria timinan v xpu maix v lah v chibalob Cayu
mil ti Jaju Chris to =   V heah David

Dauid ----- Mehente Abraham ————

Abraham ~~~ Mehente Jacob ————

Jacob ~~~~ Mehente Jodam y Judas ————

Y Chibalob pares y Saromon detanan ————

pares ~~~~ Mehente esesron ————

hesron ~~~ Mehente Aram ————

Aram ~~~ Mehente Aminadad ————

Aminadad ~~~ Mehente Nason ————

Nason ~~~ Mehente Salomon ————

Salomon ~~~ Mehente baosdarad ————

baosdarad ~~ Mehente obeter xuth ————

obeter xuth ~~ Mehente Jore ————

Jore ~~~~ Mehente dauid ahan ————

dauid ~~~ Mehente Salomon ————

Salomon ~~~ Mehente Robaan ————

Robaan ~~~ Mehente Abias ————

Abias ~~~ Mehente eSa ————

eSa ~~~ Mehente yoSapat ————

26

vidapax ~~~ Mehente Uoram _____
Uoram ~~~ Mehente oSiam _____
oSiam ~~~ Mehente Loatim _____
Loatim ~~~ Mehente Achas _____
Achas ~~~ Mehente Ezachias _____
Ezahias ~~~ Mehente Manosen _____
Manosen ~~~ Mehente Amoni _____
Amon ~~~ Mehen te Josiam _____
Josiom ~~~ Mehente the Choniam binib y yidin
babilonia tupach Eatici babiloniae lae _____
the Choniam Mehente Salatiel _____
Salatiel ~~~ Mehente Salaber _____
Saxor ~~~ Mehente Abiut _____
Abiut ~~~ Mehen te Eliachim _____
Eliachim ~~ Mehente ACono _____
ACono ~~~ Mehente Saboe _____
Saboe ~~~ Mehente AChim _____
AChim ~~~ Mehente Eliut _____
Eliut ~~~ Mehente Eliasal _____
Eliasal ~~~ Mehente Matam _____
Matam ~~~ Mehente Jacob _____
Jacob mehente Josef _____
Yespola Cacilich Colel Suhuy Sta Ma lay lihci Cayumilti

Jesuchristo Yumbilae   Amen Jesus ⹂ ⹂ ⹂

a Kinil Cabinyale Cayumil ti Jesuchristo ti alabilili
nicob : te Kinil Cabin Kuchui : hunyuk̇ xot Kine Cabin
Cabin Kuyan Cube : ti ubantal Vtebdunilob : tu jici
hetun Ah tibilbeobe tunoh Cayumilti Ds : bin
bantalob tili yalie tiobe : V ti bilil vinicob Conex
ci ci thanbil tumen yn titici Yum Conex bin
Kul Cuxtal : Meyahan olitial tex hopic Cibatcali
le avayahexpelthan = avoc sahex taueotex he cextica
Cat Valmah thanile aueuyahex Vthan : y n palieo
y Sacendoteob yn tu chitahob : tayamaexe hectice
a pi cinauoc Sahextauol Vthan xam hetevoteue v
Vboil Vinicexe lobob thanbilex tumen yn
lieh Yum penex tun tu Ka Kilmut nal : Yanil
a Sinob adoc lu lil Sahex Vthan: Maix auoce
tex tauol yuthan y V than yn pali lob : yanaix
choch Kebantex Cuctin maix hah auuaher apa
tie a Kebanex tili yalabal tex Caapat a Cilex
ay aueyan Cilex baix a Diboi Cilex atan bic yn
cham bile hetexe chuzta lexe lobob than bilex
tumen yn Cilich Yum tumen Vchil a pocticex

yn[...] mahthanile till[...] aue y[...]tilex y Chann Zile u chie
alubul [...] yabil Keban titum pelili a cucutilex
chuplale = bay xan xiblalob xan = tex ulobil xiblalexe
thubul aucitilex Patal auol ta coilex = Ci cielal a Cahex
yo Kolcab = tanaucy in ti cex atanbil [...] y yicham
Zil = hetex ulobil xiblale y chuplalexe = da a cicio
lalex yo Kolcab = xenex tu Kil nunal xenex tihun
la Kul Ci cielal hetelae = yanil Kuxcob y hun Kul
Kall = Matupben tianix u hadl yabal ti sinob num
[...]entiya titic abuain ti cex Kak y ubal tiaba lle
ex = tex xiblalex y tex chuplalex = tech xan chup
[...] tech ta haulah y[...]than = Yinthantilay unit ti Ds
y yupatie yn Keban tech Kas aunte yntantie Ds
y[...] Keban Cotentum yn cha toh tech Bay
x[...]n xan ulobil chuplale Cotentan yncha than
tech Kech tablahen yo Kol Cob Cat Sat yn ool y
y nachbil Coil y yn Keban = auctel Kolelae tolob
than bitech tumen yn Cilich Yum tumen tech tanach
Cunahen ti Cayumil ti Ds = Mata ueltate a pater
tamuK yn cicielxtie yn Keban auctel = Cat honol
u y[...]zilie u cucatilob tubatan baob = y tan
Kuxii u coob = y tan u cu biltan baob

Catun hach Hunsabaloob ti ya tumen Cizinob ti yabal KaK
tac tac Cheanob y ʋ banetail KaK: ti ʋ Cucutiloob y piblæ
loob y Chuplaloob = tu nun yaob: tu li li lie ʋ Cucutiloob y
ʋba Keloob: hach Hun ya lilix yoKaloob tamu ta tah auuatob
y ya Canob tumen ʋ yabal Hunyaa: ti metnal tam
tam yalilobe = be Kasen oxHumut Kueen bikin Ɂu ʋ
yn Hunya y yn ta Can y yntatah auat tay tumet
nale = yoKlal yan tin Ɂol paKmahi yn man sic Kin yo
yoKol Cab = Hasen oxnumut Kueen citim ʋ thanob tamuʋl
yeleloob = y tunett ʋ Ɂi Chob ti ʋ pi Cinob bay yelel ʋ hobon
Cheil hobon Chee: ʋbalma KaK tula Cal ʋ ti pi Ciloob ti nach
tu venae ʋ Cucutiloob y hach Hastae ʋ Ɂi Choob yantaae
ʋ pu uta boob tu polobe: y hach Hustae y cha Cob tu yo Cob
y tu Kabobe: ti hach Has tae ʋ Ɂi Chobe = tu batambaobe:
tanix ʋ pactie ʋ Ɂich tu batan baobe = tu huma lob = Catun
yal Cizin tiobe: hetepe yn palilex a Ɂae luK Ɂahex yn than
yoKlal ti Cuxanex Cuchie tenapay abelex ti Ɂuua Chil
ten alii abelex tenaziboltahex = tenalie a Sublar talex ley
ca Sublachiexe = Camahi a Confesar tex ti padree: ti mahie lah
Cantee a Kebanex ten chiich annt auolex Camahi apatie
a Kebanexe y aueyex Catun hopi ʋ Chiich tal yele lob:
y chil ʋ Ka Kil metnal = hetun hele lae ma mae ʋ chae ʋ

Euk ix cex tun kial = Maix bi Kin yn pat cex pany mabi Kin
v poul y num si cex ti yaa: ɔay ti met nale = ti tun v lalob than
ti v ɔey e chuplal y xiblal pam e. Ma xulumte tun yokol
y yalil v ɔiɔ bin yukkub = yt to Christianoe kaak bin
anu kiebe y ahante bay bin ɔebal a ci ciolal ɔay ɔo Kol
Cabe = ti cu xamun tan yanil ti met nale ~ ~ ~ ~ ~

Bay xan he cuyalie Cayumil ti D.s = te tula Cal xib la
lob = Sihnalob ɔay ɔo Kol Cabe = ɔaix lie a ɔaic ta Kin ti Chup
ɔale = ti a Coile Comamie v Kakkil met nal v ti a la pi xan
vaix lie a Kamie ta Kin yo Klal a Cu Cutil tech Chuplale
Ca Coñie a pi xan ti Cisin y a Cu Cutil ti u hach yail Kak
ti met nal: ti ma xulum te ɔ numyail Kakk = yanil Cusi
bca ti mix tun v Satal hun ɔit a ɔo ɔel y aba Kel tula
Cal auinicit bin xie tu Kakkil met nal = Cabin v Moluba
tula Cal vini Cob ti hunpel eha Kan Jose pat v Kaba
ti tun yalie Cayumil ti D.s = ti hun tul Angel
heu Kabae: v Angelile Sam Miguel = ɔ ya vt tu Cau
tu Kil lay Cha Kan lae: ti lie yalie yalie = Cimene xe ti
Kenex Caput cux lenex ta Cu Cu ti lex y ta pi xanex Co
nex ti xotol a Kinex y a Kamex yukil abelex y v lobil abelex
he Cabin ɔo Coc v than Angele hum Sutili bin v nuɔ lam
tic v batan ba Cob = tu batan baob = y v pi xanob
yo Kol yo Chelob = ti bay cu xanob v pi xanob

y y Cicicitilobe Cacimtali Cayumil ti D.s = ta Koh v Chicil
y ta noh te patil y ta vinicil: y tulacal Angelesob = y tu cal pixa
nob yanob tu yahaulil ciliih gloria = bin Aalalob tu pach ca
yumil ti Jesuchristo v chab v Cicicitilobe = ti mabikin v yul
y cicidlalob = tu lumilob y tu pixanob = ti banano tulacal
Ah Kebanob ti lum: hetun Ah tibil beobe. ti bananob tu
tan Cayumil ti D.s = ti lic y alabal tiobe = tumen Cayumil
ti Diose hetexe yn sihsah vinicilexe a veyahex yn than ta
Joar besahex tulacal yn valmah thanil yn patah yokol Cabe ca
Joli yntohic bal Cahe = a veyahex v than yn patilob yn Sabes
Jotesob = yanhiob yokol Cabe ani chelex helet time Conex cici
thanbilex tumen yn ciliih Yum a Joe luk sahex yn valmah thanil
v kahen cuchi = a Jahexhatun = ti heni xan y v yala benix x
ix mabulan Kalen ti mas cab = Cuchi o Kom hi amolex Cata
lex a thibinex = Catun nucab v than = tumen Ah tibil beob yn
yn ciliih yume bikin ti Jilab auk chahal y anih chahal
y allalal ti mas cab y anialalabil Cot Kom he che = Catuyalah
Cayumil ti D.s Jiob yanhi yn Hum yail Patil tibal Cahe = a Ja
hex v yatzilob tanv chic amenti cex = Conex alKamex v hel lay
tiv yahaulil ciliih gloria ti minan v yul Mix v lah = Ca
tuyalah truelobil vini Cob = hetexe A Pochdexenex ti humlukkul = xe
nextect tu kakil metnale yanil cisinobe = a Joe luk sahex v
than = v kahen Cuchi ixmabulan. Cuchi = Maix a Jahex yn
ya zil xani = penex ti hum lukkul kab = timet nal yanil
cisinob a Joe luk kahex v thane ti ma xu hmile ti a cicie
tilex

ý lapixontex= Catun v ßolah v oh ti bil beob xiblalob y Chuplalob= ti
hunhal tanukay angelesob= ti hach Cioßil y v Paxob y v tuxn petaßob
ý Cheremiasob= ti hach Cioßil v kayob tamutl v binelob ti Citih gloria
tu pach Cayumil ti Dº = ti hach lem bonac v vichob y v pixanob mabi kin v pul v Cica than talob tumenl Cayumil
ti Dº = ti minan v xul Maix v lah v ci ci v lalob y an Amen

Del qua per du Cat el Dº ui t ame ternam

um v lobil v inicobe ti ubantalob tu ruch lumee= tan v
Muxitob y v yaD lalob tan yi li Cob v na cal v tibilil vini
Cob= tu pach Cayumil ti Dº tan Yali Cob yn vi Chame In va-
le yn Chuplile yn nae= yn ßumee ta Centa pach ti Can-
Maxa ßm aui chamex=a Chuplil en = a valen cha enta pach
Ciu thanob= Catun alau bae ti ob tumen v tibilil vi ni Cob
yn Chuplile= yn vi Chame= mau Chae at atel tin pach ti
Can= hetene tu yoltah Cayumil ti Dº yn ¿ cu ti v an Hebom
yo Kol Cab hetim tech maa vuyah v ßec padre Yo Kol Cab
maa oc besah v tham Cayumil ti Dº = Maix ßa patah a Hebau
y alobil y a loil ti anech yo Kol Cab Cu chi= heled tune xo
tan a Ki nex bind ti met nal= Catun he cha hae lumee= Catun
tu bu cob tan Chumu ci tal ti met nal= Chin Chin pol y v
hu mil y v pixanob= ti yalic ti u tla palibilo be y v ßume
be= ti tiv lolob tham tiu v ßum y v Haob= hete che nac
lolob tham taac= Ym tiu chu chahe a ßa tene hete che
yn vi lah a loil ý a veyan til Cain Camah xan

heleche autah Incoil y Ve Tomalon Patie Ynvichamy Ynxinbal ʒ
Yn Keban maix abectahen ʒ maaualah Ynxi cin cuchi heldel
tune=lolob thantoae lay Ymtaʒaah ychuche Catantun Ynchatah
toch Vllobil Yn tunne baytech xan v lobil Habil baixtah panvlo
bal xiblale toch ta chum sah Insatal timetnal Catunho poc v chi
baltambaob ʒ v ʒiʒibiu cucuetilob=v naob ʒ v Tumoob caix
tal Yal tiinob numsilobti Yaa=ʒ KaaK tamuKu Telelob viuta
tilob=tuemen KaK bay v Telel vhobonchtil hobon chee vbalmaita
Ke=ʒ v Yabal KuxCo=ʒ tatah ayat timinan v xi naix vlob
v tatah aeatob tullilmetnal a a a a a a a a a a a
Ad quanos perdulat Amen Dominica: Adbentus
Cume venexit Filius Dominica 25: Capitulo
[E]than tie auuyiCexlae Bayhelae ʒibantiKaytah Alich Habil
yglesialae=ʒibantiʒolol ti Alich Sto Euangelio tunmen
Euangelio ʒiban tumen Sontalas tuhotuKal v pedel vlapi
goloit v chun ʒeee helelae lay vnah o Certiolex=Conyauinia
texe lay vnah aʒabaxianex tithan= Ynmahante bay tuauxte
lex-he CabinV luu v Altichol Suhuʒe tunohtePatile y tulocal An
gelesob=tupache Catum Aulas tusi Nail vnohtePatil v Altich
ʒayaʒitlae=binix hornotaebul Cah tutam binix vhuʒub vbaob
nachtil=tuhumalob bayli cid vhummal cintie v Canan
taman ah Canantamamobe=baytauiaʒakexe aheltexe YnYa
vinicilexe=bin aʒhaex laythan= cinʒotetae lay Dominicalae
vChuCamv DominiCail= aenuento Lae=v Lulel Cayumulti Te
Suchxistolae=Cabin Kuchuetukinil Lulel vʒabhum Kulcux
tal=ʒ hum Kul cimil lay xot Kin v Kaba laytavueyahexsa
mes= bin Tamac Chicaelob ti Kin ʒ tiV: ʒ tiekob layʒiban
tu Tanilmiyaʒ= tumen San Bernado ʒ San Jeronimo ahKinob

33

Hacx tam u kay tu lax cinex = be cil bin tac Cay u mil ti Juchau
Yo = u xoob u Hin bal Cahe bin Tanae Chi Cu Hob te Yan beil
hot hum pic Kin Chi Cul bin yanac = bay ti cil Yahe Cayume lam
San Beenado = bay ti cil Yahe San Jeronimo xane ~ ~ ~

Amen Jesus y Maria

4" **HE** u yax chun u Kinil bin yanae Chi Cul bin Tanae Kak
nab = u ho ho Chil u Cu cutil Yo Hol Vity Consol ta Cobe maix
Eu u hus ub uba tu Cuchil bay bin nac bal ham ac pe Ke

2" he tu Capel u Kinil lae bin Tanae chi Cul bin Emae tu cu
Chil ha hal tam bin Embal maix u Chac y labal tu chi u Kak
nabil ~ ~ ~ ~ ~ ~ ~ ~ ~ ~

3" hex tu yox pel u Kine bin yanae Chi Cul bin Huchuc
tu Catun te bay Yani te Yalan Kinae lae ~ ~ ~ ~ **H**

4" he tu Canpel u Kinil bin Tanae chi Cul he tu Ialal u baal
Kak na bobe lay Cayobe = bin u mol u baob Yo Hol haob
lam u tah auatob y Yacanob yo Hot haa yo K lal u Jacibob
ti Xot Kin Cutalel lae: ~ ~ ~ ~ ~ ~ ~

5" he tu ho pel u Kinil lae bin Tanae Chi Cul bin u mol uba
tu la cal chi Cheob y tu la cal bal Cheob bin ham mala Cob
tu men u Saha cil tio Ho ti Xot Kin Cutale ~ ~ ~ ~

6" he tu vae pel u Kinil bin yanae chi Cul bin ho Hot Kak
ti chi Kin ti cil u thubul Kine = y ti cil u ho Hot ti la Kine
bin ho Hoc Kak xani ~ ~ ~ ~ ~ ~ ~

7" he tu Vue pel u Kini te bin yanae chi Cul bin yanae
Yabal cume tasob y tan u len boob ti cha chac

bay lu bul v cahobe— e Kobe Ylabale ʒal ti can ʒacan

8. hetu v ax ac pel v Kinile bin Yanac chi cul bin ya
nac choc ꝛ Kot—hetu tu la cal cheobe mix tan v v a talob
ꝛ v cutalob bin v lubu cob tu vich luum ⌁ ⌁ ⌁

9. hetunbolon pis v Kinile bin Yanac chi cul he tu ni
Chobe tu la cale bin v pis v ba tan v nup tanbaob tu hu
nalob bay nu cob ꝛ me hen ta cob =bin ix hot lah cob ti
Can Cambuhob= hetu ca tene bin tu li ʒa cob tumen mac ʒit
tu la tun ⌁ ⌁ ⌁ ⌁ ⌁   ⌁ ⌁ ⌁ ⌁ ⌁ ⌁

10. hetu la hun pis v Kinile bin Yanac chi cul tu la cal
xuobeobe ꝛ cheobe bin emtahac Kii K Yo Kolob ti bay
Yemel Kii K ti bal Yaac ⌁ ⌁ ⌁ ⌁ ⌁ ⌁ ⌁ ⌁

11. hotu bulue pis v Kinile bin Yanac chi cul hetu la calal vi
ʒob ꝛ malobe ꝛ noc A cobe =paKbil tumen vini cobe
ꝛ Kaxab Comal ta cob bin lubu cob tu vich luum ⌁ ⌁ ⌁

12. hetulah cap= v Kinile bin Yanac chi cul bin v onol v ba
tu Cal bal cheob ti ʒotol v Kinob A am yo Kolob tu la cul tumen
v Sahac obob= ti xot Kin lae ⌁ ⌁ ⌁ ⌁ ⌁ ⌁ ⌁ ⌁
dia ll de Diciembre 12... 3 años Cadh pol yn canbal
ta Kie hun pel libro lensic... lal ta... lul txo ca... Causate...
Fernando...m Mar...bi... yh... pa ha... p... Temax

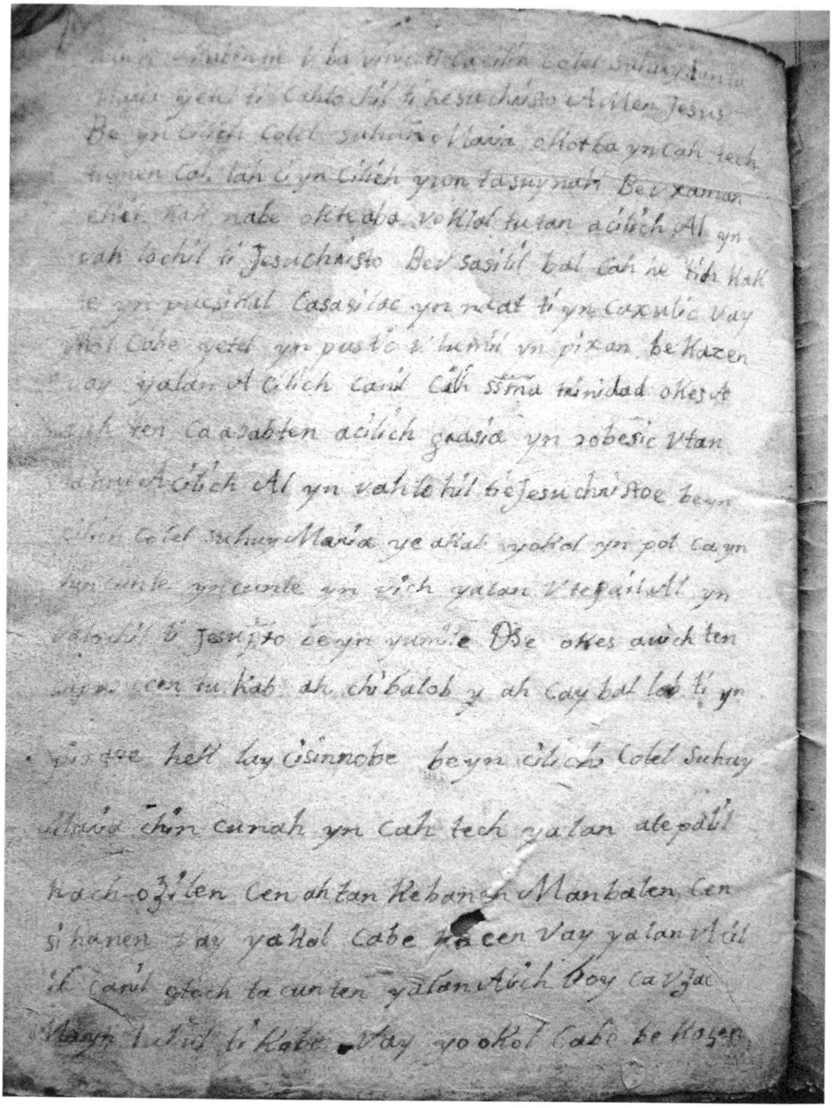

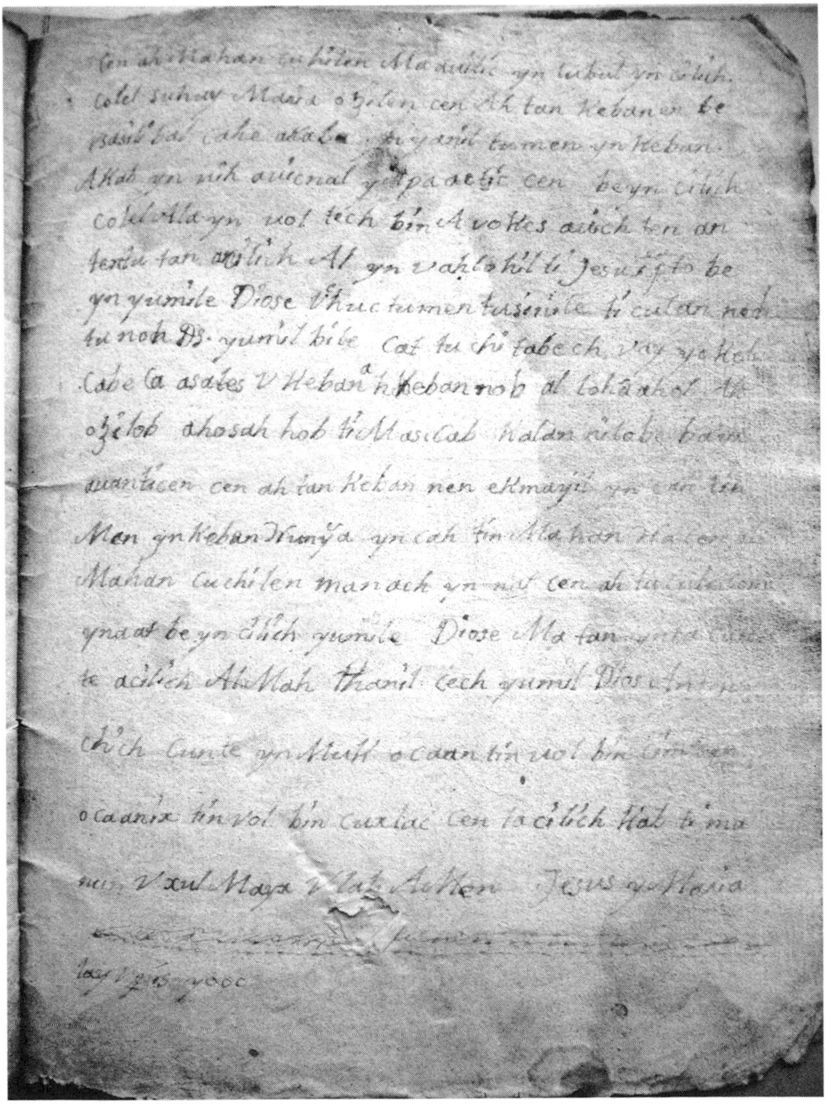

Jueves 8 Enero d 1911
para curar pasmos las mujeres
mangcuil
cascara d piscoy
alt ab su ojas
chalche
oregano
tres matas d cabascan
una mata d caballas en ic
se sancocha con miel
para un aborto
en solo menno
la raiz peregil
san cortrado
tambien
xcanbahuah con miel
su fruto d balzamito
con Anis —
habic nah can miel

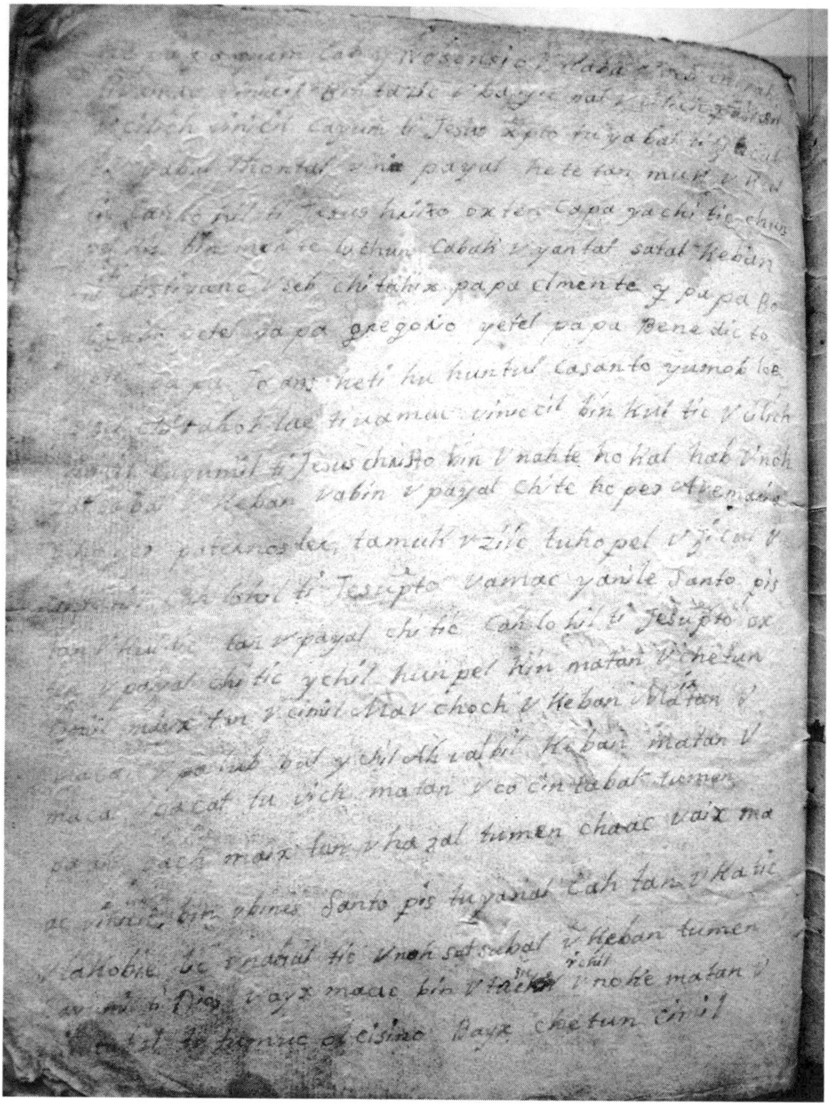

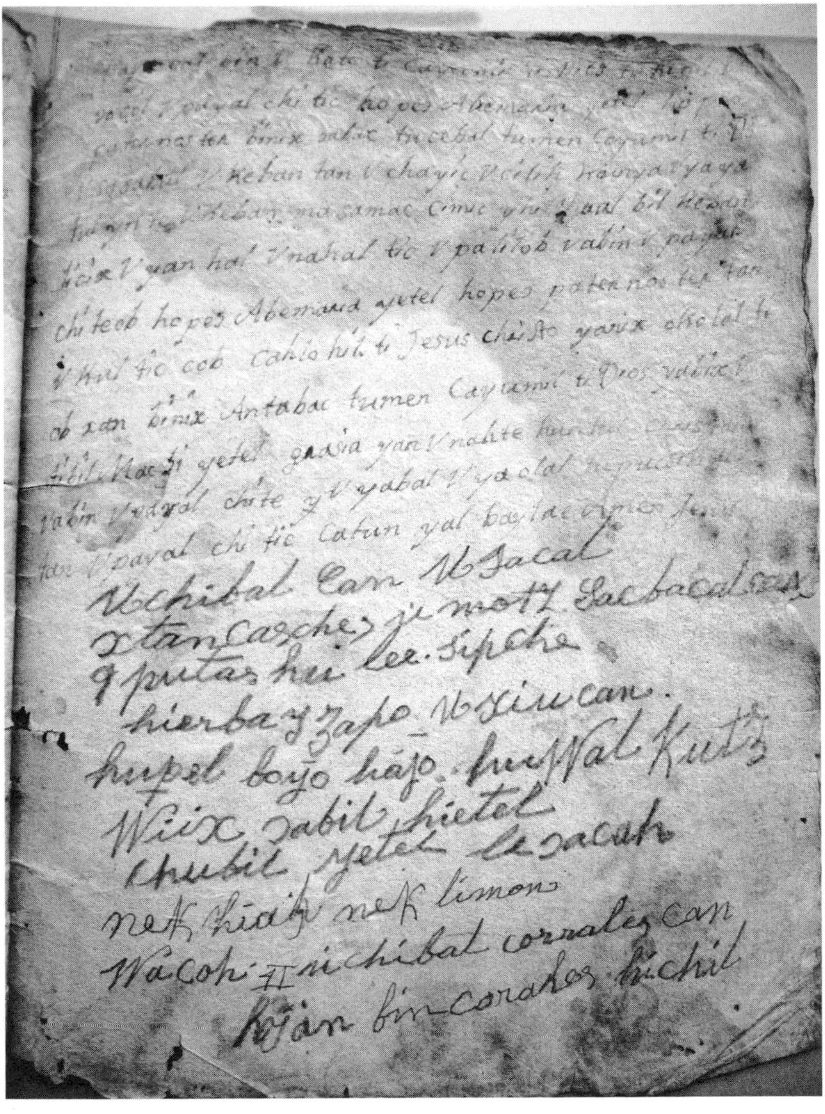

Notes

INTRODUCTION

1. Munro S. Edmonson, "The Princeton Codex of *The Book of the Chilam Balam of Chumayel*," *Princeton University Library Chronicle* 32, no. 3 (1971): 138.

2. I am referencing, of course, Michael D. Coe's seminal *Breaking the Maya Code* (New York: Thames & Hudson, 1992). For more on the Maya and their supposed doomsday prophecy regarding 2012, see Matthew Restall and Amara Solari, *2012 and the End of the World: The Western Roots of the Maya Apocalypse* (New York: Rowman & Littlefield, 2011); David Stuart, *The Order of Days: The Maya World and the Truth about 2012* (New York: Harmony Books, 2011).

3. It should be noted, however, that the colonial Maya continued to write in hieroglyphic script for a time. See Victoria Bricker, "The Last Gasp of Maya Hieroglyphic Writing in the Books of Chilam Balam of Chumayel and Chan Kan," in *Word and Image in Maya Culture: Explorations in Language, Writing and Representation*, ed. William Hanks and Don S. Rice (Salt Lake City: University of Utah Press, 1989), 39–50; John Franklin Chuchiak IV, "Writing as Resistance: Maya Graphic Pluralism and Indigenous Elite Strategies for Survival in Colonial Yucatán, 1550–1750," *Ethnohistory* 57, no. 1 (Winter 2010): 87–116. For more on the influence of hieroglyphs on colonial writing, see Kerry M. Hull, "Poetic Tenacity: A Diachronic Study of Kennings in Mayan Languages," in *Parallel Worlds: Genre, Discourse, and Poetics in Contemporary, Colonial, and Classic Period Maya Literature*, ed. Kerry M. Hull and Michael D. Carrasco (Boulder: University Press of Colorado, 2012), 73–122; Matthew Restall, "Heirs to the Hieroglyphs: Indigenous Writing in Colonial Mesoamerica," *The Americas* 54, no. 2 (1997): 239–267; John Franklin Chuchiak IV, "The Images Speak: The Survival and Production of Hieroglyphic Codices and Their Use in Post-Conquest Maya Religion, 1580–1720," in *Maya Religious Practices: Processes of Change and Adaption*, ed. Daniel Graña Behrens et al., *Acta Mesoamericana*, vol. 14 (Markt Schwaben, Germany: Verlag Anton Saurwein, 2004), 71–103.

4. I thank Russ Taylor, chair of Perry Special Collections at Brigham Young University, for providing me with the specific measurements.

5. For more on the conquest of Yucatan and, particularly, the natives' role in it, see Matthew Restall, *Maya Conquistador* (Boston: Beacon Press, 1998); John Franklin Chuchiak IV, "Forgotten Allies: The Origins and Roles of Native Mesoamerican Auxiliaries and Indios Conquistadores in the Conquest of Yucatan, 1526–1550," in *Indian Conquistadors: Indigenous Allies in the Conquest of Mesoamerica*, ed. Laura E. Matthew and Michel R. Oudijk (Norman: University of Oklahoma Press, 2007), 175–226; Michel R. Oudijk and Matthew Restall,

"Mesoamerican Conquistadors in the Sixteenth Century," in *Indian Conquistadors*, 28–64. For a succinct overview, see Victoria R. Bricker, *The Indian Christ, the Indian King: The Historical Substrate of Maya Myth and Ritual* (Austin: University of Texas Press, 1981), 13–24.

6. John D. Early, *The Maya and Catholicism: An Encounter of Worldviews* (Gainesville: University Press of Florida, 2006), 133.

7. Sergio Quezada argues for three determining factors when deciding where to place the first convents: political and administrative importance, pre-Hispanic religious significance, and density of Indian population. Sergio Quezada, *Maya Lords and Lordship: The Formation of Colonial Society in Yucatán, 1350–1600*, trans. Terry Rugeley (Norman: University of Oklahoma Press, 2014), 50.

8. Juan Francisco Molina Solís, *Historia de Yucatán durante la dominación española* (Merida: Imprenta de la lotería del estado, 1904), vol. 1, 322. See also Diego López de Cogolludo, *Historia de Yucatán* (Madrid: J. García Infanzón, 1688), Lib. 5, chs. 5–6, 254–260.

9. Molina Solís, *Historia*, 324. Within the local religious hierarchy, maestros held the top position. Existing documentation lists three types of maestros: *maestros cantores, maestros de capilla,* and *maestros de escuela.* However, it appears that more often than not these were different titles for what functioned as a single position. The presence of other positions such as *fiscales* and sacristans varied from cah to cah. Most consistent was the post of maestro. See Anne C. Collins, "The Maestros Cantores in Yucatán," in *Anthropology and History in Yucatán*, ed. Grant D. Jones (Austin: University of Texas Press, 1977), 233–247. For more on the role of maestros in the colonial structure, see Nancy M. Farriss, *Maya Society under Colonial Rule: The Collective Enterprise of Survival* (Princeton, NJ: Princeton University Press, 1984), 335–343.

10. Mendieta indicates that occasionally there was "carelessness" regarding the restriction of the schools to noble youth and that at times non-noble natives were admitted, "especially in the small towns where there are few people." Jerónimo de Mendieta, *Historia eclesiástica indiana* (Barcelona: Linkgua Ediciones, 2007), 432. However, the *Códice franciscano* (1889) encourages ecclesiastics to not make such a mistake as it would be inappropriate to make commoners the rulers of towns where the nobles had traditionally governed (62–63).

11. Although some maestros were sent to their own towns, colonial documentation suggests that others were sent to towns other than that of their origin. See Caroline Cunill, "La alfabetización de los Mayas Yucatecos y sus consecuencias sociales, 1545–1580," *Estudios de cultura Maya* 31 (2008): 163–192.

12. For example, see *Relaciones Histórico-Geográficas de la Gobernación de Yucatán: Mérida, Valladolid y Tabasco*, vol. 2 (Mexico City: Universidad Nacional Autónoma de México, 1983), 199, 226, 246, 299, 336.

13. *Códice franciscano, siglo XVI. Nueva colección de documentos para la historia de México*, ed. Joaquín García Icazbalceta (Mexico City: Imprenta de Francisco Díaz de León, 1889), 82–84; France Scholes et al., *Documentos para la historia de Yucatán*, vol. 2, *La iglesia en Yucatán* (Merida: Compañía Tipográfica Yucateca, 1938), 25–34.

14. For more details on the role of maestros and religious texts, see Mark Z. Christensen, *Nahua and Maya Catholicisms: Texts and Religion in Colonial Central Mexico and Yucatan* (Stanford and Berkeley: Stanford University Press and the Academy of American Franciscan History Press, 2013), 74–80. Interestingly, John F. Chuchiak has argued that maestros could also serve in the role of a precontact priest, or *ah kin*. See his "Pre-Conquest *Ah Kinob* in a Colonial World: The Extirpation of Idolatry and the Survival of the Maya Priesthood in Colonial Yucatán, 1563–1697," in *Maya Survivalism*, ed. Ueli Hostettler and Matthew Restall (Markt Schwaben, Germany: Verlag Anton Saurwein, 2001); see also Laura Caso Barrera, *Caminos en la selva: migración, comercio y Resistencia, mayas yucatecos e itzaes, siglos xvii–xix* (Mexico City: El colegio de México, Fondo de cultura económica, 2002), 109–122.

15. Archivo General de Indias, Seville, Mexico 105, 4a, f. 3. For more on Chi, see Matthew Restall, "Gaspar Antonio Chi: Bridging the Conquest of Yucatán," in *The Human Tradition in Colonial Latin America*, ed. Kenneth J. Andrien, 2nd ed. (Lanham, MD: Rowman & Littlefield, 2013).

16. Juan Gómez de Parada, *Constituciones sinodales del obispado de Yucatán*, ed. Gabriela Solís Robleda (Merida: Universidad Nacional Autónoma de México, 2008), 288.

17. For more on the precontact and colonial political importance of writing and the role of scribes in both adapting to Spanish formulae while preserving precontact traditions, see John Franklin Chuchiak IV, "'*Ah Dzib Cahob yetel lay u katlilob lae*': Maya Scribes, Colonial Literacy, and Maya Petitionary Forms in Colonial Yucatán," in *Text and Context: Yucatec Maya Literature in a Diachronic Perspective*, ed. Antje Gunsenheimer et al. (Aachen: Bonner Amerikanistische Studien, 2009).

18. Cunill, "La alfabetización," 178.

19. For an excellent article on the role of maestros and scribes in preserving written accounts, both official and forbidden, see Chuchiak, "Writing as Resistance"; see also Amy George-Hirons, "The Discourse of Translation in Culture Contact: 'The Story of Suhuy Teodora,' an Analysis of European Literary Borrowings in the Books of Chilam Balam" (PhD diss., Tulane University, 2004), 7–8.

20. The topic of native education is covered in other works, and I refer the reader to them, including Robert Ricard, *The Spiritual Conquest of Mexico: An Essay on the Apostolate and the Evangelizing Methods of the Mendicant Orders in New*

Spain: 1523–1572, trans. Lesley Byrd Simpson (Berkeley: University of California Press, 1966), 96–101; Martín Ramos Díaz, "Idólatras y mentores. Escuelas en el Yucatán del siglo XVI," *Estudios de Historia Novohispana* 28 (2003); Cunill, "La alfabetización"; Christensen, *Catholicisms*, 54–56; Mark Z. Christensen, *Translated Christianities: Nahuatl and Maya Religious Texts* (University Park: Pennsylvania State University Press, 2014), 7–8; William Hanks, *Converting Words: Maya in the Age of the Cross* (Berkeley: University of California Press, 2010), 59–84; Collins, "The Maestros Cantores"; *Códice franciscano*, 62–73.

21. Christensen, *Catholicisms*, 53–89.

22. As stated, printed texts required various approbations from ecclesiastical authorities. For example, one of the reasons Beltrán dedicated his *Novena* to the bishop Francisco Pablo Matos Coronado was to achieve the bishop's endorsement according to dictates of such councils. CAIHY (Centro de Apoyo a la Investigación Historica de Yucatán, Merida), SM–46, photostat reproduction of fray Pedro Beltrán de Santa Rosa María, *Novena de christo crucificado con otro oraciones en lengua maya* (Mexico City: don Francisco de Xavier Sánchez, 1740), "Dedicatoria." For more on the process and licensing of printed works, see Martin Nesvig's *Ideology and Inquisition: The World of the Censors in Early Mexico* (New Haven, CT: Yale University Press, 2009); Francisco Antonio Lorenzana, *Concilios provinciales primero, y segundo, celebrados en la muy noble y muy leal ciudad de México, presidiendo el Illmo. Y Rmo. Señor D. Fr. Alonso de Muntúfar, en los años de 1555, y 1565* (Mexico City: Imprenta del Superior Gobierno, Hogal, 1769), 143–144.

23. Such autonomous texts likewise existed outside those religious to include annals, primordial titles, and other native documentation written by natives for natives. See Kevin Terraciano, "Three Views of the Conquest of Mexico from the *Other Mexica*," in *The Conquest All Over Again: Nahuas and Zapotecs Thinking, Writing, and Painting Spanish Colonialism*, ed. Susan Schroeder (Eastbourne, UK: Sussex Academic Press, 2011), 35; James Lockhart, *The Nahuas after the Conquest: A Social and Cultural History of the Indians of Central Mexico, Sixteenth through Eighteenth Centuries* (Stanford, CA: Stanford University Press, 1992), 376–377.

24. Lorenzana, *Concilios*, 143–144. The Second Mexican Provincial Council of 1565 would later modify this condition. See ibid., 201–202. See also Barry D. Sell, "Friars, Nahuas, and Books: Language and Expression in Colonial Nahuatl Publications" (PhD diss., University of California, Los Angeles, 1993), 120–122.

25. Archivo General de la Nación (hereafter AGN), Mexico City, Inq., vol. 43, exp. 4, f. 137. For an excellent discussion, see Nesvig, *Ideology and Inquisition*, 156–163.

26. Hanks, *Converting Words*, 338. Such forbidden texts are increasingly catching the eye of scholars for their value in illustrating the natives' important role in

negotiating how Christianity fits into native worldviews. For other examples, see Ben Leeming, "'Micropetics': The Poetry of Hypertrophic Words in Early Colonial Nahuatl," *Colonial Latin American Review* 24, no. 2 (2015): 168–189; Timothy Knowlton, *Maya Creation Myths: Words and Worlds of the Chilam Balam* (Boulder: University Press of Colorado, 2010); Mark Z. Christensen, "The Tales of Two Cultures: Ecclesiastical Texts and Nahua and Maya Catholicisms," *The Americas* 66, no. 3 (2010): 353–377; Mark Z. Christensen, "The Use of Nahuatl in Evangelization and the Ministry of Sebastian," *Ethnohistory* 59, no. 4 (Fall 2012): 691–711; Laura Caso Barrera, *Chilam Balam de Ixil: Facsmiliar y estudio de un libro maya inédito* (Mexico City: Artes de México y del mundo, 2011); Victoria R. Bricker and Helga-Maria Miram, trans., ed., *An Encounter of Two Worlds: The Book of Chilam Balam of Kaua* (New Orleans: Middle American Research Institute, Tulane University, 2002).

27. Christensen, *Translated Christianities*, 4–7.

28. AGN, Inq., vol. 141, exp. 86, reproduced in Francisco Fernández del Castillo, *Libros y libreros en el siglo XVI* (Mexico City: Tip. Guerrero, 1914), 319.

29. AGN, Inq., vol. 90, exp. 42. René Acuña suggests that some of these sermons found their way into fray Juan Coronel's 1620 *Discursos predicables*. See his "Escritos Mayas inéditos y publicados hasta 1578: testimonio del obispo Diego de Landa," *Estudios de cultura maya* 21 (2001): 169. See also Cogolludo, *Historia de Yucatán*, 192–193; Pedro Sánchez de Aguilar, *Informe contra idolorum cultores de obispado de Yucatan*, 3rd ed. (Merida: E. G Triay e Hijos, 1937), 153–154, 173.

30. Barbara Tedlock, "Continuities and Renewals in Mayan Literacy and Calendrics," in *Theorizing the Americanist Tradition*, ed. Lisa Philips Valentine and Regna Darnell (Toronto: University of Toronto Press, 1999), 197. Other forbidden works, such as hieroglyphic texts, were likewise confiscated from the various Maya towns throughout the colonial period. See Chuchiak, "The Images Speak."

31. Hanks, *Converting Words*, 101.

32. For an excellent and more detailed overview of the history of studies on Maya literature, see Antje Gunsenheimer, Tsubasa Okoshi Harada, and John F. Chuchiak, "Introduction: A Brief History of the Study of Yucatec Maya Literature — Central Themes and Research Perspectives in This Volume," in Gunsenheimer, Okoshi Harada, and Chuchiak, *Text and Context*, 7–28.

33. Edmonson, "The Princeton Codex," 138.

34. For a summary of the work of earlier scholars on the Chilam Balams, see Alfred M. Tozzer, *A Maya Grammar* (1921; repr., New York: Dover, 1977), 182–194.

35. In particular, William Hanks produced notable work in this area. See, for example, his "Authenticity and Ambivalence in the Text: A Colonial Maya Case," *American Ethnologist* 13, no. 4 (1986): 721–744; and his "Grammar, Style, and

Meaning in a Maya Manuscript," *International Journal of American Linguistics* 54, no. 3 (1998): 331–369.

36. The dissertation would later be augmented by additional sources and published as Phillip C. Thompson, *Tekanto, a Maya Town in Colonial Yucatán* (New Orleans: Middle American Research Institute, Tulane University, 1999).

37. James Lockhart, "The Social History of Colonial Spanish America: Evolution and Potential," *Latin American Research Review* 7, no. 1 (Spring 1972): 36. Restall's work can be seen as a product of the school known as the New Philology and pioneered by his mentor, James Lockhart. For more on the New Philology and its impact on the Mesoamerican social histories, see Matthew Restall, "A History of the New Philology and the New Philology in History," *Latin American Research Review* 38, no. 1 (2003): 113–134. To be fair, in 1943 Roys published a rather comprehensive work on Maya society with his *The Indian Background of Colonial Yucatan*, but this was largely limited to the sixteenth century.

38. For a sample of additional works, see Gunsenheimer, Okoshi Harada, and Chuchiak, "Introduction," 10–11.

39. Chuchiak's works include but are not limited to "Pre-Conquest *Ah Kinob*"; "Secrets behind the Screens: Solicitantes in the Colonial Diocese of Yucatan and the Yucatec Maya, 1570–1785," in *Religion in New Spain*, ed. Susan Schroeder and Stafford Poole (Albuquerque: University of New Mexico Press, 2007) 83–109; "The Sins of the Fathers: Franciscan Missionaries, Parish Priests, and the Sexual Conquest of the Yucatec Maya," *Ethnohistory* 54, no. 1 (Winter 2007): 69–127; "*De Descriptio Idolorum*: An Ethnohistorical Examination of the Production, Imagery, and Functions of Colonial Yucatec Maya Idols and Effigy Censers, 1540–1700," in *Maya Worldviews at Conquest*, ed. Timothy Pugh and Leslie Cecil (Boulder: University Press of Colorado, 2009), 135–158; "Writing as Resistance."

40. Hanks, *Converting Words*, xix.

41. Here and throughout I employ "cognate" to refer to those texts that contain similar thematic content and origins. That said, I recognize that such texts parallel each other to varying degrees—the transcriptions of some texts closely mirror those of others with minor alterations, while some texts share the largest similarity in content with a loose parallel in transcription.

42. The list of studies is extensive, but some of the more recent work includes Richard N. Luxton, *The Book of Chumayel: The Counsel Book of the Yucatec Maya 1539–1638* (Laguna Hills, CA: Aegean Park Press, 1995); Richard N. Luxton, *The Book of the Chilam Balam of Tizimin* (Laguna Hills, CA: Aegean Park Press, 2010); Bricker and Miram, *Kaua*; Victoria Bricker's Morpheme Concordance studies on the Chumayel and Tizimin, *A Morpheme Concordance of the Book of Chilam Balam of Chumayel* (New Orleans: Middle American Research Insti-

tute, Tulane University, Publication 59, 1990) and *A Morpheme Concordance of the Book of Chilam Balam of Tizimin* (New Orleans: Middle American Research Institute, Tulane University, Publication 58, 1990); Antje Gunsenheimer, Tsubasa Okoshi Harada, John F. Chuchiak, eds., *Text and Context: Yucatec Maya Literature in a Diachronic Perspective* (Aachen: Bonner Amerikanistische Studien, 2009). See also the articles of Antje Gunsenheimer.

43. Exceptions, of course, do exist where a scholar makes mention of a European antecedent. See, for example, Louise Burkhart, "The Voyage of Saint Amaro: A Spanish Legend in Nahuatl Literature," *Colonial Latin American Review* 4, no. 1 (1995): 29–57; Bricker and Miram, *Kaua*; Amy George-Hirons, "Tell Me, Maiden: The Maya Adaptation of a European Riddle Sequence," *Journal of Latin American Lore* 22, no. 2 (2004): 261–277; George-Hirons, "The Discourse of Translation in Culture Contact." Yet, in general, studies are lacking that give such European works more than passing attention.

44. For example, sections of the Teabo Manuscript show the influence of Spanish syntax: interjections that appear phrase initial instead of phrase final, or adjectives that follow rather than precede nouns in unmarked constructions, as in Spanish. My thanks to Timothy Knowlton and Victoria Bricker for their insights on the matter.

45. Bricker and Miram perhaps said it best when stating that Maya-authored works allow us to better glimpse "which European texts were deemed worthy of inclusion and why, and how they were reconciled philosophically with texts of obvious New World origin." *Kaua*, 1. Furthermore, an understanding of a text's European antecedents is extremely helpful in the process of translation, as such forerunners often provide clues to otherwise arcane passages.

46. These sections are of my creation and not necessarily those of the Maya author(s) or copyists.

47. I thank Victoria Bricker for her insight into this occurrence. Personal communication, July 29, 2013.

48. The name Na can also be written as Nah, and most works reference this Chilam Balam as the Nah. However, because its compilers signed their names as Na, I, like Gubler and Bolles, use such spelling.

49. Although the Tekax has been placed in Teabo by some scholars (Munro S. Edmonson and Victoria R. Bricker, "Yucatecan Mayan Literature," in *Supplement to the Handbook of Middle American Indians*, vol. 3, *Literatures*, ed. Edmonson and Bricker [Austin: University of Texas Press, 1985], 44–63), its origins are still a topic of some debate. The first section of the Na is certainly a copy of the Tekax, thus placing the Chilam Balam in Teabo at some point. Due to the proximity of Tekax to Teabo, someone in Teabo borrowing the manuscript from Tekax is not an impossible thought, nor is the idea that the Tekax originated in Teabo

only to end up in Tekax. The lack of surviving copies of the entire manuscript contributes to the continued uncertainty. See Ruth Gubler and David Bolles, *The Book of Chilam Balam of Na* (Lancaster, CA: Labyrinthos, 2000), 11–12, 117n43; Charles Gibson and John B. Glass, "A Census of Middle American Prose Manuscripts in the Native Historical Tradition," in *Handbook of Middle American Indians*, vol. 15, *Guide to Ethnohistorical Sources*, part 4 (Austin: University of Texas Press, 1975), 385–386.

50. Jean Genet and Pierre Chelbatz, *Histoire des peuples Mayas-Quichés (Mexique, Guatemala, Honduras)* (Paris: Les Editions Genet, 1927), 42, 145, 147. Gibson and Glass use Genet and Chelbatz's work to include the *Chilam Balam of Teabo* in their "Census." Eugene Craine and Reginald Reindorp place the estimated number of extant Chilam Balams at sixteen or eighteen. See their *The Codex Pérez and The Book of Chilam Balam of Maní* (Norman: University of Oklahoma Press, 1979), xvi.

51. Alfredo Barrera Vásquez and Silvia Rendón, *El libro de los libros de Chilam Balam* (1948; repr., Mexico City: Fondo de Cultura Económica, 1974), 12.

52. One of which was certainly the Na. Bricker, personal communication, February 12, 2013; Munro S. Edmonson, trans. and ed., *The Ancient Future of the Itza: The Book of Chilam Balam of Tizimin* (Austin: University of Texas Press, 1982), xi.

53. Indeed, the prophecy of the Chilam Balam found in the Chumayel is, in fact, derived from Bernardo de Lizana's 1633 *Historia de Yucatán*. See Knowlton, *Creation Myths*, 47.

54. For an overview of the composition of Chilam Balam texts, see Antje Gunsenheimer, "Out of the Historical Darkness: A Methodological Approach to Uncover the Hidden History of Ethnohistorical Sources," *Indiana* 23 (2006): 15–49.

55. Hanks, *Converting Words*; Knowlton, *Creation Myths*; Bricker, "The Last Gasp," 39–50; Bricker and Miram, *Kaua*; Timothy Knowlton, "Dynamics of Indigenous Language Ideologies in the Colonial Redaction of a Yucatec Maya Cosmological Text," *Anthropological Linguistics* 50, no. 1 (Spring 2008), 90–112; Caso Barrera, *Ixil*.

56. Knowlton, "Dynamics"; Hanks, *Converting Words*, 341–342; Barrera Vásquez and Rendón also examine similarities in their *El libro*.

57. Portions of this discussion on the Chilam Balams derive from Christensen, "The Teabo Manuscript," *Ethnohistory* 60, no. 4 (2013): 749–753. For an excellent examination of the Chilam Balams, see Hanks, *Converting Words*, 338–364. Admittedly, it is possible, as Hanks suggests, that ecclesiastics were aware of the Books of Chilam Balam.

58. The trend to view the Chilam Balam books as village documents providing insights in colonial and postcolonial literary production is becoming increas-

ingly apparent among Maya scholars. See, for example, Gunsenheimer, Okoshi Harada, and Chuchiak, "Introduction," 14–15.

59. Gretchen Whalen, "An Annotated Translation of a Colonial Yucatec Manuscript: On Religious and Cosmological Topics by a Native Author," Foundation for the Advancement of Mesoamerican Studies, 2002, www.famsi.org/reports /01017/.

60. Knowlton, *Creation Myths*, 48.

61. Princeton University Library, Department of Rare Books and Special Collections, Garrett-Gates Mesoamerican Manuscripts (C0744) (hereafter GGMM), no. 72, "Yucatec prayers," 31r.

62. Scholes et al., *Documentos*, 30.

63. In 1722 ecclesiastics were again admonished to use "ah cambeçahs" to help others die well. Gómez de Parada, *Constituciones sinodales*, 110.

64. The story of St. Julian can be found in Jacobus de Voragine, *The Golden Legend of Jacobus de Voragine*, trans. and ed. Granger Ryan and Helmut Ripperger (New York: Longmans, Green and Co., 1941), 130–131.

65. Bricker and Miram, *Kaua*, 301–306; Marla Korlin Hires, "The Chilam Balam of Chan Kan" (PhD diss., Tulane University, 1981), 130–135. The manuscript receives brief attention in Frans Blom, ed., *Maya Research (Mexico and Central America)*, vol. 2, no. 3 (New York: Alma Egan Hyatt Foundation, 1935), 300–301. The Passion theme continued strong among the Maya beyond the colonial period. See Bricker, *The Indian Christ, the Indian King*, 155–162.

66. For example, once trained in reading and writing, the Maya Miguel Canchan was reportedly seen always with the work. Caso Barrera, *Caminos*, 295. This genre of text was popular and numerous authors produced works with similar names, although some fell under the prohibition of the Inquisition. In fact, the convents of sixteenth-century Merida contained the prohibited *Ramillete de flores espirituales* by Manuel de Gaya. Fernández del Castillo, *Libros y libreros*, 325.

67. These final pages are missing from the original copy at Princeton, but are included in the photostatic copy held at Brigham Young University, L. Tom Perry Special Collections (LTPSC), MSS 279, box 74, folder 2, "Para ayudar a buen morir en lengua yucateca." For the signature of Na, see Gubler and Bolles, *Na*, 224–225, 237; for the lineage, see the same, 2n9.

68. I thank Victoria Bricker for alerting me to and providing digital images of this manuscript.

69. Personal communication, July 24, 2013.

70. Hanks, *Converting Words*, 346.

71. In reality, the sheer numbers of ecclesiastics vis-à-vis their Maya parishioners, coupled with the constant fear of uprisings, rebellion, flight, and "losing the

province," demanded such leniency in most cases. For more on the Spaniards' tenuous position, see Adriana Rocher Salas, "Un baluarte diferente: iglesia y control social en Yucatán durante el período colonial," *Península* 3, no. 1 (2008): 65–81. For an example of Category 3 texts and the concern they caused ecclesiastics among the Zapotec in Villa Alta, see David Tavárez, "Representations of Spanish Authority in Zapotec Calendrical and Historical Genres," in Schroeder, *The Conquest All Over Again.*

72. Knowlton, *Creation Myths*; Whalen, "Annotated Translation."

73. For a 1581 account of Teabo by its encomendero, Juan Bote, see *Relaciones*, vol. 1, 317–321. For its visita/cabecera status, see Hanks, *Converting Words*, 43, 45.

74. Crescencio Carrillo y Ancona, *Vida del v. padre fray Manuel Martínez, célebre franciscano yucateco, ó sea studio historico sobre la extinción de la orden franciscana en yucatán y sobre sus consecuencias* (Merida: Gamboa Guzman y Hermano, 1883), 53.

75. AGN, México 3072, "El intendente de Yucatán Lucas de Gálvez al rey sobre remoción de fray José Perdomo, Mérida, 18 de mayo de 1792." For more on Perdomo, see Rocher Salas, "Un baluarte diferente," 75–76.

76. José Javier González Puc, *El campesino maya de Teabo, Yucatán* (Mexico City: Secretaría de Educación Pública, Instituto Nacional Indigenista, 1982), 200–202.

77. Hanks, *Converting Words*, 101.

78. Caso Barrera, *Ixil*, 29, 98, 99.

79. Ibid., 17.

80. LTPSC, MSS 279, box 74, folder 3, "Christian doctrine" (hereafter Teabo MS), 35. The sentence appears incomplete.

81. GGMM no. 66, "Discourses on the Passion of Christ and other Texts," 44.

82. The Passion text exists in its original form in GGMM no. 66, "Passion of Christ," and also in photostats at LTPSC, MSS 279, box 74, folder 10, "Pasión de Jesucristo." Interestingly, when Jóse Secundino Na signed the Chilam Balam of Na, he used a similar, although somewhat different, phrase as Baltasar Mutul: "Here I have finished copying the notebook on the 15th day of August of the current year of 1863. It is I who will see if there is anything forgotten or wrong. It is not my fault because my education is not complete. This I swear by my word, I José Secundino Na." Gubler and Bolles, *Na*, 224–225. Gubler and Bolles use the date 1873. However, this seems to be an error as the manuscript reads "mil ochocientos sesenta y tres años."

CHAPTER 1: CREATING THE CREATION

1. LTPSC, MSS 279, box 74, folder 3, "Teabo MS," 1.

2. Bricker and Miram, *Kaua*, 283–284.

3. Hires, "Chan Kan," 198. Hires's transcription and translation of the Chan Kan

has the Creation occurring in "uuc p'el kin," or seven days (p. 38). This is either an error in transcription, as "six" in Maya is "uac" and the "a" can often appear as a "u" in these manuscripts, or it is an example of a variation, albeit quite unorthodox, on the traditional story. I am inclined toward the former.

4. For further insights into creation myths and their universality, see Munro Edmonson, *Lore: An Introduction to the Science of Folklore and Literature* (New York: Holt, Rinehart, and Winston, 1971), particularly chap. 3.

5. Knowlton, *Creation Myths*, 17.

6. Knowlton's *Creation Myths* is most effective in examining the dialogical processes involved in producing the colonial creation myths in the Chilam Balams and their connection to precontact cosmogonies and iconography.

7. Stuart, *Order of Days*, 209.

8. For a general overview, see Enrique Florescano, *National Narratives in Mexico: A History*, trans. Nancy T. Hancock (Norman: University of Oklahoma Press, 2006), 3–31; Miguel León-Portilla, *Native Mesoamerican Spirituality: Ancient Myths, Discourses, Stories, Doctrines, Hymns, Poems from the Aztec, Yucatec, Quiche-Maya and Other Sacred Traditions* (New York: Paulist Press, 1980), 27–30; Restall and Solari, *2012*, 7–26. Knowlton provides a more detailed discussion of the metaphysics of Maya cosmogonies in his *Creation Myths*, 16–31.

9. Allen J. Christenson, *Popol Vuh — The Sacred Book of the Maya: The Great Classic of Central American Spirituality, Translated from the Original Maya Text* (Norman: University of Oklahoma Press, 2007), 205n525.

10. The *Título de Totonicapan* is another example of a different creation story among the K'iche' Maya. My thanks to Frauke Sachse for sharing her work with me on this topic.

11. Christenson, *Popol Vuh*, 199.

12. See, for example, the myth of Katun 11 Ahau in the Chumayel recounting the Creation. Katun 11 Ahau is the first of thirteen katun rounds, each consisting of twenty-year periods, which compose what is commonly called the Short Count appearing in the Late Classic and continuing to the early colonial period. For an elucidation of this text, see Knowlton, *Creation Myths*, chap. 4. For a general overview of Maya texts and their creation myths, see J. Eric S. Thompson, *Maya History and Religion* (Norman: University of Oklahoma Press, 1970), 337–342. Some of Thompson's interpretations are dated, but helpful nonetheless.

13. Munro S. Edmonson, *Heaven Born Mérida and Its Destiny: The Book of Chilam Balam of Chumayel* (Austin: University of Texas Press, 1986), 153. Because I find it to be more accurate, I use Knowlton's translation of the passage in his *Creation Myths*, 37.

14. For an excellent study employing objectives for a different text, see George-Hirons, "Discourse of Translation."

15. Genesis 2:20.

16. Genesis 3:16.

17. Genesis 3:18. For the Creation account, see Genesis, chaps. 1–4.

18. The proper veneration of God included myriad forms and changed over time. The children of Adam and Eve, Cain and Abel, made offerings to God in the forms of fruit and animals. Yet after the death of Christ, other nonsacrificial forms such as charitable acts, devotion, and prayer became more evident. For the ending of animal sacrifices in Christianity, see Acts 6:13–14, 1 Corinthians 5:7, 1 Corinthians 10:18.

19. With the possible exception being a passage in Genesis 1:26 that uses the plural first-person pronoun, "Let us make man in our image." Such plurality would later be explained by theologians as evidence of the Trinity.

20. Fray Luis de Granada, *Introducción del símbolo de la Fe* (Salamanca: Herederos de Matías Gast, 1583), chap. 38, II.

21. See Hanks's *Converting Words* for more on ecclesiastics' efforts to instill the *policía cristiana* among the Yucatec Maya.

22. Although the acknowledged author of the work, Sahagún composed the text with four elderly Nahua and other native assistants. Studies on the *Colloquios* are extensive, but especially noteworthy are fray Bernardino de Sahagún, *Coloquios y doctrina cristiana*, ed. and trans. Miguel León-Portilla (Mexico City: Fundación de Investigaciones Sociales, Universidad Nacional Autónoma de México, 1986); and J. Jorge Klor de Alva, "La historicidad de los colloquios de Sahagún," *Estudios de cultura Náhuatl* 15 (1982): 147–184. Succinct summaries of the work can be found in Viviana Díaz Balsera, *The Pyramid under the Cross: Franciscan Discourses of Evangelization and the Nahua Christian Subject in Sixteenth-Century Mexico* (Tucson: University of Arizona Press, 2005), 15–21; and Louise M. Burkhart, *Holy Wednesday: A Nahua Drama from Early Colonial Mexico* (Philadelphia: University of Pennsylvania Press, 1996), 68.

23. Sahagún, *Coloquios*, 163–205.

24. Fray Martín de León, *Camino del cielo en lengua mexicana* (Mexico City: Emprenta de Diego Lopez Daualos, 1611), 7v–11r, 15v–25r. Fernando Cervantes observes ecclesiastics' desire to connect devils with fallen angels in his "How to See Angels: The Legacy of Early Mendicant Spirituality," in *Angels, Demons, and the New World*, ed. Fernando Cervantes and Andrew Redden (New York: Cambridge University Press, 2013), 81–83 (69–98).

25. For the sermons, see *Doctrina cristiana en lengua española y mexicana por los religiosos de la orden de Santo Domingo*, Colección de Incunables Americanos, vol. 1 (Madrid: Ediciones Cultura Hispánica, 1944), 138r–146r.

26. Ignacio de Paredes, *Promptuario manual mexicano* (Mexico City: Bibliotheca mexicana, 1759), 9–16.

27. Although a distant second to Coronel's work, Francisco Eugenio Domínguez y Argáiz discusses, briefly, God's creation of man in his *Pláticas de los principales mysterios de nvestra Sta fee* (Mexico City: Colegio de S. Ildefonso, 1758), 18–21.

28. Fray Juan Coronel, *Discursos predicables, con otras diuersas materias espirituales, con la doctrina xpna, y los articulos de la fé* (Mexico City: Pedro Gutiérrez en la emprenta de Diego Garrido, 1620), 1r–38r.

29. Ibid., xv.

30. Regarding what Bibles ecclesiastics and trained Maya had access to, the most common, post-Trent, was the Vulgata Sixto-Clementina. This revised 1592 edition of a 1590 predecessor had its origins in Trent and the order of Pope Sixtus to issue a definitive edition of the Vulgate. Experiencing multiple publications throughout the colonial period, it was the only authorized version of the Bible until the twentieth century. That certain Maya received training in the Bible and its stories is made clear by not only the Teabo Manuscript, but others such as the Ixil, which contains Maya redactions of the Sacrifice of Isaac and the Exodus among others. Caso Barrera notes that these redactions followed biblical originals rather closely, suggesting a careful referencing of the original, in this case the Vulgate translated into Spanish by Scio de San Miguel. See Caso Barrera, *Ixil*, 19–23.

31. In a similar fashion, Antje Gunsenheimer notes that the European and Maya sources formed a pool of information of sorts from which the Maya drew to compose their manuscripts. Gunsenheimer, "Out of the Historical Darkness," 27.

32. Gunsenheimer makes a similar observation of the Books of Chilam Balam. Ibid., 20.

33. For one example concerning the Dresden, Madrid, and Paris Codices, see Gabrielle Vail, "Creation Narratives in the Postclassic Maya Codices," in *Parallel Worlds: Genre, Discourse, and Poetics in Contemporary, Colonial, and Classic Period Maya Literature*, ed. Kerry M. Hull and Michael D. Carrasco (Boulder: University Press of Colorado, 2012).

34. Restall and Solari, *2012*, 107.

35. An excellent overview of the Genesis Commentary and its possible European connections is found in Bricker and Miram, *Kaua*, 34–35. Dante's popular *Divine Comedy* likewise perpetuated a layered concept of the universe and his work traveled across the Atlantic to New World libraries. See Irving A. Leonard, *Books of the Brave: Being an Account of Books and of Men in the Spanish Conquest and Settlement of the Sixteenth-Century New World* (New York: Gordian Press, 1964), 362, 365.

36. John L. Heilbron, "Censorship of Astronomy in Italy after Galileo," in *The*

Church and Galileo, ed. Ernan McMullin (Notre Dame, IN: University of Notre Dame Press, 2005), 307.

37. For more on these heavens, see Bricker and Miram, *Kaua*, 12–13. James M. Lattis provides a detailed analysis of the creation of this cosmology in his *Between Copernicus and Galileo: Christoph Clavius and the Collapse of Ptolemaic Cosmology* (Chicago: University of Chicago Press, 1994). For the influence of such a model on European authors, see Manuel Duran, *Luis de León* (Boston: Twayne Publishers, 1971), 36–48. For an intriguing article exploring the likelihood of a layered pre-Columbian universe of the Nahua and Maya having derived from European and Dantean worldviews, see Kesper Nielsen and Toke Sellner Reunert, "Dante's Heritage: Questioning the Multi-layered Model of the Mesoamerican Universe," *Antiquity* 83 (2009): 399–413.

38. LTPSC, MSS 279, box 74, folder 3, "Teabo MS," 1.

39. Ibid., 3.

40. Ibid., 3.

41. Knowlton, *Creation Myths*, 55–81; Restall and Solari, *2012*, 22–25.

42. Edmonson, *Chumayel*, 120–126; Knowlton, *Creation Myths*, chap. 7. Bricker expertly illustrates the hybrid discourse of the text and the ability for the Maya to incorporate Christianity into their preexisting worldview in her "The Mayan *Uinal* and the Garden of Eden," *Latin American Indian Literatures Journal* 18, no. 1 (2002): 1–20.

43. I thank Stephen Houston for his insight on the matter. Also, see his "Crafting Credit: Authorship among Classic Maya Painters and Sculptors," paper presented at Dumbarton Oaks Fall Symposium, October 12, 2013.

44. Matthew Restall describes both the letters and the primordial titles at length in his *Maya Conquistador* (Boston: Beacon Press, 1998), chaps. 6 and 9 respectively.

45. Hanks, *Converting Words*, 341; Knowlton, *Creation Myths*, 3–4. For a philological comparison of the Genesis Commentary in the Kaua, Chan Kan, and Morley Manuscript (hearafter MM), see Knowlton, "Dynamics."

46. Although the entire work is important in understanding the matter, see Hanks, *Converting Words*, 112–117, and chap. 11.

47. As is evidenced in Knowlton's "Dynamics"; Hanks, *Converting Words*; Bricker and Miram, *Kaua*; and Antje Gunsenheimer, "En contra del ovido y en pro de la continuidad: las crónicas de los *Libros del Chilam Balam* en su context colonial," in *Escondido en la selva: arqueología en el morte de Yucatán*, ed. Hanns J. Prem (Mexico City: Universidad de Bonn, Instituto Nacional de Antropología e Historia), 371–414; Gunsenheimer, "Out of the Historical Darkness"; and John F. Chuchiak, "Los mayas y el pirate: tributo indígena, corsarios renegados, y la misteriosa identidad del capitán Antonio Martínez, personaje de los libros de chilam balam," in *Memorias del XXII encuentro internacional los investigadores*

de la cultura maya (Campeche: Universidad Autónoma de Campeche, 2014), 15–50.

48. Gunsenheimer makes a similar observation in her analysis of various cognate sections of the Chilam Balams. Here, she posits that authors of such texts fell between two extreme models of text production: one being the faithful reproduction of an original text, and the other being a creative reproduction with personal additions and omissions. See her "En contra del olvido," 376–377; and "Out of the Historical Darkness," 25, 29–30.

49. LTPSC, MSS 279, box 74, folder 3, "Teabo MS," 5.

50. Bricker and Miram, *Kaua*, 152 of ms; Hires, "Chan Kan," 53 of ms.

51. LTPSC, MSS 279, box 74, folder 3, "Teabo MS," 5.

52. Ibid., 11.

53. An example is found in ibid., 15–22, and Whalen, "Annotated Translation," 200–213 of ms.

54. LTPSC, MSS 279, box 74, folder 3, "Teabo MS," 24.

55. Cogolludo, *Historia de Yucatán*, 192–193.

56. Sánchez de Aguilar, *Informe contra idolorum cultores de obispado de Yucatán*, 181.

57. Ibid., 172.

58. Knowlton discusses this in his *Creation Myths*, 42.

59. For more on these myths, see ibid., 53–55.

60. Although the Spanish catechism of Jerónimo de Ripalda served as a model for numerous Nahuatl catechisms. See Christensen, *Catholicisms*, 68–69, 72, 80.

61. The transcriptions and translations remain faithful to the text of origin. Occasionally, I alter capitalization and spacing to facilitate the comparison.

62. Bricker reads this as *bala* (*Kaua*, 226n896). The cognate text in the MM has *bala*, thus confirming the reading of *bla* as *bala*. Whalen, "Annotated Translation," 183 of ms.

63. Reading as *pot chakanhal*.

64. LTPSC, MSS 279, box 74, folder 3, "Teabo MS," 4.

65. Whalen, "Annotated Translation," 183–184 of ms. (transcription and translation by Whalen).

66. Bricker and Miram, *Kaua*, 288–289 (transcription and translation by Bricker and Miram).

67. Hires, "Chan Kan," 62–63 (transcription and translation by Hires).

68. Whalen, "Annotated Translation," 183 of ms (transcription and translation by Whalen).

69. Bricker and Miram, *Kaua*, 289n1532.

70. Whalen, "Annotated Translation," note 213.

71. Rodrigo Zamorano, *Cronología y reportorio de la razón de los tiempos* (Seville: Rodrigo Cabrera, 1594), 13r.

72. Ibid., 12v. The theory that both the Prime Mover and Crystalline layers moved appeared to explain precession, or the gradual, conical motion of the axis of rotation of the earth. This phenomenon was observed as early as 128 BC by Hipparchus, the Greek astronomer. The Prime Mover's movement was fast when compared to that of Crystalline, which moved one degree every one hundred years.

73. LTPSC, MSS 279, box 74, folder 3, "Teabo MS," 3. Although, admittedly, this could be a simple scribal error, as six and seven in Maya are written similarly as *uac* and *uuc* respectively.

74. Christensen, "Tales of Two Cultures," 372.

75. Pedro J. Rueda Ramírez, *Negocio e intercambio cultural: el comercio de libros con América en la Carrera de Indias (siglo XVII)* (Seville: Universidad de Sevilla, consejo superior de investigaciones científicas, 2005), 427–428; Fernández del Castillo, *Libros y libreros*, 344, 417; Leonard, *Books of the Brave*, 202, 341, 348, 360, 371; Efraín Castro Morales, "Libros del siglo XVI en la ciudad de Puebla de los Angeles," in *Libros europeos en la Nueva España a fines del siglo XVI*, ed. Wilhelm Lauer, Das Mexico-Projekt der Deutschen Forschungsgemeinschaft, vol. 5 (Wiesbaden: Franz Steiner, 1973), 114.

76. Soledad González Díaz, "Guaman Poma y el *repertorio* anónimo (1554): una nueva Fuente para las edades del mundo en la *Nueva corónica y buen gobierno*," *Chungara, Revista de Antropología Chilena* 44, no. 3 (2012): 377–388.

77. W. Michael Mathes, *The America's First Academic Library: Santa Cruz de Tlatelolco* (Sacramento: California State Library Foundation, 1985), 32.

78. Brian Murdoch, *The Medieval Popular Bible: Expansions of Genesis in the Middle Ages* (Rochester, NY: D. S. Brewer, 2003), 3.

79. Rueda Ramírez, *Negocio e intercambio*, 146.

80. Leonard, *Books of the Brave*, 249, 339, 363; Rueda Ramírez, *Negocio e intercambio*, 299; Helga Kropfinger von Kügelgen, "Exportación de libros europeos de Sevilla a la Nueva España en el año de 1586," in *Libros europeos*, 27. For examples of Genesis commentaries held in the College of Tlatelolco, see Mathes, *First Academic Library*, 56, 100.

81. For a discussion of the sermon, see Jospeh Hirst Lupton, *St. John of Damascus* (New York: E. & J. B. Young, 1882), 121–128. For a translation and commentary of the *Fountain*, see Frederic H. Chase, trans., *St. John of Damascus, Writings*, vol. 37, *The Fathers of the Church* (Washington, DC: Catholic University of America Press, 1958).

82. Otis H. Green and Irving A. Leonard, "On the Mexican Booktrade in 1600: A Chapter in Cultural History," *Hispanic Review* 9, no. 1 (1941): 6n19. For examples of Aquinas's works, see 15, 17, 19, 29; Leonard, *Books of the Brave*, 348–349; Kropfinger von Kügelgen, "Exportación de libros," 91–92. For Aquinas's

works in the College of Tlatelolco, see Mathes, *First Academic Library*, 30, 35, 53, 55.

83. Thomas Aquinas, *Summa theologica*, First Part, Question 91, Article 3.

84. LTPSC, MSS 279, box 74, folder 3, "Teabo MS," 9.

85. Ibid., 23–24.

86. Aquinas, *Summa*, Second Part, Question 164, Article 2.

87. LTPSC, MSS 279, box 74, folder 3, "Teabo MS," 2.

88. *Bolon*, meaning "nine," could also mean "many" or "great" to convey the meaning of "he of the great soul." For insight into the meaning of "bolon" in hieroglyphic texts, see J. Eric S. Thompson, "The Rise and Fall of Maya Civilization," in *The Decipherment of Ancient Maya Writing*, ed. Stephen Houston, Oswaldo Chinchilla Mazariegos, and David Stuart (Norman: University of Oklahoma Press, 2001), 183.

89. LTPSC, MSS 279, box 74, folder 3, "Teabo MS," 5. For additional examples, see Christensen, *Catholicisms*, 46–48.

90. Again, see Nielsen and Reunert's "Dante's Heritage" for the possibility of the multilayered Maya universe deriving from European sources.

91. Hanks, *Converting Words*, 152. René Acuña produced a wonderful facsimile of the dictionary in his *Bocabulario de maya than: Codex Vindobonesis N.S. 3833* (Mexico City: Instituto Nacional Autónoma de México, 1993).

92. For more on parallel constructions in Maya, see Luis Enrique Sam Colop, "Poetics in the *Popol Wuj*," in Hull and Carrasco, *Parallel Worlds*, 283–310; Victoria Bricker, "The Ethnographic Context of Some Traditional Mayan Speech Genres," in *Explorations in the Ethnography of Speaking*, eds. Richard Bauman and Joel Sherzer (Cambridge, UK: Cambridge University Press, 1974), 369–388. For a general discussion of occurrences in Nahuatl, see J. Richard Andrews, *Introduction to Classical Nahuatl*, rev. ed., vol. 1 (Norman: University of Oklahoma Press, 2003), 556–558.

93. LTPSC, MSS 279, box 74, folder 3, "Teabo MS," 12.

94. Lockhart, *The Nahuas*, 366.

95. Following the Latin Vulgate, Virago is the name Adam gives to Eve and carries the meaning of a heroic woman or female warrior. From the Latin *vir*, man, and the suffix *–ago* denoting relationship or resemblance.

96. LTPSC, MSS 279, box 74, folder 3, "Teabo MS," 16.

97. Timothy Knowlton and Gabrielle Vail, "Hybrid Cosmologies in Mesoamerica: A Reevaluation of the *Yax Cheel Cab*, a Maya World Tree," *Ethnohistory* 57, no. 4 (2010): 709–739. See also Knowlton, *Creation Myths*, 121–152.

98. Today, some scholars hold the view that there was one tree. See Tryggve N. D. Mettinger, *The Eden Narrative: A Literary and Religio-historical Study of Genesis*

2–3 (Winona Lake, IN: Eisenbrauns, 2007), 5–11. "Do not touch . . ." quotation, LTPASC, MSS 279, box 74, folder 3, "Teabo MS," 18.

99. For its use in idolatry rites, see John F. Chuchiak, "'It Is Their Drinking that Hinders Them': Balché and the Use of Ritual Intoxicants among the Colonial Yuctaec Maya, 1550–1780," *Estudios de cultura Maya* 24 (Fall 2003): 137–171.

100. LTPSC, MSS 279, box 74, folder 3, "Teabo MS," 20 82r; Whalen, "Annotated Translation," 209 of ms.

101. Edmonson, *Tizimin*, 143; Coronel, *Discursos*, 82r.

102. I discuss this connection in detail in *Catholicisms*, 205–206, and "Tales of Two Cultures."

103. Mark 8:22–26 also recounts a miracle that included Christ's saliva.

104. An online translation of St. Anthony's sermons can be found at www.basilica .org/pages/ebooks/St.%20Anthony%20of%20Padua-The%20Sermons%20 of%20Saint%20Anthony.pdf. The referenced passage derives from Septuagesima from his Sunday sermons.

105. See John L. Phelan's *The Millennial Kingdom of the Franciscans in the New World*, 2nd ed. (Berkeley: University of California Press, 1970), 8.

106. For more on the significance of seats, see Kevin Terraciano, *The Mixtecs of Colonial Oaxaca: Ñudzahui History, Sixteenth through Eighteenth Centuries* (Stanford, CA: Stanford University Press, 2001), 32–38.

107. LTPSC, MSS 279, box 74, folder 3, "Teabo MS," 19.

108. Ana M. Juárez and Jon McGee, "A Mayan Version of the Adam and Eve Story," *Latin American Literatures Journal* 19, no. 1 (Spring 2003): 1–18.

109. Throughout the manuscript, watermarks and wear render certain passages unreadable. Obvious omissions are indicated in brackets. Occasionally, bracketed insertions derive from cognate texts, and I indicate in the notes where such is the case.

110. Here begins the cognate text with the Kaua, 146 of ms., and Chan Kan, 26 of ms. All references to the Kaua derive from Bricker and Miram 2002, and the Chan Kan from Hires 1981.

111. Wear on the page makes these syllables unreadable. The bracketed portion is from the Kaua, 146 of ms.

112. This entry appears in ballpoint pen and certainly dates to the twentieth century. The meaning, however, is unclear.

113. Here begins the cognate text in the MM, 178 of ms.

114. Read *ca*.

115. The true intended meaning is the space directly below the celestial firmament.

116. Various theologians commented on the creation of the angels. See, for example, St. Damascus's discussion in Chase, *St. John of Damascus*, 205–210.

117. This is from *caa' sut*, "to return," with *sut* carrying a meaning of revolving or orbiting.

118. This appears to be referencing, quite loosely, St. John of Damascus's sermon on Holy Saturday. See Lupton, *St. John of Damascus*, 123.

119. This seems to be a metaphor for the "light" God created on the first day. Aquinas explains, "First, because light gives a name to the air, since by it the air actually becomes luminous." Aquinas, *Summa*, First Part, Question 67, Article 3. This seems to be in reference to clouds.

120. This is coming from *oci*, but in the Kaua (285n1500) Bricker translates it as *toci* after the Chan Kan. However, seeing that it appears as *oci* in the Teabo, Kaua, and MM, I translate it as such.

121. This, most likely, refers to the stars that composed the eighth layer of the Ptolemaic model.

122. Again, this would be in reference to the eighth layer and its role of holding the stars.

123. From Kaua, 148 of ms.

124. As in the MM (181 of ms.), the author uses a bilingual couplet for "hours," *oras U kintzil*.

125. Here we have an interesting intrusion of Spanish orthography with the "ll" replacing the "y" as a phonetic parallel. The word should read "yanob."

126. Should be "uactas."

127. Derived from *tuba tu hunal*, which Knowlton suggests is a couplet demonstrating "colonial Maya theology rooted in the autochthonous metaphysics of complementary dualism." *Creation Myths*, 109.

128. This ordering of the planets and their assigned positions differs from that stated by St. John of Damascus. See Chase, *St. John of Damascus*, 216.

129. Bricker reads this as a contraction of *bala* in the Kaua (289n1530). However, again the cognate text in the MM (182 of ms.) has *bala*, thus confirming the reading of *bla* as *bala*.

130. Reading as *pot chakanhal*.

131. Here the author divides what appears in the MM and Kaua to be a continued treatise. Yet in this division, the author should have made "sihsah" to be "sihsahilob." The cognate text in the Chan Kan likewise breaks here (33 of ms.).

132. In other words, no one calls the Crystalline "water," although that is how it appears in the scriptures.

133. The Crystalline is in the ninth heaven, not the sixth as the Maya author indicates. Bricker reads this as *uaxac*, but I am hesitant to do so, primarily because, as noted earlier, the author wrote "eighth" as *uaxac* and had previously used *uactas caan* for "sixth layer of heaven." Moreover, the MM has the text as *uactas* (184 of ms.).

134. From MM, 184 of ms.
135. Here again we see the "ll" being used for the "y."
136. Aquinas promulgates this theory, and I believe it may be in reference to Isaiah 30:26. Aquinas, *Summa*, Supplement, Question 91, Article 3.
137. The cognate text with the Kaua breaks here.
138. This "their" is puzzling and could be used to refer to the "other" wise men, or the European wise men.
139. It seems as though the intended meaning is to illustrate how the creations were different from each other. See MM, 186 of ms. for another version of this line.
140. This idea of light entering the form of the Sun appears in Aquinas's *Summa*, First Part, Question 67, Article 4. See also Question 70. It helps explain why God created "light" on the first day, yet the sun wasn't created until day four. Essentially, the sun is a vessel of light, not the creator of it. In this sense, the light created on the first day was spiritual, and the sun on the fourth day was its corporal manifestation.
141. From Kaua, 155 of ms.
142. Again, God did not want the Sun to give off light at first.
143. Here ends the cognate text with the MM, 189 of ms.
144. Here ends the cognate text with the Kaua, 57 of ms., and with the Chan Kan, 61 of ms.
145. This use of *pal* carries with it a sexual connotation that certainly strays from the traditional story.
146. Perhaps an approximation of *delante*.
147. Reading as *chayan*.
148. This insertion of the Trinity into the biblical record reflects the opinion of many scholars such as Aquinas in his *Summa*, First Part, Question 45, Articles 6 and 7, and their attempt to make sense of the "we" in Genesis.
149. This is meant to illustrate how man was the greatest, most esteemed creation of God.
150. Again, the author seems familiar with Aquinas's *Summa*, First Part, Question 91, Article 3 in which he states, "Nevertheless, though of erect stature, man is far above plants. For man's superior part, his head, is turned towards the superior part of the world, and his inferior part is turned towards the inferior world; and therefore he is perfectly disposed as to the general situation of his body. Plants have the superior part turned towards the lower world, since their roots correspond to the mouth; and their inferior part towards the upper world."
151. This is St. Thomas Aquinas, who is considered the Doctor of Angels due to how much of his *Summa* is dedicated to them. Here, then, the author plainly states he is deriving inspiration from Aquinas.

152. See Chase, *St. John of Damascus*, 264–266. Moreover, this aligns with the *Summa* saying Adam was created in grace. Aquinas, *Summa*, First Part, Question 95, Article 1.

153. Here begins again the cognate text with the MM, 194 of ms.

154. Read *uinbail*.

155. Read *kax*. Here, as in other places, "u" is used interchangeably with "a."

156. From, for example, Aquinas, *Summa*, First Part, Question 93, Article 5.

157. This is in reference to Revelation 22:1–2: "Then the angel showed me the river of life-giving water, sparkling like crystal, flowing from the throne of God and of the Lamb down the middle of its street. On either side of the river grew the tree of life that produces fruit twelve times a year, once each month; the leaves of the trees serve as medicine for the nations."

158. It is possible that this and other similar occurances of repeated words are a result of copying from a written text.

159. This author/copyist seldom employs the "j" for the syllable final "h."

160. This is in reference to the New Jerusalem and Revelation 21:12.

161. This is in reference to Revelation 22:1.

162. For more on this concept, see Phelan, *The Millennial Kingdom*, 72. This was also taught to the Nahuas. See, for example, León, *Camino*, 17r; also fray Juan de la Anunciación, *Doctrina christiana muy cumplida* (Mexico City: Pedro Balli, 1575), 25v.

163. It was believed, particularly in the Eastern Orthodox Church, that the Garden of Eden was located in the East. Many medieval and early modern scholars believed the specific location to be Hebron, and that Adam was formed from the earth of the Damascene field. See Rev. James H. Defouri, "The Location of the Early Paradise," *The Catholic World* 36 (1883): 778–795. In his *Summa*, Aquinas likewise expressed the belief that the Garden of Eden was located in the East. Aquinas, *Summa theologica*, First Part, Question 102, Article 1.

164. From *may to oCooc haa yokol*. *Oc haa* and its variants are frequently used for "baptism." However, the Morley Manuscript reads *may to othaac yokol*, which Whalen translates as "before he had skin above" (197 of ms.). Later, the Teabo Manuscript mentions the creation of Adam's skin using *yothal*.

165. From Mark 7:34.

166. From "yah sihsahule." *Sih* is a verb for creation relating to females. See Knowlton, *Creation Myths*, 73, 108. Other Maya texts pair this female creation verb with its male counterpart, *chab*: Edmonson, *Tizimin*, 40; MM, 151 of ms.

167. This addition seems to be in much darker ink and was possibly added at a much later date.

168. See Genesis 2:20.

169. Reading as *hunɔit*.
170. It is unusual that in *kaMycex* the "y" is not an "i."
171. The beginning of this word is badly faded and represents my best guess. If I am correct, this is a scribal error in repeating the previous phrase.
172. Read *nahma*.
173. Here begins a different hand.
174. Although *tzeCan* here probably means "castigated," I am unsure of the following *joul tean*.
175. Reading *chiltabal*.
176. From *toh olal*, which when combined with *cuxtal* reads more poetically as "health." My thanks to Timothy Knowlton for his insights.
177. Read *Miayatz*.
178. This phrase is likely a scribal error as the MM (207 of ms.) reads *U lubesob. ti keban*, "they fall into sin," which I think would be the intended meaning here.
179. Read *ti yan*.
180. The word "will" comes from *yol* or *wol*, which is similar to "spirit" and originated from the deity Hunab Itzamna. See Christensen, *Catholicisms*, 45.
181. In this last portion of dialogue, the author switches between the first and third person—a not entirely uncommon trait of Maya manuscripts.
182. From *u kohbilan*, which means a representative of something or someone.
183. Reading as *Bayx*.
184. Here the text reads *Ca a ualab tech*, "Then you say to you." I believe that Eve is the speaker here and that the "a" should have been the first-person "in."
185. "Warrior" is from *holcan*. The word means "head of the serpent," and it referred to those warriors who served under the chief Maya military captain. It also appears in the MM, 211 of ms.; see Christensen, *Translated Christianities*, 32–35.
186. Here ends the cognate text in the MM, 212 of ms.
187. From *sip*, which can relay a meaning of any error, while the more typical word for "sin," or *keban*, commonly appears with religious meaning, although both often appear as synonymous. See Christensen, *Catholicisms*, 43; Hanks, *Converting Words*, 196–202, 265. Interestingly, throughout the Teabo Manuscript, its authors prefer the use of keban when referencing sin. Indeed, sip appears primarily in the Fall of Adam and Eve. This could be authorial preference, or it could reflect an intended meaning of an "error" or "mistake" committed by two beings lacking a full knowledge.
188. Here is a prime example of how multiple renditions of a similar text can provide fruitful insights. In the MM the passage appears as *ox muchix u thanalob*, and Whalen, "Annotated Translation," note 262, states her struggle in translating the phrase, eventually arriving at "multitudinous the recriminations by God to Adam back then." However, because the Teabo Manuscript has the phrase as *ox*

tenhi u thanal, we can see that the intended meaning was closer to that of the biblical text, as *ten* is a classifier for a count of times (*hun ten*, one time; *ox ten*, three times).

189. As mentioned, the bark of this tree is frequently used by H-Men for its medicinal purposes. For examples of such in colonial texts, see Ralph L. Roys, *The Ethno-Botany of the Maya* (New Orleans: Department of Middle American Research, Tulane University, 1931), 242.

190. It seems like the negative *ma* is missing here.

191. Inserted between the lines is *Bay alabtic tiob tumen Ca ymil ti Dios tan u peniten-siaob catal.*

192. Inserted between the lines is "As it is said to them by our lord God, 'You [will] go through penances.'"

CHAPTER 2: GENEALOGIES, PARABLES, AND THE FINAL JUDGMENT

1. Acts 1:11.

2. For more on the matter, see Knowlton, *Creation Myths*, chap. 4.

3. Zamorano, *Cronología y reportorio*, 323r. The reportorio notes that some divide the world into seven ages by splitting the third age into two separate ages. An example of the six-age view can be found in Jerónimo de Chaves, *Chronographia o reportorio de los tiempos* (Seville: 1576), 56v–64r.

4. It is also possible, although somewhat less likely, that the illustration of Christ's genealogy was to connect him with his role as Judge and the "Lion of the tribe of Juda, the Root of David" who removes the seven seals in the last days (Revelation 5:5).

5. Matthew Restall, *The Maya World: Yucatec Culture and Society, 1550–1850* (Stanford, CA: Stanford University Press, 1997), 28.

6. Such is illustrated in Mark Christensen, "The Spoils of the Pech Conquistadors," in *Native Wills from the Colonial Americas: Dead Giveaways in a New World*, ed. Mark Christensen and Jonathan Truitt (Salt Lake City: University of Utah Press, 2016). For additional insights on marriage patterns, see Philip C. Thompson, *Tekanto, A Maya Town in Colonial Yucatán* (New Orleans: Tulane University Middle American Research Institute, 1999), 210–216.

7. For an excellent work illustrating the matter, see Restall, *Maya Conquistador*; see also Quezada's discussion in his *Maya Lords*, 27–32.

8. Christenson, *Popol Vuh*, 292–305.

9. LTPSC, MSS 279, box 74, folder 4 "Christian Genealogy in Maya." The text appears to be a model of how to compose a genealogy. The "Xiu Family Tree" forms part of the larger *Xiu Family Chronicle*, which, in essence, was a *probanza de hidalguía* designed to prove the nobility status of the Xiu lineage. The family

tree receives attention in various works, including fray Diego de Landa, *Yucatan before and after the Conquest by Friar Diego De Landa: With Other Related Documents, Maps and Illustration*, trans. William Gates (New York: Dover Publications, 1978; first published in 1937 by the Maya Society, Baltimore), 120–132; Restall, *Maya Conquistador*, chap. 8.

10. For the Damascene's discussion, see Chase, *St. John of Damascus*, 361–366. Like John of Damascus, various Church Fathers employed the genealogy to prove Mary as having descended from David, thus allowing Christ to be called "son of David."

11. Here and throughout I employ a less contemporary spelling of the names as found in the King James Version of the Bible to facilitate a phonetic comparison between the Maya transcription and English translation of the names.

12. Onan, a child of Judah, marries Tamar. After Onan's death and the death of Judah's wife, Tamar deceives Judah into fathering twins with her.

13. Bricker and Miram, *Kaua*, 11.

14. The right hand throughout the Bible was meant to exude a righteous state of approval and authority. The sixth article of faith of the Catholic Church states that Christ ascends to heaven to sit at the right hand of God (see also Mark 16:19). This reference to the right hand proved problematic when instructing natives about the noncorporal nature of God. When discussing the matter, fray Domingo de la Anunciación's 1565 *Doctrina* reminds the Nahua pupil that "God does not have a right hand like us, but that God glorifies Christ." Fray Domingo de la Anunciación, *Doctrina Xpiana breue y cōpendiosa* (Mexico City: Pedro Ocharte, 1565), 26r.

15. Edmonson, *Chumayel*, 249–252. Roys and Edmonson posit that the author of this particular section is a Spanish priest presumably due to its highly Catholic content and other reasons. However, the text's misspelling of common Spanish terms and its use of couplets suggests the contribution of a Maya hand.

16. For a Nahuatl counterpart to the Maya sermon, see fray Juan de la Anunciación, *Doctrina christiana muy cumplida* (Mexico City: Pedro Balli, 1575), 54–66, and its discussion in Louise Burkhart, "Death and the Colonial Nahua," in *Death and Life in Colonial Nahua Mexico*, vol. 1 of *Nahuatl Theater*, ed. Barry D. Sell and Louise Burkhart (Norman: University of Oklahoma Press, 2004), 41–42.

17. LTPSC, MSS 279, box 74, folder 3, "Teabo MS," 27. Such a distinction is also made in MM in its exposition of the "Our Father," 275 of ms.

18. Hanks, *Converting Words*, 129–132, 188–193.

19. The manual was likely employed by a Yucatecan friar administering in the parish of Tixcacalcupul. Folio 9r gives some indication of the manual being specifically used in Tekom. University of Pennsylvania, Rare Books and Manuscript Library Collection 700, item 26, "Modo de confesar en lengua maya, año de 1803." For

more on the topic of sexual sin, see John Franklin Chuchiak IV, "The Sins of the Fathers: Franciscan Missionaries, Parish Priests, and the Sexual Conquest of the Yucatec Maya," *Ethnohistory* 54, no. 1 (Winter 2007): 78–80; Chuchiak, "Secrets behind the Screens: Solicitantes in the Colonial Diocese of Yucatan and the Yucatec Maya, 1570–1785," in *Religion in New Spain*, ed. Susan Schroeder and Stafford Poole (Albuquerque: University of New Mexico Press, 2007), 83–109.

20. LTPSC, MSS 279, box 74, folder 3, "Teabo MS," 29.

21. Coronel's *Discursos* provides the lengthiest exposition on hell and its torments in Maya; see 81v–93r, 148r–149v. For an excellent summary of Nahuatl texts on the Final Judgment, see Louise M. Burkhart, "Death and the Colonial Nahua," in *Death and Life in Colonial Nahua Mexico*, vol. 1 of *Nahuatl Theater*, ed. Barry D. Sell and Louise Burkhart (Norman: University of Oklahoma Press, 2004), 39–43. Ignacio de Paredes's 1759 *Promptuario manual mexicano* (Mexico City: Bibliotheca mexicana, 1759) devotes significant space to describing the torments of hell in Nahuatl (XLVIII–LX), as does fray Juan de la Anunciación's 1575 *Doctrina*, 60–66. Regarding the moralistic plays, see Sell and Burkhart, *Death and Life in Colonial Nahua Mexico*. Vol. 1 of *Nahuatl Theater*, 190–209.

22. See Restall and Solari, *2012*, 82–86.

23. Matthew 25:40.

24. A double-reed pipe similar to an oboe.

25. For a list of the colonial uses of keban in the Motul and San Francisco Part 1 dictionaries, see Hanks, *Converting Words*, 196–202.

26. For more on tlatlacolli, keban, and *sip*, see Christensen, *Catholicisms*, 42–43.

27. Grupo Dzíbil, *Chilam Balam of Tuzik* (Mexico City: n.p., 1996), 31–34.

28. LTPSC, MSS 279, box 74, folder 3, "Teabo MS," 33.

29. Ibid., 28.

30. See, for example, Numbers 15:38, Ezekiel 7:2, Isaiah 11:12, and Revelation 7:1.

31. See Knowlton and Vail, "Hybrid Cosmologies," 711–722. For the trees in creation myths, see Knowlton, *Creation Myths*, 54–81.

32. For an example of the primordial title genre, see the *Title of Calkini* in Restall, *Maya Conquistador*, 93.

33. Archivo Histórico del Arzobispado de Yucatán, Oficios 1748–1749, 1801–1884, vol. 1, "Peten Itza," "Francisco Itza."

34. Ralph L. Roys, *The Titles of Ebtun* (Washington, DC: Carnegie Institution, 1939), 253; see also Restall, *Maya World*, 196.

35. An example of which is related in the *Popol Vuh*. See Christenson, *Popol Vuh*, 122n258.

36. LTPSC, MSS 279, box 74, folder 3, "Teabo MS," 33.

37. Restall, *Maya World*, 88.

38. This is likely intended to reference the number of years from the Creation to

the birth of Christ. Most reportorios included a section detailing the ages of the world and their date of initiation since the Creation. In Zamorano's 1594 reportorio, the birth of Christ is dated at year 3967. Zamorano, *Cronología y reportorio*, 353r. Regardless, the Bible states that Adam died at the age of 930 (Genesis 5:5).

39. Here the lineage follows that found in Matthew 1:1–16, which outlines the genealogy of Jesus to Abraham. Luke 3:23–38 gives a different genealogy, that of Jesus to Adam.

40. Actually, Abraham begat Isaac and Isaac begat Jacob, thus making Abraham Jacob's grandfather.

41. Here the manuscript is badly faded and the wording is uncertain.

42. Here the manuscript is badly faded and the translation is my best approximation.

43. From *choch keban*, "untie sin."

44. Reading as *tanlic*. In the following line the scribe writes *yn tanlic dios*, and I believe this is what he means here.

45. Reading *hach lobil*.

46. This is from "bak" which can also refer to the genitals.

47. Reading *bal tail*.

48. Reading this as Ɔoc.

49. Also referred to as Jehoshaphat, which means "God judges." This is in reference to the Valley of Jehoshaphat referenced in Joel 3:2: "I will assemble all the nations and bring them down to the Valley of Jehoshaphat, and I will enter into judgment with them there on behalf of my people and my inheritance, Israel; Because they have scattered them among the nations, and divided my land." Also in Joel 3:12: "Let the nations bestir themselves and come up to the Valley of Jehoshaphat; For there I will sit in judgment upon all the neighboring nations."

50. Should read "ad quam nos perducat ad uitam aeternam," "bring us to everlasting life."

51. This reference to mothers and their nursing is reflected in the Bible in instances of both blessing and cursing. See, for example, Luke 11:27 and Luke 23:29.

CHAPTER 3: DOOMSDAY AND THE MAYA

1. William W. Heist, *The Fifteen Signs before Doomsday* (East Lansing: Michigan State College Press, 1952), 2.

2. Luke 21:25–28.

3. Fray Juan Bautista, *Sermonario en lengua mexicana* (Mexico City: Diego López Dávalos, 1606), 160. Valeriano is attributed with the abundant glosses found throughout the sermonary.

4. Johannes Fried, "Awaiting the Last Days . . . Myth and Disenchantment," in

    Apocalyptic Time, ed. Albert I. Baumgarten (Leiden, Netherlands: Brill, 2000), 283.

5. See Luke 21:7–28.

6. For an excellent study of apocryphal apocalypses, see Heist, *Fifteen Signs*.

7. Regarding the Franciscans, see Bert Roest, *Franciscan Literature of Religious Instruction before the Council of Trent* (Leiden, Netherlands: Brill, 2004), 246, 306, 388–389, 440, 452.

8. Likely a rendition of *The Apocalypse of Philip*. Heist, *Fifteen Signs*, 64n7.

9. Martin McNamara, "The (Fifteen) Signs before Doomsday in Irish Tradition," *Warszawskie Studia Teologiczne* 20, no. 2 (2007): 223–254.

10. The Gelasian decree determined those scriptures that would be included in the canon of the Church.

11. Máire Herbert and Martin McNamara, *Irish Biblical Apocrypha: Selected Texts in Translation* (London: T&T Clark, 2004), xxii.

12. Heist, *Fifteen Signs*, 200–203.

13. For more on this text, see Christensen, "Tales of Two Cultures"; Christensen, *Translated Christianities*, 15–24.

14. This poem would later see print as early as 1780. Heist, *Fifteen Signs*, 36. The signs in the subsequent *Flos sanctorum* (Castile, ca. 1472–1475) are extremely similar to those in the poem.

15. Heist, *Fifteen Signs*, 36; William Pettas, *A Sixteenth-Century Spanish Bookstore: The Inventory of Juan de Junta* (Philadelphia: American Philosophical Society, 1995), 69, 72, 122, 159, 211, 218, 220, passim. Eschatological material was so popular it even appeared in dramas. For an overview, see Daniel Mosquera, "Nahuatl Catechistic Drama: New Translations, Old Preoccupations," in *Death and Life in Colonial Nahua Mexico*, ed. Barry D. Sell and Louise Burkhart (Norman: University of Oklahoma Press, 2004), 71–73.

16. See *Hamlet*, act 1 scene 1; *Julius Caesar*, act 1 scene 2. Also, see C. H. Conley, "An Instance of the Fifteen Signs of Judgment in Shakespeare," *Modern Language Notes* 30, no. 2 (1915): 41–44.

17. Heist, *Fifteen Signs*, 109. For more on the "types" of versions of the signs, see ibid. The signs in the tables that follow are shortened representations of their lengthier originals.

18. Regarding their libraries, see Mathes, *First Academic Library*, 5, 19, 29, 35, 53, 58; Leonard, *Books of the Brave*, 373; Pettas, *Bookstore*, 47, 69, 72, 122, 159. For examples of medieval Franciscans employing these works in their sermons and personal literature, see Roest, *Franciscan Literature*, 107, 111. The popularity of Voragine and the subsequent *Flos sanctorum* can be seen in Rueda Ramírez, *Negocio e intercambio*, 312–316. The *Flos* also influenced murals and images painted

in the churches. See Eleanor Wake, *Framing the Sacred: The Indian Churches of Early Colonial Mexico* (Norman: University of Oklahoma Press, 2009), 187, 224. Scriptural commentaries on the book of Revelation were popular in New Spain. See Rueda Ramírez, *Negocio e intercambio*, 300–302.

19. Heist, *Fifteen Signs*, 27–28.

20. Again, for more on Nahuatl texts discussing the Final Judgment, see Burkhart, "Death and the Colonial Nahua," in *Death and Life in Colonial Nahua Mexico*, 39–43.

21. Medieval theologians and early modern authors of religious texts, including those native-language texts of New Spain, list fourteen articles of faith: seven pertaining to the Godhead, and seven pertaining to the humanity of Christ. Today, the Catholic Church employs twelve articles of faith identified in the Creed.

22. Heist, *Fifteen Signs*, 26.

23. Jacobus de Voragine, *The Golden Legend*, 4.

24. Aquinas, *Summa*, Supplement, Question 73, Article 1.

25. Fray Diego de Córdova Salinas, *Crónica franciscana de las provincias del Perú*, notes and introduction by Lino G. Canedo, OFM (Washington, DC: Academy of American Franciscan History, 1957), 1113. I thank Jaime Lara for informing me of this reference.

26. *Flos sanctorum*, 280r–280v.

27. For an excellent examination of the *Sermonario*, see Sell, "Friars, Nahuas, and Books," 142–165.

28. Bautista, *Sermonario*, 160–178.

29. Ibid., 160.

30. Ibid., 171.

31. Fray Juan de la Anunciación, *Sermonario en lengua mexicana* (Mexico City: Antonio Ricardo, 1577), f. 3r–4v. I thank Ben Leeming for alerting me to this entry. Interestingly, fray Martín de León's 1614 *Sermonario* employs portions of Anunciación's sermon—sometimes verbatim—in its own first sermon for the first Sunday of Advent.

32. Sell, "Friars, Nahuas, and Books," 142.

33. Anunciación, *Sermonario*, f. 3r.

34. For some direct biblical citations, see Acts 2:20, Isaiah 13:10, Revelation 6:12, Matthew 24:29, Mark 13:24, and Luke 21:25.

35. Horacio Carochi, S.J., *Grammar of the Mexican Language, with an Explanation of Its Adverbs*, bilingual ed. by James Lockhart (Stanford, CA: Stanford University Press and UCLA Latin American Center Publications, 2001), ix.

36. Bancroft Library M–M 464, "Santoral en Mexicano," "*De Judicio Finali*,"

276r–280r. I thank Louise Burkhart for providing me with copies of the index to the manuscript. I also thank Ben Leeming for his generosity in sharing this document with me.

37. Read *tletzintli*.
38. Bancroft Library M-M 464, "Santoral en Mexicano," "*De Judicio Finali*," 277r.
39. Ibid., 277v.
40. *Doctrina*, 44r–44v.
41. Ignacio de Paredes, *Promptuario*, XLIV.
42. Fray Juan Bautista, *Libro de la miseria y brevedad de la vida del hombre y de sus cuatro postrimerías, en lengua mexicana* (Mexico: Diego López Dávalos, 1604), 82v–86r.
43. Knowlton, *Creation Myths*, 81–83; Whalen, "Annotated Translation."
44. GGMM no. 65, "Maya Sermons," 14–15.
45. For more on the ah kin in colonial Yucatan, see Chuchiak, "Pre-Conquest *Ah Kinob* in a Colonial World"; Caso Barrera, *Caminos*, 109–122.
46. Jacobus de Voragine, *The Golden Legend*, 250–255; *Flos sanctorum*, 217v–218r.
47. The last sign appears at the bottom of a page, but space exists to have included another sign or, at the very least, continue the list on the back of the page. The author could have forgotten or chosen not to include the remaining three signs, or perhaps was recording an incomplete oral version.
48. Here, I employ the facsimile of the Chilam Balam that appears in Grupo Dzíbil, *Chilam Balam of Tuzik* (Mexico City: n.p., 1996). Although the work provides a transcription and a Spanish translation of the Maya, damage and wear to various pages of the surviving manuscript renders difficult an accurate transcription and translation. The cognate passages of the "Maya Sermons" text, then, play an important role in providing missing words and context that alters, at times considerably, the existing transcription and translation.
49. Had the Teabo Manuscript included a thirteenth sign, it most certainly would have contained the phrase "yoklal mactzil."
50. Paul Sullivan, *Unfinished Conversations: Mayas and Foreigners between Two Wars* (New York: Knopf, 1989), 205–210. See also Whalen, "Annotated Translation."
51. See Christensen, *Translated Christianities*, chap. 2.
52. MM, 104 of ms.
53. See Revelation 22:2. For more on the medieval and early modern origins, as well as an excellent discussion of the evolution of the belief among colonial Maya, see Knowlton and Vail, "Hybrid Cosmologies."
54. For more, see Terry Rugeley, *Yucatán's Maya Peasantry and the Origins of the Caste War* (Austin: University of Texas Press, 1996).
55. See Coronel, *Discursos*, 87r.

56. *Flos sanctorum*, 280v–283r.

57. Fernández del Castillo, *Libros y libreros*, 319. For a list of prohibited books discovered circulating in Yucatan in 1586, see the same, 317–326.

58. Grupo Dzíbil, *Tuzik*, 30–31; GGMM no. 65, "Maya Sermons," 18.

59. Grupo Dzíbil, *Tuzik*, 31–34; LTPSC, MSS 279, box 74, folder 3, "Teabo MS," 32–33.

60. GGMM no. 65, "Maya Sermons," 19–20; Coronel, *Discursos*, 29v–30r. The close parallel begins with *Likenex cimenexe*.

61. Jehoshaphat means "The Lord judges."

62. Coronel, *Discursos*, 58v–59v; GGMM no. 65, "Maya Sermons," 19–20.

63. GGMM no. 65, "Maya Sermons," 19–20; *Doctrina*, 77r–77v.

64. Coronel, *Discursos*, vii.

65. Large sections of the MM are also found in the *Discursos*. The MM includes the date 1576 within its pages and portions of the manuscript do seem to originate from the early colonial period, although the paper dates to the late eighteenth century; see Whalen, "Annotated Translation," and Knowlton, "Dynamics." That said, the frequent recopying and redacting of such texts frustrates any definitive statement.

66. GGMM no. 65, "Maya Sermons," 17–18.

67. Grupo Dzíbil, *Tuzik*, 25–26. Here I use the transcription of Grupo Dzíbil, but my own translation of the Maya. The group's transcription and translation of the Tusik is a wonderful contribution. However, occasionally their Spanish translation goes awry and illustrates the importance of understanding the European context of such texts to provide accurate translations, particularly in regard to *The Fifteen Signs*.

68. Here I use Whalen's transcription (MM, 101 of ms.) while employing my own translation for purposes of consistency when comparing the four translated passages.

69. For more on the similar yet distinct translations of basic Catholic doctrine, see Christensen, *Catholicisms*, chap. 3.

70. Knowlton, *Creation Myths*, 123.

71. Whalen, "Annotated Translation."

72. Rugeley's *Maya Peasantry* provides an excellent study of the Caste War. For additional connections between the Caste War and apocalyptic beliefs, see Restall and Solari, *2012*, 107–110.

73. Phelan, *The Millennial Kingdom*, 21–23. The entire work is monumental for understanding the millenarianism of the early Franciscans.

74. Here the text deviates from what is in Maya Sermons and only has the "we/us" from "us Christians."

75. Interestingly, the text uses the Latin form for Sunday, "Dominica," and not the

Spanish "Domingo," which surely all Maya were familiar with. Notwithstanding, the Maya modified the Latin somewhat by adding the suffix "-il" to "Dominica" to express attributive relationship.

76. The Chilam Balam of Tusik has a similar text, pp. 25–29; so does the MM, pp. 101–106; as does "Maya Sermons" no. 65 from Princeton. Although different, the Teabo text is most similar to that found in "Maya Sermons."

77. Both the "Maya Sermons" text and the Tusik have *balcheob* here. It is likely that the Teabo MS should read likewise.

78. As mentioned, if the missing lines existed, we would likely find the name of the author here.

CHAPTER 4: MARY, CHRIST, AND THE POPE

1. See also Stafford Poole, *Our Lady of Guadalupe: The Origins and Sources of a Mexican National Symbol, 1531–1797* (Tucson: University of Arizona Press, 1995), 20.

2. For an excellent overview on the birth of the Marian cult in Spain, see Linda B. Hall, *Mary, Mother and Warrior: The Virgin in Spain and the Americas* (Austin: University of Texas Press, 2004), 19–44.

3. William A. Christian Jr., *Local Religion in Sixteenth-Century Spain* (Princeton, NJ: Princeton University Press, 1981), 21, 73, 182–184.

4. Hall, *Mary*, 51 (for the devotion of Columbus to Mary, 45–57).

5. John D. Early describes this as the "Cortés model." See his *Maya and Catholicism*, 197–198. For an excellent overview of Mary, her introduction to the Nahuas, and her treatment in Nahuatl texts, see Louise M. Burkhart, *Before Guadalupe: The Virgin Mary in Early Colonial Nahuatl Literature* (Austin: University of Texas Press, 2001), 1–7. See also William B. Taylor, "The Virgin of Guadalupe in New Spain: An Inquiry into the Social History of Marian Devotion," *American Ethnologist* 14, no. 1 (February 1987): 9–33.

6. Mendieta, *Historia*, 42.

7. Ibid., 475.

8. Landa, *Yucatan*, 6–7.

9. See Burkhart, *Before Guadalupe*.

10. Coronel, *Discursos*, 38r–42r.

11. Christian, *Local Religion*, 15–16.

12. France Scholes et al., *La iglesia en Yucatán* (Merida: Compañía Tipográfica Yucateca, 1938), 28. See also Mendieta, *Historia*, 225–227. William Hanks also provides important insights on Toral and his involvement in the Maya's education in his *Converting Words*, 66–70.

13. For more on the feast days required of the natives, see France Scholes et al., *La iglesia en Yucatán*, 34; Mendieta, *Historia*, 279–283.

14. For an overview of Our Lady of Izamal, see Cogolludo, *Historia de Yucatán*,

Lib. 6, chaps. 2–4, Lib. 12, chaps. 12–13; Luis Weckmann, *The Medieval Heritage of Mexico*, trans. Frances M. López-Morillas (New York: Fordham University Press, 1992), 281. For a lengthier discussion of Marian images venerated throughout central Mexico and Yucatan, see the same, 278–287. Christian's *Local Religion* remains the essential work on the cult of the saints in Spain.

15. Nancy M. Farriss details the influence of Mary upon the naming of Maya cahob in her *Maya Society under Colonial Rule: The Collective Enterprise of Survival* (Princeton, NJ: Princeton University Press, 1984), 513n46.

16. For a detailed comparison between Nahua and Maya adoption of the cult of the saints as seen through testaments, see Christensen, *Catholicisms*, chap. 8.

17. The literature on the Guadalupe legend is extensive, but see Poole, *Our Lady* and Lisa Sousa, Stafford Poole, C.M., and James Lockhart, eds. and trans., *The Story of Guadalupe: Luis Laso de la Vega's 'Huei tlamahuiçoltica' of 1649* (Stanford, CA: Stanford University Press/UCLA Latin American Center Publications, 1998).

18. For a general discussion, see Virginia Reinburg, *French Books of Hours: Making an Archive of Prayer, c. 1400–1600* (Cambridge, UK: Cambridge University Press, 2012), 15–18; Charity Scott-Stokes, *Women's Books of Hours in Medieval England* (Cambridge, UK: D. S. Brewer, 2006), 1–24.

19. For examples of Nahuatl prayers to Mary, see Burkhart, *Before Guadalupe*, 115–130.

20. Bricker and Miram, *Kaua*, 295–296.

21. St. John Damascene, *St. John Damascene on Holy Images followed by Three Sermons on the Assumption*, trans. Mary H. Allies (London: Thomas Baker, 1898), 147–211. He is also known for his support of images in the face of the Iconoclastic Controversy.

22. A discussion of exempla and this and various other examples can be found in Christensen, *Translated Christianities*, 27–42. Whalen, "Annotated Translation," 346 of ms.; Coronel, *Discursos*, 201v–202r.

23. Here I employ the term "co-essence" after Houston and Stuart (1989). Yet the concept also appears referred to as *nagual* or *tonal*, both Nahuatl in origin. For an excellent overview of the matter, see Stephen Houston and David Stuart, "The *Way* Glyph: Evidence for 'Co-essences' among the Classic Maya," *Research Reports on Ancient Maya Writing* 30 (Washington, DC: Center for Maya Research, 1989). See also J. Eric S. Thompson, *Maya History and Religion* (Norman: University of Oklahoma Press, 1970), 167, 202, 315–317.

24. Sullivan, *Unfinished Conversations*, 201. See also the fieldwork of Marianna Appel Kunow in her *Maya Medicine: Traditional Healing in Yucatan* (Albuquerque: University of New Mexico Press, 2003), 17, 44–45.

25. "Then spake Jesus again unto them, saying, I am the light of the world: he that followeth me shall not walk in darkness, but shall have the light of life."

26. Hall, *Mary*, 47.
27. I thank Stafford Poole, C.M. and fray Roger Corriveau, A.A. for their thoughts on the matter.
28. Bricker and Miram, *Kaua*, 297–299.
29. For an overview, see R. N. Swanson, *Indulgences in Late Medieval England: Passports to Paradise?* (Cambridge, UK: Cambridge University Press, 2007), 8–76.
30. Patrick J. O'Banion, *The Sacrament of Penance and Religious Life in Golden Age Spain* (University Park: Pennsylvania State University Press, 2012), 93.
31. Ibid., 101–104.
32. Gómez de Parada, *Constituciones sinodales*, 104.
33. For an excellent account of the colonial sale of indulgences among the Maya, see Patch, *Maya and Spaniard in Yucatan*, 82–83, 157–158.
34. John Franklin Chuchiak IV, "Papal Bulls, Extirpators, and the Madrid Codex: The Content and Probable Provenience of the M. 56 Patch," in *The Madrid Codex: New Approaches to Understanding an Ancient Maya Manuscript*, ed. Gabrielle Vail and Anthony Aveni (Boulder: University Press of Colorado, 2009), 72. See also Pedro Bracamonte y Sosa, *La conquista inconclusa de Yucatán: los mayas de la montaña, 1560–1680* (Mexico City: Centro de investigaciones y estudios superiors en antropología social, Universidad de Quintana Roo, 2001), 156–158.
35. Chuchiak, "Papal Bulls," 76–78.
36. Ibid.
37. Nahuatl texts likewise preserved such bulls in their copybooks. One such example appears as the initial pages of a bound Nahuatl manuscript housed in LTPSC, MSS 279, box 83, folder 7, "Christian text."
38. Bricker and Miram, *Kaua*, 297n1602, 299.
39. LTPSC, MSS 279, box 74, folder 3, "Teabo MS," 40.
40. Karl A. Taube, *The Major Gods of Ancient Yucatan* (Washington, DC: Dumbarton Oaks, 1992), 17–27.
41. Relics of saint's clothing appear in Europe, although I am hesitant to believe that Teabo possessed such an important item.
42. Luke 8:40–56.
43. This and the following page also are disconnected from the discussion on *The Fifteen Signs*. Also, the Maya seems to be of a different quality. Due to water damage, various sections are illegible, thus removing some context that proves vital for translations. I have done my best notwithstanding.
44. Reading as *tacunte*.
45. Similar to the one previous, this page suffers from water damage, particularly along the right side, which makes certain words and phrases unreadable.
46. Here are a few words rendered illegible by repeated strikethroughs.
47. This line, "do not see me fall," is similar to that found in the Our Father.

48. From "uchuc tumen tusinile."

49. It is likely that there is something behind the expression *piz oc* which we fail to grasp, as it also appears in the Chumayel in relation to the creation of the world. Edmonson, *Chumayel*, 121.

50. This page is in the same hand as that which composed the prayers to Mary and Christ.

51. This page again is badly faded on the left side, making some words and phrases illegible.

52. As Bricker and Miram mention (*Kaua*, 297n1601), this is likely in reference to the twelfth-century Pope Innocent II, who authorized indulgences to those supporting the construction of churches.

53. I agree with Bricker and Miram that these names likely are in reference to popes Clement VI, Boniface VIII, Gregory the Great, and John XXII.

54. Indulgences are of two types: plenary, or a complete forgiveness of the temporal punishment required to expiate sin, including punishment in purgatory; and partial, which only remits a portion of the punishment.

55. From *payal chi*. Hanks observes how this phrase contains the literal meaning of "pulling mouth," which presents the intended meaning of drawing the divine to the speaker. Interestingly, the root *pay* also appears in relation to idolatry as *pay cizin* or "pulling devil" and drawing him. For more on payal chi, see Hanks, *Converting Words*, 150, 158.

56. From *Santo pis*. See Bricker and Miram, *Kaua*, 137.

57. In other words, before his time.

CHAPTER 5: RECORDS OF DEATH AND HEALING

1. Archivo Histórico del Arzobispado de Yucatán, Oficios 1748–1749, 1801–1884, vol. 1, "Peten Itza," "Ignasio Pech."

2. Gubler and Bolles, *Na*, 55 of ms.

3. Kunow, *Maya Medicine*, 24.

4. *Relaciones Histórico-Geográficas de la Gobernación de Yucatán: Mérida, Valladolid y Tabasco* (Mexico City: Universidad Nacional Autónoma de México, 1983), vol. 1, 288.

5. Davild Bolles makes this connection in his "Edited Version and Translation of the Na Manuscript," available at http://alejandrasbooks.org/www/Maya /NATRANS.pdf. Here, Bolles notes that "The death of a child, José Eladio Na, son of Secundino Na and Petrona Moó, is recorded for April 3, 1874 in the death records of Teabo for the years 1872–1875 (volume 3, page 36 #148). Archivo Histórico del Arzobispado de Yucatán, Merida. Therein it is stated that he died of natural causes and was buried 24 hours later" (207n531).

6. Gómez de Parada, *Constituciones sinodales*, 106–107.

7. Ibid., 110.

8. Although studies on Nahuatl testaments abound, those examining the limited corpus Yucatan offers are few in comparison. That said, see Matthew Restall, *Life and Death in a Maya Community: The Ixil Testaments of the 1760s* (Lancaster, CA: Labyrinthos Press, 1995); Restall, *The Maya World: Yucatec Culture and Society, 1550–1850* (Stanford, CA: Stanford University Press, 1997), 229–250; Philip C. Thompson, *Tekanto, a Maya Town in Colonial Yucatán* (New Orleans: Middle American Research Institute, Tulane University, 1999); Victoria R. Bricker and Rebecca E. Hill, "Climatic Signatures in Yucatecan Wills and Death Records," *Ethnohistory* 56, no. 2 (2009): 227–268. For a comparison between Nahuatl and Maya testaments, see Christensen, *Catholicisms*, 213–257.

9. For an example of the recording of deaths in cofradía records, see Archivo Histórico del Arzobispado de Yucatán, caja 221, San Ramon, 1424, "Libro de cuentas de la cofradía de las animas."

10. For examples of marriage records, see Hires, "Chan Kan," 128 of ms; Gubler and Bolles, *Na*, 239.

11. See Christensen, *Catholicisms*, 213–240.

12. For more on the itz'aat, see Daniel Graña-Behrens, "*Itz'aat* and *Tlamatini*: The 'Wise Man' as Keeper of Maya and Nahua Collective Memory," in *Mesoamerican Memory: Enduring Systems of Remembrance*, ed. Amos Megged and Stephanie Wood (Norman: University of Oklahoma Press, 2012), 17.

13. Here, testaments recording the bequeathed goods of individuals would greatly assist in determining socioeconomic status. An example of employing Maya wills to achieve such an end is Christensen, "The Spoils," in *Native Wills from the Colonial Americas: Dead Giveaways in a New World*, ed. Mark Z. Christensen and Jonathan Truitt (Salt Lake City: University of Utah Press, 2016).

14. Gómez de Parada, *Constituciones sinodales*, 74.

15. Matthew Restall demonstrates the important role Afro-Yucatecans played as healers in his *The Black Middle: Africans, Mayas, and Spaniards in Colonial Yucatan* (Stanford, CA: Stanford University Press, 2009), 247–277. Indeed, in the *Relaciones* a response from the province of Tabasco stated that both the Maya and *negros* employed local herbs in their healing. *Relaciones*, vol. 2, 429.

16. Caso Barrera, *Ixil*, 29, 98, 99.

17. University of Pennsylvania, Rare Books and Manuscript Library, Collection 700, item 26, "Modo de confesar en lengua maya, año de 1803," 1r; fray Alonso de Molina, *Confesionario mayor en la lengua mexicana y castellana (1569)*, with an introduction by Roberto Moreno (Mexico City: Instituto de Investigaciones Filológicas, Instituto de Investigaciones Históricas, Universidad Nacional Autónoma de México, 1984), 20v.

18. Landa, *Yucatan*, 72; Cogolludo, *Historia de Yucatán*, Lib. 4, chap. 8, 196.

19. Landa, *Yucatan*, 63. For an excellent discussion on medicinal healing in both the New and Old Worlds, see Ruth Gubler, *Fuentes herbolarias yucatecas del siglo XVIII: El libro de medicinas muy seguro y Quaderno de medicinas* (Merida: Universidad Nacional Autónoma de México, 2010), 9–28. See also John Franklin Chuchiak IV, "The Medicinal Practices of the Yucatec Maya and their Influence on Colonial Medicine in Yucatán, 1580–1780," in *Change and Continuity in Mesoamerican Medicinal Practice*, ed. John F. Chuchiak and Bodil Liljefors Persson, special ed., *Acta Americana* 10, nos. 1–2 (2006): 5–19.
20. Christian, *Local Religion*, 42–43, 48–49, 206–208.
21. *Relaciones*, vol. 1, 10.
22. Ibid., 443.
23. For further descriptions of these works and their contributions, see Ruth Gubler, "Antiguos documentos de medicina Maya," *Anales de antropología* 34 (2000): 321–349; Gubler and Bolles, *Na*, 9–12. See also a discussion of Maya medicine in Caso Barerra, *Ixil*, 23–36.
24. Personal communication, September 20, 2015. See also Christensen, *Catholicisms*, 43.
25. Hanks, *Converting Words*, 369.
26. Kunow, *Maya Medicine*, 48. Another particularly revealing example is in Hanks, *Converting Words*, 368–371.
27. For example, Hires, "Chan Kan," 109 of ms.
28. In other texts, such as the Kaua and Na, *pasmos* could refer to spasms. See Bricker and Miram, *Kaua*, 338, 410, 427; Gubler and Bolles, *Na*, 124–25.
29. Gubler likewise observes as much in her *Fuentes herbolarias*, 27.
30. Bricker and Miram, *Kaua*, 447; Roys, *Ethno-Botany*, 27.
31. For more on the uses of such plants and their employment for snakebites, see Roys, *Ethno-Botany*, 302; Kunow, *Maya Medicine*, 134, 136. For some examples of homeopathic remedies in Kaua, see Bricker and Miram, *Kaua*, 351, 360, 412.
32. Kunow, *Maya Medicine*, 33–34.
33. For insights into the modern healer in Yucatan, see Ruth Gubler, "El papel del curandero y la medicina tradicional en Yucatán," *Alteridades* 6, no. 12 (1996): 11–18.
34. The handwriting is different and is in pencil throughout the entire page.
35. The idea being the abortion of a deformed or abnormal fetus.
36. Considering that the author tends to use the phrase "con miel" with plants, *habac naah* could also be in reference to an unregistered plant name or perhaps even "abaca," *Musa textiles*.
37. Reading *tsap*.
38. Reading *ya*.
39. Today, Maya healers frequently use the tips, or *puntas*, of plants, claiming their

higher concentration in medicinal value. See Walter Randolph Adams and John P. Hawkins, *Health Care in Maya Guatemala: Confronting Medical Pluralism in a Developing Country* (Norman: University of Oklahoma Press, 2007), 60.

40. Roys cites a similar remedy employing garlic and tobacco for bites in his *Ethno-Botany*, 27.

41. Roys states that this plant is commonly used in snakebite remedies; see *Ethno-Botany*, 291.

42. No entry has been found for this vine. *Ek u ne* is supposedly a very venomous snake. I thank David Bolles for his assistance in this identification.

CONCLUSION

1. Alfonso Villa Rojas, "The Maya of Yucatan," in *Estudios etnológicos: los mayas*, ed. Alfonso Villa Rojas (Mexico City: Universidad Nacional Autónoma de México, 1985), 230–231.

2. Louise Burkhart notes as much in her *The Slippery Earth: Nahua-Christian Moral Dialogue in Sixteenth-Century Mexico* (Tucson: University of Arizona Press, 1989), 190.

3. William Christian sees this as a negotiation between two separate Catholicisms, that of the Church Universal and local religion. Christian, *Local Religion*.

4. For an excellent work embodying such ideas, see Robert Bireley, *The Refashioning of Catholicism, 1450–1700: A Reassessment of the Counter Reformation* (Washington, DC: Catholic University of America Press, 1999).

5. For examples of the preambles from Ixil, Tekanto, Ebtun, and Cacalchen, see Christensen, *Catholicisms*, 213–240.

6. Lockhart, *The Nahuas after the Conquest*, 366.

Selected Bibliography

Acuña, René. *Bocabulario de maya than: Codex Vindobonesis N.S. 3833.* Mexico City: Instituto Nacional Autónoma de México, 1993.

———. "Escritos Mayas inéditos y publicados hasta 1578: testimonio del obispo Diego de Landa." *Estudios de cultura maya* 21 (2001): 165–171.

Adams, Walter Randolph, and John P. Hawkins. *Health Care in Maya Guatemala: Confronting Medical Pluralism in a Developing Country.* Norman: University of Oklahoma Press, 2007.

Andrews, J. Richard. *Introduction to Classical Nahuatl.* Rev. ed. Norman: University of Oklahoma Press, 2003.

Andrien, Kenneth, ed. *The Human Tradition in Colonial Latin America.* Wilmington, DE: Scholarly Resources, 2002.

Anunciación, fray Domingo de la. *Doctrina Xpiana breue y cōpendiosa.* Mexico City: Pedro Ocharte, 1565.

Anunciación, fray Juan de la. *Doctrina christiana muy cumplida.* Mexico City: Pedro Balli, 1575.

———. *Sermonario en lengua mexicana.* Mexico City: Antonio Ricardo, 1577.

Aquinas, Thomas. *Summa theologica.*

Barrera Vásquez, Alfredo, and Silvia Rendón. *El libro de los libros de Chilam Balam.* 1948. Repr., Mexico City: Fondo de Cultura Económica, 1974.

Bautista, fray Juan. *Libro de la miseria y brevedad de la vida del hombre y de sus cuatro postrimerías, en lengua mexicana.* Mexico: Diego López Dávalos, 1604.

———. *Sermonario en lengua mexicana.* Mexico City: Diego López Dávalos, 1606.

Beltrán de Santa Rosa María, Pedro. *Novena de christo crucificado con otro oraciones en lengua maya.* Mexico City: don Francisco de Xavier Sánchez, 1740. Photostat reproduction, Centro de Apoyo a la Investigación Historica de Yucatán.

Bireley, Robert. *The Refashioning of Catholicism, 1450–1700: A Reassessment of the Counter Reformation.* Washington, DC: Catholic University of America Press, 1999.

Blom, Frans, ed. *Maya Research (Mexico and Central America).* Vol. 2, no. 3. New York: Alma Egan Hyatt Foundation, 1935.

Bolles, David. "Edited Version and Translation of the Na Manuscript." Accessed October 14, 2014. http://alejandrasbooks.org/www/Maya/NATRANS.pdf.

Bracamonte y Sosa, Pedro. *La conquista inconclusa de Yucatán: los mayas de la montaña, 1560–1680.* Mexico City: Centro de investigaciones y estudios superiors en antropología social, Universidad de Quintana Roo, 2001.

Bricker, Victoria R. "The Ethnographic Context of Some Traditional Mayan Speech Genres." In *Explorations in the Ethnography of Speaking,* edited by Richard

Bauman and Joel Sherzer, 369–388. Cambridge, UK: Cambridge University Press, 1974.

———. *The Indian Christ, the Indian King: The Historical Substrate of Maya Myth and Ritual.* Austin: University of Texas Press, 1981.

———. "The Last Gasp of Maya Hieroglyphic Writing in the Books of Chilam Balam of Chumayel and Chan Kan." In *Word and Image in Maya Culture: Explorations in Language, Writing and Representation,* edited by William Hanks and Don S. Rice, 39–50. Salt Lake City: University of Utah Press, 1989.

———. "The Mayan *Uinal* and the Garden of Eden." *Latin American Indian Literatures Journal* 18, no. 1 (2002): 1–20.

———. *A Morpheme Concordance of the Book of Chilam Balam of Chumayel.* New Orleans: Middle American Research Institute, Tulane University, Publication 59, 1990.

———. *A Morpheme Concordance of the Book of Chilam Balam of Tizimin.* New Orleans: Middle American Research Institute, Tulane University, Publication 58, 1990.

Bricker, Victoria R., and Rebecca E. Hill. "Climatic Signatures in Yucatecan Wills and Death Records." *Ethnohistory* 56, no. 2 (2009): 227–268.

Bricker, Victoria R., and Helga-Maria Miram, trans. and eds. *An Encounter of Two Worlds: The Book of Chilam Balam of Kaua.* New Orleans: Middle American Research Institute, Tulane University, 2002.

Burkhart, Louise M. *Before Guadalupe: The Virgin Mary in Early Colonial Nahuatl Literature.* Austin: University of Texas Press, 2001.

———. "Death and the Colonial Nahua." In *Death and Life in Colonial Nahua Mexico,* vol. 1 of *Nahuatl Theater,* edited by Barry D. Sell and Louise Burkhart, 29–54. Norman: University of Oklahoma Press, 2004.

———. *Holy Wednesday: A Nahua Drama from Early Colonial Mexico.* Philadelphia: University of Pennsylvania Press, 1996.

———. *The Slippery Earth: Nahua-Christian Moral Dialogue in Sixteenth-Century Mexico.* Tucson: University of Arizona Press, 1989.

———. "The Voyage of Saint Amaro: A Spanish Legend in Nahuatl Literature." *Colonial Latin American Review* 4, no. 1 (1995): 29–57.

Carochi, Horacio. *Grammar of the Mexican Language, with an Explanation of Its Adverbs.* Bilingual edition by James Lockhart. Stanford, CA, and Los Angeles: Stanford University Press and UCLA Latin American Center Publications, 2001.

Carrillo y Ancona, Crescencio. *Vida del v. padre fray Manuel Martínez, célebre franciscano yucateco, ó sea studio histórico sobre la extinción de la orden franciscana en yucatán y sobre sus consecuencias*. Merida: Gamboa Guzman y Hermano, 1883.

Caso Barrera, Laura. *Caminos en la selva: migración, comercio y Resistencia, mayas yucatecos e itzaes, siglos xvii–xix*. Mexico City: El colegio de México, Fondo de cultura económica, 2002.

———. *Chilam Balam de Ixil: Facsmiliar y estudio de un libro maya inédito*. Mexico City: Artes de México y del mundo, 2011.

Castro Morales, Efraín. "Libros del siglo XVI en la ciudad de Puebla de los Angeles." In *Libros europeos en la Nueva España a fines del siglo XVI*, edited by Wilhelm Lauer, Das Mexico-Projekt der Deutschen Forschungsgemeinschaft, vol. 5, 114. Wiesbaden: Franz Steiner, 1973.

Cervantes, Fernando. "How to See Angels: The Legacy of Early Mendicant Spirituality." In *Angels, Demons, and the New World*, edited by Fernando Cervantes and Andrew Redden, 69–98. New York: Cambridge University Press, 2013.

Chase, Frederic H., trans. *St. John of Damascus, Writings*, vol. 37, *The Fathers of the Church*. Washington, DC: Catholic University of America Press, 1958.

Chaves, Jerónimo de. *Chronographia o reportorio de los tiempos*. Seville: n.p., 1576.

Christensen, Mark Z. *Nahua and Maya Catholicisms: Texts and Religion in Colonial Central Mexico and Yucatan*. Stanford, CA, and Berkeley, CA: Stanford University Press and the Academy of American Franciscan History Press, 2013.

———. "The Spoils of the Pech Conquistadors." In *Native Wills from the Colonial Americas: Dead Giveaways in a New World*, edited by Mark Z. Christensen and Jonathan Truitt, 119–137. Salt Lake City: University of Utah Press, 2016.

———. "The Tales of Two Cultures: Ecclesiastical Texts and Nahua and Maya Catholicisms." *The Americas* 66, no. 3 (January 2010): 353–377.

———. "The Teabo Manuscript." *Ethnohistory* 60, no. 4 (2013): 749–753.

———. *Translated Christianities: Nahuatl and Maya Religious Texts*. University Park: Pennsylvania State University Press, 2014.

———. "The Use of Nahuatl in Evangelization and the Ministry of Sebastian." *Ethnohistory* 59, no. 4 (Fall 2012): 691–711.

Christenson, Allen J. *Popol Vuh—The Sacred Book of the Maya: The Great Classic of Central American Spirituality, Translated from the Original Maya Text*. Norman: University of Oklahoma Press, 2007.

Christian, William A., Jr. *Local Religion in Sixteenth-Century Spain*. Princeton, NJ: Princeton University Press, 1981.

Chuchiak, John Franklin, IV. "'*Ah Dzib Cahob yetel lay u katlilob lae*': Maya Scribes, Colonial Literacy, and Maya Petitionary Forms in Colonial Yucatán." In

Text and Context: Yucatec Maya Literature in a Diachronic Perspective, edited by Antje Gunsenheimer, Tsubasa Okoshi Harada, and John F. Chuchiak, 159–184. Aachen: Bonner Amerikanistische Studien, 2009.

———. "*De Descriptio Idolorum*: An Ethnohistorical Examination of the Production, Imagery, and Functions of Colonial Yucatec Maya Idols and Effigy Censers, 1540–1700." In *Maya Worldviews at Conquest*, edited by Timothy Pugh and Leslie Cecil, 135–158. Boulder: University Press of Colorado, 2009.

———. "Forgotten Allies: The Origins and Roles of Native Mesoamerican Auxiliaries and Indios Conquistadores in the Conquest of Yucatan, 1526–1550." In *Indian Conquistadors: Indigenous Allies in the Conquest of Mesoamerica*, edited by Laura E. Matthew and Michel R. Oudijk, 175–226. Norman: University of Oklahoma Press, 2007.

———. "The Images Speak: The Survival and Production of Hieroglyphic Codices and Their Use in Post-Conquest Maya Religion, 1580–1720." In *Maya Religious Practices: Processes of Change and Adaption*, edited by Daniel Graña Behrens, Nikolai Grube, Christian M. Prager, Frauke Sachse, Stefanie Teufel, and Elisabeth Wagner, 71–103. *Acta Mesoamericana*, vol. 14. Markt Schwaben, Germany: Verlag Anton Saurwein, 2004.

———. "Los mayas y el pirate: tributo indígena, corsarios renegados, y la misteriosa identidad del capitán Antonio Martínez, personaje de los libros de chilam balam." In *Memorias del XXII encuentro internacional los investigadores de la cultura maya*, 15–50. Campeche: Universidad Autónoma de Campeche, 2014.

———. "The Medicinal Practices of the Yucatec Maya and their Influence on Colonial Medicine in Yucatán, 1580–1780." In *Change and Continuity in Mesoamerican Medicinal Practice*, edited by John F. Chuchiak and Bodil Liljefors Persson. Special ed., *Acta Americana* 10, nos. 1–2 (2006): 5–19.

———. "Papal Bulls, Extirpators, and the Madrid Codex: The Content and Probable Provenience of the M. 56 Patch." In *The Madrid Codex: New Approaches to Understanding an Ancient Maya Manuscript*, edited by Gabrielle Vail and Anthony Aveni, 57–88. Boulder: University Press of Colorado, 2009.

———. "Pre-Conquest *Ah Kinob* in a Colonial World: The Extirpation of Idolatry and the Survival of the Maya Priesthood in Colonial Yucatán, 1563–1697." In *Maya Survivalism*, edited by Ueli Hostettler and Matthew Restall, 135–160. Markt Schwaben, Germany: Verlag Anton Saurwein, 2001.

———. "Secrets behind the Screens: Solicitantes in the Colonial Diocese of Yucatan and the Yucatec Maya, 1570–1785." In *Religion in New Spain*, edited by Susan Schroeder and Stafford Poole, 83–109. Albuquerque: University of New Mexico Press, 2007.

———. "The Sins of the Fathers: Franciscan Missionaries, Parish Priests, and the Sexual Conquest of the Yucatec Maya." *Ethnohistory* 54, no. 1 (Winter 2007): 69–127.

———. "Writing as Resistance: Maya Graphic Pluralism and Indigenous Elite Strategies for Survival in Colonial Yucatán, 1550–1750." *Ethnohistory* 57, no. 1 (Winter 2010): 87–116.

Códice franciscano, siglo XVI. Nueva colección de documentos para la historia de México, edited by Joaquín García Icazbalceta. Mexico City: Imprenta de Francisco Díaz de León, 1889.

Coe, Michael D. *Breaking the Maya Code*. New York: Thames & Hudson, 1992.

Cogolludo, Diego López de. *Historia de Yucatán*. Madrid: J. García Infanzón, 1688.

Collins, Anne C. "The Maestros Cantores in Yucatán." In *Anthropology and History in Yucatán*, edited by Grant D. Jones, 233–247. Austin: University of Texas Press, 1977.

Conley, C. H. "An Instance of the Fifteen Signs of Judgment in Shakespeare." *Modern Language Notes* 30, no. 2 (1915): 41–44.

Córdova Salinas, fray Diego de. *Crónica franciscana de las provincias del Perú*. Notes and introduction by Lino G. Canedo, OFM. Washington, DC: Academy of American Franciscan History, 1957.

Coronel, fray Juan. *Discursos predicables, con otras diuersas materias espirituales, con la doctrina xpna, y los articulos de la fé*. Mexico City: Pedro Gutiérrez en la emprenta de Diego Garrido, 1620.

Craine, Eugene R., and Reginald C. Reindorp. *The Codex Pérez and The Book of Chilam Balam of Maní*. Norman: University of Oklahoma Press, 1979.

Díaz Balsera, Viviana. *The Pyramid under the Cross: Franciscan Discourses of Evangelization and the Nahua Christian Subject in Sixteenth-Century Mexico*. Tucson: University of Arizona Press, 2005.

Doctrina cristiana en lengua española y mexicana por los religiosos de la orden de Santo Domingo. Colección de Incunables Americanos, vol. 1. Madrid: Ediciones Cultura Hispánica, 1944.

Domínguez y Argáiz, Francisco Eugenio. *Pláticas de los principales mysterios de nvestra Sta fee con una breve exortación al fin del modo con que deben excitarse al dolor de las culpas*. Mexico City: Colegio de S. Ildefonso, 1758.

Duran, Manuel. *Luis de León*. Boston: Twayne Publishers, 1971.

Early, John D. *The Maya and Catholicism: An Encounter of Worldviews*. Gainesville: University Press of Florida, 2006.

Edmonson, Munro S., trans. and ed. *The Ancient Future of the Itza: The Book of Chilam Balam of Tizimin*. Austin: University of Texas Press, 1982.

———. *Heaven Born Mérida and Its Destiny: The Book of Chilam Balam of Chumayel*. Austin: University of Texas Press, 1986.

————. *Lore: An Introduction to the Science of Folklore and Literature*. New York: Holt, Rinehart, and Winston, 1971.

————. "The Princeton Codex of *The Book of the Chilam Balam of Chumayel*." *Princeton University Library Chronicle* 32, no. 3 (1971): 137–142.

Edmonson, Munro S., and Victoria R. Bricker. "Yucatecan Mayan Literature." In *Supplement to the Handbook of Middle American Indians*, vol. 3, *Literatures*, edited by Munro S. Edmonson and Victoria R. Bricker, 44–63. Austin: University of Texas Press, 1985.

Farriss, Nancy M. *Maya Society under Colonial Rule: The Collective Enterprise of Survival*. Princeton, NJ: Princeton University Press, 1984.

Fernández del Castillo, Francisco. *Libros y libreros en el siglo XVI*. Mexico City: Tip. Guerrero, 1914.

Florescano, Enrique. *National Narratives in Mexico: A History*. Translated by Nancy T. Hancock. Norman: University of Oklahoma Press, 2006.

Flos sanctorum. Castile, ca. 1472–1475.

Fried, Johannes. "Awaiting the Last Days . . . Myth and Disenchantment." In *Apocalyptic Time*, edited by Albert I. Baumgarten, 283–303. Leiden: Brill, 2000.

Genet, Jean, and Pierre Chelbatz. *Histoire des peuples Mayas-Quichés (Mexique, Guatemala, Honduras)*. Paris: Les Editions Genet, 1927.

George-Hirons, Amy. "The Discourse of Translation in Culture Contact: 'The Story of Suhuy Teodora,' an Analysis of European Literary Borrowings in the Books of Chilam Balam." PhD diss., Tulane University, 2004.

————. "Tell Me, Maiden: The Maya Adaptation of a European Riddle Sequence." *Journal of Latin American Lore* 22, no. 2 (2004): 261–277.

Gibson, Charles, and John B. Glass, "A Census of Middle American Prose Manuscripts in the Native Historical Tradition." In *Handbook of Middle American Indians*, vol. 15, *Guide to Ethnohistorical Sources*, part 4, 322–400. Austin: University of Texas Press, 1975.

Gómez de Parada, Juan. *Constituciones sinodales del obispado de Yucatán*. Edited by Gabriela Solís Robleda. Merida: Universidad Nacional Autónoma de México, 2008.

González Díaz, Soledad. "Guaman Poma y el *repertorio* anónimo (1554): una nueva Fuente para las edades del mundo en la *Nueva corónica y buen gobierno*." *Chungara, Revista de Antropología Chilena* 44, no. 3 (2012): 377–388.

González Puc, José Javier. *El campesino maya de Teabo, Yucatán*. Mexico City: Secretaría de Educación Pública, Instituto Nacional Indigenista, 1982.

González Rodríguez, Jaime. "La difusión manuscrita de ideas en Nueva España (siglo XVI)." *Revista complutense de historia de América* 18 (1992): 89–116.

Graña-Behrens, Daniel. "*Itz'aat* and *Tlamatini*: The 'Wise Man' as Keeper of Maya and Nahua Collective Memory." In *Mesoamerican Memory: Enduring Sys-*

tems of Remembrance, edited by Amos Megged and Stephanie Wood, 15–32. Norman: University of Oklahoma Press, 2012.

Granada, fray Luis de. *Introducción del símbolo de la Fe*. Salamanca: Herederos de Matías Gast, 1583.

Green, Otis H., and Irving A. Leonard. "On the Mexican Booktrade in 1600: A Chapter in Cultural History." *Hispanic Review* 9, no. 1 (1941): 1–40.

Grupo Dzíbil. *Chilam Balam of Tuzik*. Mexico City: n.p., 1996.

Gubler, Ruth. "Antiguos documentos de medicina Maya." *Anales de antropología* 34 (2000): 321–349.

———. *Fuentes herbolarias yucatecas del siglo XVIII: El libro de medicinas muy seguro y Quaderno de medicinas*. Merida: Universidad Nacional Autónoma de México, 2010.

———. "El papel del curandero y la medicina tradicional en Yucatán." *Alteridades* 6, no. 12 (1996): 11–18.

Gubler, Ruth, and David Bolles. *The Book of Chilam Balam of Na*. Lancaster, CA: Labyrinthos, 2000.

Gunsenheimer, Antje. "La historia de don Andrés Cocom en los libros del Chilam Balam." *Indiana* 17/18 (2000/2001): 269–288.

———. "Out of the Historical Darkness: A Methodological Approach to Uncover the Hidden History of Ethnohistorical Sources." *Indiana* 23 (2006): 15–49.

Gunsenheimer, Antje, Tsubasa Okoshi Harada, and John F. Chuchiak, eds. *Text and Context: Yucatec Maya Literature in a Diachronic Perspective*. Aachen: Bonner Amerikanistische Studien, 2009.

Hall, Linda B. *Mary, Mother and Warrior: The Virgin in Spain and the Americas*. Austin: University of Texas Press, 2004.

Hanks, William F. "Authenticity and Ambivalence in the Text: A Colonial Maya Case." *American Ethnologist* 13, no. 4 (1986): 721–744.

———. *Converting Words: Maya in the Age of the Cross*. Berkeley: University of California Press, 2010.

———. "Grammar, Style, and Meaning in a Maya Manuscript." *International Journal of American Linguistics* 54, no. 3 (1998): 331–369.

Heilbron, John L. "Censorship of Astronomy in Italy after Galileo." In *The Church and Galileo*, edited by Ernan McMullin, 279–322. Notre Dame, IN: University of Notre Dame Press, 2005.

Heist, William W. *The Fifteen Signs before Doomsday*. East Lansing: Michigan State College Press, 1952.

Herbert, Máire, and Martin McNamara. *Irish Biblical Apocrypha: Selected Texts in Translation*. London: T&T Clark, 2004.

Hires, Marla Korlin. "The Chilam Balam of Chan Kan." PhD diss., Tulane University, 1981.

Hostettler, Ueli, and Matthew Restall, eds. *Maya Survivalism*. Markt Schwaben, Germany: Verlag Anton Saurwein, 2001.

Houston, Stephen. "Crafting Credit: Authorship among Classic Maya Painters and Sculptors." Paper presented at Dumbarton Oaks Fall Symposium, October 12, 2013.

Houston, Stephen, and David Stuart. "The *Way* Glyph: Evidence for 'Co-essences' among the Classic Maya." *Research Reports on Ancient Maya Writing* 30. Washington, DC: Center for Maya Research, 1989.

Hull, Kerry M. "Poetic Tenacity: A Diachronic Study of Kennings in Mayan Languages." In *Parallel Worlds: Genre, Discourse, and Poetics in Contemporary, Colonial, and Classic Period Maya Literature*, edited by Kerry M. Hull and Michael D. Carrasco, 73–122. Boulder: University Press of Colorado, 2012.

Hull, Kerry M., and Michael D. Carrasco, eds. *Parallel Worlds: Genre, Discourse, and Poetics in Contemporary, Colonial, and Classic Period Maya Literature*. Boulder: University Press of Colorado, 2012.

Jacobus de Voragine. *The Golden Legend of Jacobus de Voragine*. Translated and edited by Granger Ryan and Helmut Ripperger. New York: Longmans, Green and Co., 1941.

Jones, Grant D. *Maya Resistance to Spanish Rule: Time and History on a Colonial Frontier*. Albuquerque: University of New Mexico Press, 1989.

Juárez, Ana M., and Jon McGee. "A Mayan Version of the Adam and Eve Story." *Latin American Literatures Journal* 19, no. 1 (Spring 2003): 1–18.

Klor de Alva, J. Jorge. "La historicidad de los colloquios de Sahagún." *Estudios de cultura Náhuatl* 15 (1982): 147–184.

Knowlton, Timothy. "Dynamics of Indigenous Language Ideologies in the Colonial Redaction of a Yucatec Maya Cosmological Text." *Anthropological Linguistics* 50, no. 1 (Spring 2008): 90–112.

———. *Maya Creation Myths: Words and Worlds of the Chilam Balam*. Boulder: University Press of Colorado, 2010.

Knowlton, Timothy, and Gabrielle Vail. "Hybrid Cosmologies in Mesoamerica: A Reevaluation of the *Yax Cheel Cab*, a Maya World Tree." *Ethnohistory* 57, no. 4 (2010): 709–739.

Kropfinger von Kügelgen, Helga. "Exportación de libros europeos de Sevilla a la Nueva España en el año de 1586." *Libros europeos*, 27.

Kunow, Marianna Appel. *Maya Medicine: Traditional Healing in Yucatan*. Albuquerque: University of New Mexico Press, 2003.

Landa, fray Diego de. *Yucatan before and after the Conquest, by Friar Diego De Landa: With Other Related Documents, Maps and Illustration*. Translated by William Gates. New York: Dover Publications, 1978. First published in 1937 by the Maya Society, Baltimore.

Lattis, James M. *Between Copernicus and Galileo: Christoph Clavius and the Collapse of Ptolemaic Cosmology*. Chicago: University of Chicago Press, 1994.

León, fray Martín de. *Camino del cielo en lengua mexicana*. Mexico City: Emprenta de Diego Lopez Daualos, 1611.

León-Portilla, Miguel. *Native Mesoamerican Spirituality: Ancient Myths, Discourses, Stories, Doctrines, Hymns, Poems from the Aztec, Yucatec, Quiche-Maya and Other Sacred Traditions*. New York: Paulist Press, 1980.

Leonard, Irving A. *Books of the Brave: Being an Account of Books and of Men in the Spanish Conquest and Settlement of the Sixteenth-Century New World*. New York: Gordian Press, 1964.

Lockhart, James. *The Nahuas after the Conquest: A Social and Cultural History of the Indians of Central Mexico, Sixteenth through Eighteenth Centuries*. Stanford, CA: Stanford University Press, 1992.

———. "The Social History of Colonial Spanish America: Evolution and Potential." *Latin American Research Review* 7, no. 1 (Spring 1972): 6–45.

Lorenzana, Francisco Antonio. *Concilios provinciales primero, y segundo, celebrados en la muy noble y muy leal ciudad de México, presidiendo el Illmo. Y Rmo. Señor D. Fr. Alonso de Muntúfar, en los años de 1555, y 1565*. Mexico City: Imprenta del Superior Gobierno, Hogal, 1769.

Luxton, Richard N. *The Book of the Chilam Balam of Tizimin*. Laguna Hills, CA: Aegean Park Press, 2010.

———. *The Book of Chumayel: The Counsel Book of the Yucatec Maya 1539–1638*. Laguna Hills, CA: Aegean Park Press, 1995.

Manning, Patricia. *Voicing Dissent in Seventeenth-Century Spain: Inquisition, Social Criticism and Theology in the Case of El Criticón*. Leiden: Brill, 2009.

Mathes, W. Michael. *The America's First Academic Library: Santa Cruz de Tlatelolco*. Sacramento: California State Library Foundation, 1985.

McNamara, Martin. "The (Fifteen) Signs before Doomsday in Irish Tradition." *Warszawskie Studia Teologiczne* 20, no. 2 (2007): 223–254.

Mendieta, Jerónimo de. *Historia eclesiástica indiana*. Barcelona: Linkgua Ediciones, 2007.

Mettinger, Tryggve N. D. *The Eden Narrative: A Literary and Religio-historical Study of Genesis 2–3*. Winona Lake, IN: Eisenbrauns, 2007.

Molina, fray Alonso de. *Confesionario mayor en la lengua mexicana y castellana (1569)*. With an introduction by Roberto Moreno. Mexico City: Instituto de Investigaciones Filológicas, Instituto de Investigaciones Históricas, Universidad Nacional Autónoma de México, 1984.

Molina Solís, Juan Francisco. *Historia de Yucatán durante la dominación española*. Merida: Imprenta de la lotería del estado, 1904.

Mosquera, Daniel. "Nahuatl Catechistic Drama: New Translations, Old Preoccupations." In *Death and Life in Colonial Nahua Mexico*, edited by Barry D. Sell and Louise Burkhart, 55–84. Norman: University of Oklahoma Press, 2004.

Murdoch, Brian. *The Medieval Popular Bible: Expansions of Genesis in the Middle Ages.* Rochester, NY: D. S. Brewer, 2003.

Nesvig, Martin Austin. *Ideology and Inquisition: The World of the Censors in Early Mexico.* New Haven, CT: Yale University Press, 2009.

Nielsen, Kesper, and Toke Sellner Reunert. "Dante's Heritage: Questioning the Multi-layered Model of the Mesoamerican Universe." *Antiquity* 83 (2009): 399–413.

O'Banion, Patrick J. *The Sacrament of Penance and Religious Life in Golden Age Spain.* University Park: Pennsylvania State University Press, 2012.

Oudijk, Michel R., and Matthew Restall. "Mesoamerican Conquistadors in the Sixteenth Century." In *Indian Conquistadors: Indigenous Allies in the Conquest of Mesoamerica*, edited by Laura E. Matthew and Michel R. Oudijk, 28–64. Norman: University of Oklahoma Press, 2007.

Paredes, Ignacio de. *Promptuario manual mexicano.* Mexico City: Bibliotheca mexicana, 1759.

Patch, Robert W. *Maya and Spaniard in Yucatan, 1648–1812.* Stanford, CA: Stanford University Press, 1993.

Pettas, William. *A Sixteenth-Century Spanish Bookstore: The Inventory of Juan de Junta.* Philadelphia: American Philosophical Society, 1995.

Phelan, John L. *The Millennial Kingdom of the Franciscans in the New World.* 2nd ed. Berkeley: University of California Press, 1970.

Poole, Stafford, C.M. *Our Lady of Guadalupe: The Origins and Sources of a Mexican National Symbol, 1531–1797.* Tucson: University of Arizona Press, 1995.

Quezada, Sergio. *Maya Lords and Lordship: The Formation of Colonial Society in Yucatán, 1350–1600.* Translated by Terry Rugeley. Norman: University of Oklahoma Press, 2014.

Ramos Díaz, Martín. "Idólatras y mentores. Escuelas en el Yucatán del siglo XVI." *Estudios de Historia Novohispana* 28 no. 28 (2003): 37–60.

Reinburg, Virginia. *French Books of Hours: Making an Archive of Prayer, c. 1400–1600.* Cambridge, UK: Cambridge University Press, 2012.

Relaciones Histórico-Geográficas de la Gobernación de Yucatán: Mérida, Valladolid y Tabasco. Vols. 1 and 2. Mexico City: Universidad Nacional Autónoma de México, 1983.

Restall, Matthew. *The Black Middle: Africans, Mayas, and Spaniards in Colonial Yucatan.* Stanford, CA: Stanford University Press, 2009.

———. "Gaspar Antonio Chi: Bridging the Conquest of Yucatán." In *The Human*

Tradition in Colonial Latin America, 2nd ed., edited by Kenneth J. Andrien, 6–21. Lanham, MD: Rowman & Littlefield, 2013.

———. "Heirs to the Hieroglyphs: Indigenous Writing in Colonial Mesoamerica." *The Americas* 54, no. 2 (1997): 239–267.

———. "A History of the New Philology and the New Philology in History." *Latin American Research Review* 38, no. 1 (2003): 113–134.

———. *Life and Death in a Maya Community: The Ixil Testaments of the 1760s.* Lancaster, CA: Labyrinthos Press, 1995.

———. *Maya Conquistador.* Boston: Beacon Press, 1998.

———. *The Maya World: Yucatec Culture and Society, 1550–1850.* Stanford, CA: Stanford University Press, 1997.

Restall, Matthew, and Amara Solari. *2012 and the End of the World: The Western Roots of the Maya Apocalypse.* New York: Rowman & Littlefield, 2011.

Ricard, Robert. *The Spiritual Conquest of Mexico: An Essay on the Apostolate and the Evangelizing Methods of the Mendicant Orders in New Spain: 1523–1572.* Translated by Lesley Byrd Simpson. Berkeley: University of California Press, 1966.

Rocher Salas, Adriana. "Un baluarte diferente: iglesia y control social en Yucatán durante el período colonial." *Península* 3, no. 1 (2008): 65–81.

Roest, Bert. *Franciscan Literature of Religious Instruction before the Council of Trent.* Leiden, Netherlands: Brill, 2004.

Roys, Ralph L. *The Ethno-Botany of the Maya.* New Orleans: Department of Middle American Research, Tulane University, 1931.

———. *The Indian Background of Colonial Yucatan.* Washington, DC: Carnegie Institution, 1943.

———. *The Titles of Ebtun.* Washington, DC: Carnegie Institution, 1939.

Rueda Ramírez, Pedro J. *Negocio e intercambio cultural: el comercio de libros con América en la Carrera de Indias (siglo XVII).* Seville: Universidad de Sevilla, consejo superior de investigaciones científicas, 2005.

Rugeley, Terry. *Yucatán's Maya Peasantry and the Origins of the Caste War.* Austin: University of Texas Press, 1996.

Sahagún, fray Bernardino de. *Coloquios y doctrina cristiana.* Edited and translated by Miguel León-Portilla. Mexico City: Fundación de Investigaciones Sociales, Universidad Nacional Autónoma de México, 1986.

Sam Colop, Luis Enrique. "Poetics in the *Popol Wuj*." In *Parallel Worlds: Genre, Discourse, and Poetics in Contemporary, Colonial, and Classic Period Maya Literature*, edited by Kerry M. Hull and Michael D. Carrasco, 283–309. Boulder: University Press of Colorado, 2012.

Sánchez de Aguilar, Pedro. *Informe contra idolorum cultores de obispado de Yucatán.* 3rd ed. Merida: E. G. Triay e Hijos, 1937.

Scholes, France, Carlos Menéndez, J. Rubio Mañé, and E. Adams, eds. *Documentos para la historia de Yucatán*. Vol. 2, *La iglesia en Yucatán*. Merida: Compañía Tipográfica Yucateca, 1938.

Scott-Stokes, Charity. *Women's Books of Hours in Medieval England*. Cambridge, UK: D. S. Brewer, 2006.

Sell, Barry D. "Friars, Nahuas, and Books: Language and Expression in Colonial Nahuatl Publications." PhD diss., University of California, Los Angeles, 1993.

Sell, Barry D., and Louise M. Burkhart, eds. *Death and Life in Colonial Nahua Mexico*. Vol. 1 of *Nahuatl Theater*. Norman: University of Oklahoma Press, 2004.

———. *Nahuatl Theater*. 4 vols. Norman: University of Oklahoma Press, 2004–2009.

Singer, Charles, ed. *Studies in the History and Method of Science*. Vol. 1. Oxford, UK: Oxford University Press, 1917.

Sousa, Lisa, Stafford Poole, C.M., and James Lockhart, ed. and trans. *The Story of Guadalupe: Luis Laso de la Vega's 'Huei tlamahuiçoltica' of 1649*. Stanford, CA: Stanford University Press/UCLA Latin American Center Publications, 1998.

Stuart, David. *The Order of Days: The Maya World and the Truth about 2012*. New York: Harmony Books, 2011.

Sullivan, Paul. *Unfinished Conversations: Mayas and Foreigners between Two Wars*. New York: Knopf, 1989.

Swanson, R. N. *Indulgences in Late Medieval England: Passports to Paradise?* Cambridge, UK: Cambridge University Press, 2007.

Taube, Karl A. *The Major Gods of Ancient Yucatan*. Washington, DC: Dumbarton Oaks, 1992.

Tavárez, David. *The Invisible War: Indigenous Devotions, Discipline, and Dissent in Colonial Mexico*. Stanford, CA: Stanford University Press, 2011.

———. "Representations of Spanish Authority in Zapotec Calendrical and Historical Genres." In *The Conquest All Over Again: Nahuas and Zapotecs Thinking, Writing, and Painting Spanish Colonialism*, edited by Susan Schroeder, 206–225. Eastbourne, UK: Sussex Academic Press, 2011.

Taylor, William B. "The Virgin of Guadalupe in New Spain: An Inquiry into the Social History of Marian Devotion." *American Ethnologist* 14, no. 1 (1987): 9–33.

Tedlock, Barbara. "Continuities and Renewals in Mayan Literacy and Calendrics." In *Theorizing the Americanist Tradition*, edited by Lisa Philips Valentine and Regna Darnell, 195–208. Toronto: University of Toronto Press, 1999.

Terraciano, Kevin. *The Mixtecs of Colonial Oaxaca: Ñudzahui History, Sixteenth through Eighteenth Centuries*. Stanford, CA: Stanford University Press, 2001.

Thompson, J. Eric S. *Maya History and Religion*. Norman: University of Oklahoma Press, 1970.

———. "The Rise and Fall of Maya Civilization." In *The Decipherment of Ancient Maya Writing*, edited by Stephen Houston, Oswaldo Chinchilla Mazariegos, and David Stuart, 180–188. Norman: University of Oklahoma Press, 2001.

Thompson, Philip C. *Tekanto, a Maya Town in Colonial Yucatán*. New Orleans: Middle American Research Institute, Tulane University, 1999.

Tozzer, Alfred M. *A Maya Grammar*. Cambridge, MA: Peabody Museum of American Archaeology and Ethnology, Harvard University, 1921. Repr., New York: Dover, 1977.

Vail, Gabrielle. "Creation Narratives in the Postclassic Maya Codices." In *Parallel Worlds: Genre, Discourse, and Poetics in Contemporary, Colonial, and Classic Period Maya Literature*, edited by Kerry M. Hull and Michael D. Carrasco, 223–251. Boulder: University Press of Colorado, 2012.

Vail, Gabrielle, and Anthony Aveni, ed. *The Madrid Codex: New Approaches to Understanding an Ancient Maya Manuscript*. Boulder: University Press of Colorado, 2009.

Villa Rojas, Alfonso. "The Maya of Yucatan." In *Estudios etnológicos: los mayas*, edited by Alfonso Villa Rojas, 199–242. Mexico City: Universidad Nacional Autónoma de México, 1985.

Wake, Eleanor. *Framing the Sacred: The Indian Churches of Early Colonial Mexico*. Norman: University of Oklahoma Press, 2009.

Weckmann, Luis. *The Medieval Heritage of Mexico*. Translated by Frances M. López-Morillas. New York: Fordham University Press, 1992.

Whalen, Gretchen. "An Annotated Translation of a Colonial Yucatec Manuscript: On Religious and Cosmological Topics by a Native Author." Foundation for the Advancement of Mesoamerican Studies, 2002. www.famsi.org /reports/01017/.

Zamorano, Rodrigo. *Cronología y reportorio de la razón de los tiempos*. Seville: Rodrigo Cabrera, 1594.

Index

Page numbers in *italics* refer to tables and figures.

buletas (bulls), 179–180

Burkhart, Louise, 175

cabecera de doctrina (principal town of a district), 18

cabildo (town council), 4–5

Camino del cielo (León), 29

Campeche, 4, 18

Carillo y Ancona, Crescencio, 8

Carochi, Horacio, 146–148, 157

cartapacios (copybooks), 8. See also Maya Christian copybooks

Caso Barrera, Laura, 10, 45

Caste War (1847–1901), 154, 163

categories of native-language religious texts, 5–8, 17, 29, 30

Catherwood, Frederick, 1

Catholicism: Articles of Faith, 29, 51, 158; creation story and, 28–29; Index Librorum Prohibitorum, 31; indulgences and, 179; man's fall and, 47–48; Mary and, 174–177; Mass, 16, 28, 38–39, 216; Maya and, 4–5, 11, 30, 45; medicinal remedies and, 199–201; schools, 4–5; sexual desire and, 109. See also Dominicans; Franciscans

Chelbatz, Pierre, 13

Chi, Gaspar Antonio, 4

chibal (lineage), 19, 105–106, 196. See also genealogy of Christ

chibal can (snakebite), 200

Chilam Balams, 1, 2, 7, 9–11; apocalyptic discourse, 108–113; authorship, 17, 19, 22; category of, 12–17; Chan Kan, 25, 35, 35; chronological sequence of, 35; Chumayel, 12, 27, 33, 38, 104, 108, 216; contents, 13–14; cosmology and, 48; creation myths in, 26–27, 34; eschatological discourse (Fifteen Signs before Doomsday), 149–151, 153, 155–158, 155–158, 162; Genesis Commentary in, 35, 38; Ixil, 10, 198; Kaua, 2, 10, 11, 13, 25, 35, 35; Na, 13, 17, 18, 19, 22, 192, 194, 195, 196, 196, 197, 198, 200, 201, 216; naming of, 12–13; Tekax, 13, 18, 200, 201; Tizimin, 12, 27, 33, 38, 50, 104; towns where extant Books of Chilam Balam were found, 14; Tusik, 12, 15, 104, 112–113, 149–150, 151, 151, 153, 155–156, 156, 158, 199, 213, 216, 216

Chuchiak, John, 10, 180

City of God, The (Augustine), 46

Códice Pérez, 27, 33, 38, 104, 198

Cogolludo, Diego López de, 8, 37, 176, 198

Colloquios (Sahagún), 29

colonial Maya texts, 3–8, 104, 214; ethnohistory, 8–12; origins of, 52

Columbus, Christopher, 163, 175

Comestor, Peter, 46, 140, 142, 157

confession, 4, 28, 179

confessional manuals, 7, 109, 157, 198

Conkal, 19

convents, 3–4, 18–19, 29, 52

conversion. See religious conversion

copybooks. See Maya Christian copybooks

Córdova Salinas, Diego de, 143

Coronel, Juan, 29, 34, 50, 155–156, 156, 157, 175, 177, 216

Cortés, Hernán, 175

Cortés y Lárraz, Pedro, 8

cosmology, 31–33, 48, 50–51; Michelangelo Caetani's diagram of Dante's layered cosmos, 32; Ptolemaic, 30–33, 44, 108; spherical model of the universe, 31 creation stories, 52; Birth of the Uinal, 33; in Chilam Balams, 26–27, 34–38, 48; Katun 11 Ahau myth, 33; precontact era, 26–27, 30, 33–34, 44–45, 48, 50. *See also* Genesis Commentary

Cronología y reportorio (Zamorano), 105

Cross of Jesus, 154, 175

cruzada (crusade), 179–180

Damian, Peter, 140, *141*, 145, 156–157

death records, 14, 15, *16*, 21–22, 192–196, 201, 216

"de Judicio Finali," 147, *147*

De los signos que aparecerán ante del juicio (Berceo), 140

De novissimis et Antichristo (Damian), 140, *141*, 145, 156–157

despoblado (uninhabited), 3

Discursos predicables (Coronel), 29, 34, 50, 155–156, *156*, 157, 175, 177, *216*

Doctrina (Dominican text), 149, 156

doctrinas (catechisms), 7, 18, 29, 156, 175, 177

Dominicans, 29, 149, 156

doomsday prophecies. See *Fifteen Signs before Doomsday*; parable of sheep and goats

Dresden Codex, 104

Dürer, Albrecht, 109, *111*

earthquakes, 139, *142–145*, *147*, 149, *152*, *154*

Edmonson, Munro S., 1, 9, 13, 33

eschatological discourse, 150–151, 153, 155–158, 162. See also *Fifteen Signs before Doomsday*

escribanos (scribes), 4–5, 15

ethnohistory, 8–12

Eugubino, Augustino, 46

evangelism, 3–4, 7, 11, 18, 27–30, 42, 156, 163. *See also* John the Evangelist; religious conversion

Evernew Tongue, The, 139

exempla, 177–178, *216*

Farriss, Nancy, 9

Fifteen Signs before Doomsday, The, 2, 12, 138–164; in Chilam Balams, 112, 149–151, *151*, 153, 155–158, 162; cognate passages, 155–156, *156*, *216*; concluding sermons, 155–156; in "de Judicio Finali," 147, *147*; in *De novissimis et Antichristo* (Damian), 140, *141*; in *Flos sanctorum*, 140, *144*; in *Golden Legend* (Jacobus de Voragine), 140, *142*; in *Historia scholastica* (Comestor), 140, *142*; in Maya Christian copybooks, 15, *16*; in Maya Sermons, 149–151, *152*, 153, 155–156, *156*, 158–159, 161–162; Maya texts, 149–155, *156*, 156–159; Morley Manuscript and, 149–150, 152–155, *156*, 156–159; Nahuatl texts, 144–150, 156–157; origins of, 138–141; renditions of, 141–155; in *Sermonario* (Anunciación), 146, *147*, 157; in Sermonario (Bautista), 138, 144–145, 145, *147*, 148, 157; in *Summa theologica* (Aquinas), 140, *143*; in Teabo Manuscript and, 20, 138, 144, 149–151, *152*, 152–164

Final Judgment, 104–105, 108, 111–113, 139, 141–150, 155–161

Florentine Codex (Sahagún), 148, 199

Flos sanctorum, 15, 16, 140, *144*, 145, 150, 155, 157

Fountain of Wisdom (John of Damascus), 46–47

Fourth Book of Ezra, 139

Josephus, Flavius, 46
Juárez, Ana M., 52
Julius Caesar (Shakespeare), 140

keban thanil (betrayal), 111
keban uol (to be sad), 111
K'iche' Codex, 8
Knowlton, Timothy, 10, 14, 26, 34, 44, 50, 149
Kunow, Marianna Appel, 199

Landa, Diego de, 8, 34, 175, 176, 198
Last Judgment, The (Dürer), *111*
León, Martín de, 29
Liber sententiarum (Lombard), 140
Lockhart, James, 10, 49, 147
Lombard, Peter, 140

Madrid Codex, 180
maestro (instructor, choirmaster), 4–5, 8, 13, 15, 37, 155, 162, 194, 199, 217
Mani, 4, 18, 19
Marcos Chan of Ebtun, 113
Mary, mother of Jesus, 2, 174–181, 214; Catholicism and, 174–177; Maya and, 174–179; in Teabo Manuscript, 177–181
Maya Christian copybooks: *Arte de bien morir* (GGMM no. 70a), *16*, 17, *18*, 180, 193–194, *195*, 216; authorship, 19–22; category of, 12–18; examples of, *16*; GGMM no. 72, 15, *16*; Maya Sermons (GGMM no. 65), 15, *16*, 149–151, *152*, 153, 155–156, *156*, 158–159, 161–162, 177, 181, *216*; Passion text (GGMM no. 66), *16*, *18*, 20–21, 38, 180, 194, *195*, *196*, *216*; text sharing and, 34; Yucatec Prayers (GGMM no. 71), 15, *16*, *18*, *195*.

See also Morley Manuscript; Teabo Manuscript
McNamara, Martin, 139
medicinal remedies, 197–201
Merida, 3–4, 18, 176, 192
Mexican Provincial Councils (1555 and 1565), 6
miracles, 152–153, 175, 176, 199
Miram, Helga-Maria, 10, 11, 38, 43, 44–45, 108, 179, 180, 198
Molina Solís, Juan Francisco, 3–4, 7, 198
Morley Manuscript, 11–17, *16*, *35*, 35–37, 41–43, 47, 50, 149–150, 152–159, *156*, 177, *216*
Motul, 19
Murdoch, Brian, 46
Mutul, Baltasar, *16*, *21*, 20–22

Na, José María, 17, 19, 194
Na, Secundino (José Secundino), 17, 18, 19, 22, 192, 194, *195*, 216
New Spain, 11, 12, 19, 45, 104, 110, 138, 140, 155, 175, 180, 199
New Testament. *See* Bible; biblical references
Nueva corónica y buen gobierno (Poma), 45

O'Banion, Patrick, 179
Old Testament. *See* Bible; biblical references; Genesis; Genesis Commentary
orthography, 19–21, 35, 38–39, 112, 149, 159, 162, 174, 194, 215
Oxkutzcab, 19

parable of sheep and goats, 31–46, 104, 108–113, 139, 149–150, 156, 162, 163, *216*